Bewitched Again

Bewitched Again

Supernaturally Powerful Women on Television, 1996–2011

JULIE D. O'REILLY

McFarland & Company, Inc., Publishers
Jefferson, North Carolina, and London

LIBRARY OF CONGRESS CATALOGUING-IN-PUBLICATION DATA

O'Reilly, Julie D., 1971–
　Bewitched again : supernaturally powerful women on television, 1996–2011 / Julie D. O'Reilly.
　　p.　cm.
　Includes bibliographical references and index.

　ISBN 978-0-7864-4711-4
　softcover : acid free paper ∞

　1. Women heroes on television.　2. Women prophets on television.　3. Witches on television.　4. Women psychics on television.　I. Title.
PN1992.8.W65O75 2013
791.45'67—dc23　　　　　　　　　　　　　　　2013023044

BRITISH LIBRARY CATALOGUING DATA ARE AVAILABLE

© 2013 Julie D. O'Reilly. All rights reserved

No part of this book may be reproduced or transmitted in any form or by any means, electronic or mechanical, including photocopying or recording, or by any information storage and retrieval system, without permission in writing from the publisher.

On the cover: *left to right* Holly Marie Combs, Rose McGowan and Alyssa Milano in *Charmed*, 2005 (Warner Bros. Television/Photofest); *background image* leather bound cover (Hemera/Thinkstock)

Manufactured in the United States of America

McFarland & Company, Inc., Publishers
　Box 611, Jefferson, North Carolina 28640
　　www.mcfarlandpub.com

To my nieces and nephew by family and by friendship
(Lauren, Anne-Elizabeth, Camille, Monica, and Luke),
for sharing their superpowers

AND

To my spouse, Marc, for believing in my abilities—
even though I am not always superpowered

Table of Contents

Acknowledgments ix
Introduction 1

CHAPTER 1
Samantha as Archetype 23

CHAPTER 2
Misreading the Superpowerful Female Body 44

CHAPTER 3
Masquerade of Selflessness 68

CHAPTER 4
Surveillance of Female Superpower 95

CHAPTER 5
Female Empowerment on Trial 122

CHAPTER 6
Sacrifice and Sanctuary 151

Conclusion 187
Chapter Notes 201
Bibliography 209
Television Episodes, Telefilms and Feature Films Cited 219
Index 229

Acknowledgments

Writing a book about television has been a lifelong aspiration. Television has always intrigued, frustrated, and, most of all, intellectually engaged me. As antithetical as it may sound to some, television makes me think, even television programming that is considered "bad," "mindless," or "forgettable." And, when it is done well, television programming makes me think long after I have turned off the set or closed the browser window. The thing television makes me think most about? How gender is depicted within its fictional realms.

One of the series that has made me think the most over the last sixteen years is *Buffy the Vampire Slayer*. So, I thank its creator, Joss Whedon, for conceiving of the incredible world that is Sunnydale and its complex protagonist, who sometimes makes me feel like I can kickbox and other times makes me yell, "Seriously?!?" Whedon has an amazing ability to come *this close* to depicting what I would deem female empowerment and then turning the narrative in a different direction. Even though I have no right to critique his artistic vision, I often do, because his work *almost* presents the powerful *and* empowered female characters I long for on television. (P.S. Joss, why did Echo have to drop the chip containing all of her memories? And why did Paul have to catch it? You might as well have put him on a white horse and called it a day. P.P.S. I love you anyway. Please make more television.)

Buffy, of course, is not the only show that makes me think, and *Buffy* came along near the start of a wave of similarly powerful characters who also energized and aggravated me. Therefore, in the process of writing this book — *my* book — on television, I watched series after series and then started researching what others had written about these characters and their predecessors and which theories would serve as the best frameworks for analysis. For assisting me with that research, I thank the staffs at Bowling Green State University's Jerome Library (including the impressive Browne Popular Culture Library) and Heidelberg University's Beeghly Library, especially Nainsí Houston, as well as all those who make OhioLINK possible.

I also thank Heidelberg University for awarding me an Aigler Grant, which allowed for the inclusion of images to complement my writing. Thanks also to the staff at Photofest for locating my desired images, answering my questions, and working with my grant deadlines. In addition, thanks go to the members of the Heidelberg University Communication and Theatre Arts (CTA) Department for their collegiality, especially Irene Frisch, for making my work life easier on a daily basis.

Additional thank yous go to Julie Hada, for being an amazing editorial assistant and all-around example of "schwankee-ness"; to April Beisaw, for being a benevolent drill sergeant and model of productivity; to Kathy Bradshaw, for being a great mentor and friend through every incarnation of this project; to Jeff Brown, Vickie Rutledge Shields, and Jim Foust, for providing guidance on a previous incarnation of this project; to Leona Fisher, for offering encouragement at just the right time; to the Legion of Doom (Tony, Peg, Lisa, Stefan, Charlie, Stevie, Michael ... and Heather, my best friend of nearly twenty years who also found time to read a very long chapter), for serving as a great support system; to the Fighting Quills (Christine, Frank, Colleen, Mike/The Baffler, and Cousin Heather), for continuing the laughs over Facebook; to my Millikin crew (especially Nank, Ang, Fermon, Stubby, Shel, Hokampo, Davy, and Johnnnn), for being forever friends; to Heather and Paul Grover, for inspiring me with their writing and composing, respectively; to Lisa Elliott Johnson (the Isa to my Hul), for sharing her awesomeness and motivating me to work on another book (even though she stills owes me a title written on a pastry bag); to Ginny Gregg and Traci Stark, for making Aigler second floor a great first Heidelberg home; to numerous friends I do not have room to name here, for ongoing interest in and encouragement for this project; and to my Heidelberg students past and present (especially the CTA Department majors and minors, the Women's and Gender Studies minors, and the Women's Leadership Initiative members), for making me love what I do and for indulging me when I get on my soapbox about writing, television, or gender ... or some combination thereof.

And, finally, a special thank you and much love to my spouse, Marc, and all of my family ... mom, Sue; sister, Vicki; and all the rest of the Stevensons, Roots, Cromartys, Cooleys, O'Reillys, Gendrons, Desjardins, and all offshoots thereof, including heaven-directed thanks to my father, Larry, and grandparents, Lloyd, Helen, C.R., and Eva.

Introduction

"Well, not that part"

In "Lost and Bound," the 31 January 2002 episode of *Charmed* (WB, 1998–2006), Phoebe Halliwell, one of a trio of sister witches who comprise the "Power of Three," explains to her fiancé, Cole, that *Bewitched* was her preferred television viewing as a child. *Bewitched* (ABC, 1964–72) featured a newlywed witch named Samantha Stephens, who, for the sake of domestic harmony, promises her husband, Darrin, that she will no longer use her supernatural powers. For Phoebe, who often has to conceal her own abilities, Samantha's plight is especially poignant — a sentiment she conveys to Cole:

> I mean, I like Samantha, but I never actually wanted to become her.[1] See, Samantha, she was married to a human, Darrin. Darrin completely repressed Samantha's magic, completely denied who she was, and it wasn't because he didn't love her, it was just that's the way it had to be.

When Cole then, logically, asks, "And this was one of your favorite shows?," Phoebe, perhaps not so logically but truthfully, replies, "Well, not that part." Although Phoebe's less-than-positive description of *Bewitched* and her professed fondness for that series are seemingly incongruous, her "Well, not that part" simply and accurately encapsulates both the appeal and the limitations of that particular series and those series that have followed featuring super-powered women, including *Charmed* and Phoebe herself.

1964–1996

Bewitched premiered in fall 1964, featuring the aforementioned Samantha Stephens, a seemingly average housewife who happens to be a witch; Samantha's magical machinations, although benign, unnerve her husband, Darrin, which leads to his "repression" of her magic, as lamented by Phoebe. *Bewitched*, since it followed on the heels of *Mr. Ed* (CBS, 1961–65), which featured a talking horse, and *My Favorite Martian* (CBS, 1963–66), which featured an alien main character, was not the first series to highlight an element of the supernatural in a primarily domestic setting. However, it was the first to connect the supernatural with the feminine,[2] but far from the last. Additional sitcoms featuring superpowered women, including *I Dream of Jeannie* (NBC, 1965–70), with its magic-wish-granting protagonist, aired in the 1960s. Series featuring superpowered female characters in the subsequent decade broke from the half-hour format and the confines of domesticity; these 1970s superpowered women, most notably Jaime Sommers of *The Bionic Woman* (ABC and NBC, 1976–78) and Amazonian princess Diana of *Wonder Woman* (ABC and CBS, 1976–79), headlined adventure series in which they employ their powers beyond the home but are guided by or motivated by the men in their lives, a more subtle form of repression that, nevertheless, would probably cause Phoebe angst. Following the final episode of *Wonder Woman*, superpowered women experienced a lull in their television popularity; despite a continuing stream of sitcoms and dramas featuring this character type, only a few captured enough of an audience to air for multiple seasons, such as kid friendly comedies *Small Wonder* (Syndicated, 1985–89) and *Out of This World* (Syndicated, 1987–91) and the spiritual *Touched by an Angel* (CBS, 1994–2003). The superpowered women in the 1980s and 1990s faced constraints, just as their predecessors had, only now such constraints included proving themselves to male authority figures, using their powers to serve others, and fearing repercussions if their powers were revealed.

1996–2006

By the mid–1990s, female television characters with supernatural or superhuman abilities experienced what should have been a "golden age," as 1996 to 2006 delivered an increased presence of superpowered women on television and was bookended by two of the longest-running series of this type: *Sabrina, the Teenage Witch* (ABC and WB, 1996–2003) and Phoebe's series, *Charmed*. During that decade, series featuring women with innate — bodily or mental — power predominated the small screen, introducing viewers to protagonists who materialize objects and change their appearance with the twirl of a finger like Sabrina of the aforementioned *Sabrina, the Teenage Witch*, slay vampires and defeat evil like Buffy of *Buffy the Vampire Slayer* (WB and UPN, 1997–2003), levitate and have premonitions like Phoebe of the aforementioned *Charmed*, avenge injustice and armor themselves via a magical gauntlet like Sara of *Witchblade* (TNT, 2001–02), speak to the dead and travel back in time to save lives like Tru of *Tru Calling* (FOX, 2003–05), or even see and talk to God like Joan of *Joan of Arcadia* (CBS, 2003–05). These superpowered women, and the many others from this time period, possess extraordinary physical and mental abilities, thereby illustrating resistance to traditional gender roles. However, these same characters continuously face challenges to and infringements upon their abilities, as their empowerment — their agency — is limited through various social mores and institutions. Sabrina, Phoebe, and company are called freaks, held to an impossible standard of self-sacrifice, kept under surveillance, and regularly put on trial. In short, their power does not translate into empowerment within their fictional universes; despite their potential to be symbols of resistance, these characters reinforce the same hegemonic power structures that they challenge. Or, as Mary Magoulick writes in "Frustrating Female Heroism: Mixed Messages in *Xena*, *Nikita*, and *Buffy*,"[3] "[T]hese female heroes [from *Buffy the Vampire Slayer*, *Xena: Warrior Princess* (Syndicated, 1995–2001), and *La Femme Nikita* (USA, 1997–2001)], conceived of and written mostly by men in a still male-dominated world, present male fantasies and project the *status quo* more than they fulfill feminist hopes" (729). During this decade it seemed, to borrow a phrase from Phoebe, "that's the way it had to be" ("Lost and Bound"). Hence, what should have been a golden age can be described more accurately as a "gilded age," as television's superpowered women from 1996 to 2006 presented a veneer of empowerment while facing constraint after constraint. These ultra-powerful female characters have the capacity to save the world, but they often are pressured and/or need permission to do so.

Regardless of the feminist theoretical lens employed to read these television texts, the limitations of these gilded-age characters are apparent, as their agency is diminished in multiple ways. While conflict is, of course, necessary to maintain the comedic or dramatic tension within series television, the conflicts faced by superpowered women during this decade often differed greatly from those faced by their male counterparts. Consequently, superpowers within these female-centered series serve as a mechanism of marginalization more so than of empowerment. As Danny Fingeroth proposes in *Superman on the Couch: What Superheroes Really Tell Us About Ourselves and Our Society*, "You don't have to be Sigmund Freud to figure out that the fantasy of the superhero involves empowerment" (119). Therefore, superpowers within these television series are a narrative technique to disenfranchise these female characters both socially and culturally. Superpowered women on U.S. television from 1996 to 2006, then, illustrate a paradox of women's power: can these female characters truly be considered powerful, much less superpowerful, if they do not have the opportunity to embrace, develop, or utilize their abilities fully and/or freely? It is a question that applies to series after series from 1996 to 2006, as well as many that followed over the next five television seasons.

2006–2011

Some series that aired after 2006 seemed to be an extension of the previous decade, most notably *Medium* (NBC and CBS, 2005–11) and *Ghost Whisperer* (CBS, 2005–10), which both debuted near the end of *Charmed*'s run (in January and September 2005, respectively), as well as *Saving Grace* (TNT, 2007–10). In these series, each of the protagonists, *Medium*'s Allison, *Ghost Whisperer*'s Melinda, and *Saving Grace*'s title character, are compelled — and at times conscripted — to assist others because of their abilities (Allison and Melinda communicate with the dead, and Grace communes with an angel), often at great sacrifice to their personal and/or familial happiness. For Grace, her connection to the supernatural even demands the ultimate sacrifice — her death — to combat evil. Once again, as in the previous decade, extraordinary abilities require superhuman selflessness.

Medium, *Ghost Whisperer*, and *Saving Grace* were not the only series from 2006 to 2011 to feature superpowered women, as evidenced by programs such as the re-envisioned (and short-lived) *Bionic Woman* (NBC, 2007),[4] with its titular cyborg, Jaime; the high-profile *True Blood* (HBO, 2008–), with its telepathic protagonist, Sookie; and the not-long-for-the-airwaves *Eastwick* (ABC, 2009), with its supernatural trio of the element-influencing Kat, the future-predicting Roxy, and the will-bending Joanna. However, during this more contemporary era, series featuring superpowered male protagonists or mixed-sex superpowered ensembles outnumbered series headlined by superpowered women. Thus, television viewers could follow the weekly exploits of the laboratory-created title character of *Kyle XY* (ABC Family, 2006–09), who has prodigious strength, speed, and intellect; the extraordinarily abled ensemble of *Heroes* (NBC, 2006–10), which includes Hiro, Matt, Claire, and Peter, whose powers range from time travel to mind reading to self-healing to mirroring the powers of others; the quirky lead character of *Pushing Daisies* (ABC, 2007–09), Ned, who can raise the dead with a single touch (or make them forever dead with a second touch); the human-internet-download title character of *Chuck* (NBC, 2007–12), who can "flash" on virtually any information, from bomb schemata to martial arts moves; the undead leads of *The Vampire Diaries* (CW, 2009–), Stefan and Damon, who have superior strength and speed; and the unusual housemates of *Being Human* (SyFy, 2011–), Aidan, Josh, and Sally, whose respective identities as a vampire, werewolf, and ghost imbue them with superhuman abilities. Despite a decrease in female-led series since 2006, superpowered women have continued to serve pivotal roles in numerous male-led and ensemble series, such as the immortal Dr. Helen Magnus of *Sanctuary* (SyFy, 2007–11), who is the protector of a safe house for supernatural creatures.

While plots and themes are less unified in these more recent series, the superpowered women within them face many of the same challenges as their gilded-age predecessors, but, unlike in the previous era, their male counterparts may struggle more in kind (especially in regard to being called freaks ... apparently superpowered women were freaks before freaks were cool). Therefore, many superpowered characters from 2006 to 2011, regardless of biological sex or gender, seem resigned to their limited social agency and seek community with one another, with superpowered women often serving as the catalyst for and/or focal point of such communities. In this new era, superpowered women's abilities, in many ways, incorporate them into a reimagined domestic sphere. This reimagining illustrates a new-old paradox of women's power, presenting the appearance of choice while associating women with and employing their abilities for traditional roles. Instead of needing permission to save the world, these "new" superpowered women (and occasionally "normal" female characters who are pulled into the supernatural world) are choosing to protect their families at all costs, however nontraditional those families may be.

Powerful Women in the Popular and Academic Presses

The proliferation of superpowered women on television beginning in 1996 with *Sabrina, the Teenage Witch* paralleled a larger media trend that focused on a range of superpowerful and powerful female icons, including comic book superheroes, movie action heroines, and even popular musicians, in particular the British pop band the Spice Girls. "Girl power," the mainstream, *i.e.*, highly commercialized, mantra most closely associated with the Spice Girls, offered teen and pre-teen girls on both sides of the Atlantic a late–twentieth-century version of consciousness raising, albeit of the bubblegum variety. Girl power encompassed both an affirmation of the physical and emotional strength of women and a celebration of traditionally feminine appearances and attitudes—third-wave feminism for the junior high school crowd.[5] In Rachel Fudge's "Girl, Unreconstructed: Why Girl Power Is Bad for Feminism," she describes the Spice Girls as a "prefabricated" and "plasticized" group that "prattl[ed] about girl power—which was never really defined, but seemed to sum up as 'Be yourself (and wear a Wonderbra if you wanna!)'"

(156). Furthermore, Fudge points out that the riot grrrl movement in the early 1990s, which initially developed from punk rock scenes in Washington, D.C.; Olympia, Washington; and London, England, had been "loudly claiming the revolutionary power of girlhood" before the Spice Girls gained popularity (155–56); likewise, Andi Zeisler, in *Feminism and Pop Culture*, notes the implicit irony in the "riot grrrls' raw emotion and conscious rejection of the mainstream" being "candy-coated and repackaged" by the Spice Girls (107).

Other cultural critics, however, perceive the Spice Girls more favorably. Juliana Tringali, in "Remembering the Spice Wars: Can the Spice Girls Live Up to Their Girl Power Legacy?," considers the positive messages about diversity and friendship that the Spice Girls offered their young audience and commends the creative control exerted by the band members (29). In *OverLoaded: Popular Culture and the Future of Feminism*, Imelda Whelehan acknowledges that even detractors of the Spice Girls recognized that the band members were, to their teenage fans, icons of "women achieving success on their own terms" (40); however, the keys to that achievement were superficial and suspect, as Whelehan notes that the band members' glamorous appearances were essential to their appeal (41) and their "credentials as models of female empowerment [we]re distinctly dubious" (8). The girl power phenomenon, therefore, while perhaps rhetorically empowering for young female audiences, failed to address, as Whelehan indicates, the social and cultural institutions that continued to prevent or, at the very least, problematize women's attainment of personal and/or professional goals (41). Fudge summarizes this sentiment as, "Girl power slaps them [young women] on the back and says, 'You go, girl,' even if it's not at all clear where or why they should be going, and it certainly doesn't say that they might face significant obstacles along the way" ("Girl, Unreconstructed" 161). Or, as Whelehan asks, "what do girls really have the power to do?" (8).

Kathleen Rowe Karlyn answers Whelehan's question, in part, in "*Scream*, Popular Culture, and Feminism's Third Wave: 'I'm Not My Mother.'" In this article, Karlyn explains that girls may not have gained greater social power in the 1990s, which she refers to as "the decade of Girl Culture and Girl Power," but they, as a demographic group, did gain the attention of popular culture producers who now were interested in meeting girls' consumer preferences, since girls now had greater disposable income. So girls, apparently, now had the power to buy or, perhaps more importantly, the power to influence what was available for purchase. Thus, girl power never could be separated fully from commercialism, as it more directly targeted girls' allowances than their burgeoning feminist sensibilities.[6]

Although media coverage of the Spice Girls quickly dwindled in the late 1990s as the band members explored solo careers, the impact of their catch-phrase continued to be felt, as powerful girls — or women — in film, comic books, young adult and adult fiction, video games, and, as noted previously, television gained recognition throughout the end of that decade and beyond. While mainstream news and entertainment sources such as *Psychology Today* and *Good Housekeeping*, respectively, questioned why the "Warrior Women" of television were gaining popularity (Ventura 59) and when and how television's "Girls Who Fight Back" had become a new type of role model for young girls (Moy 86), media and cultural studies scholars considered the feminist implications of this surge of "tough girls," "action heroines," "warrior women" (reminiscent of the popular press), "fantasy girls," "Athena's daughters," and "action chicks."

Sherrie A. Inness's *Tough Girls: Women Warriors and Wonder Women in Popular Culture* analyzes representations of "tough girls" — a term she uses interchangeably with "tough women" — across media and genres, including television, women's magazines, film, science fiction, and comic books. Through her analysis, she examines such characters and individuals as Emma Peel from *The Avengers* (ITV, 1961–69), Jaime Sommers from *The Bionic Woman*, Jodie Foster (specifically her role in *The Silence of the Lambs* [1991]), Martha Washington from the graphic novel *Give Me Liberty: An American Dream* (1992), and the title character from *Xena: Warrior Princess*. Inness also considers the level of toughness such individuals and characters exhibit as well as the contexts within which they exhibit that toughness. She concludes that, despite the growing number of tough girls in popular culture, the mainstream media remain conservative in their depictions of gender roles. For this reason, tough girls such as Xena or Ripley (the protagonist from the *Alien* film series [1979, 1986, 1992, 1997]) occupy positions as cultural "outsider[s]"; this outsider status, therefore, reinforces "the cult of femininity" and "separates [women] from authority and power" (181). Inness's work, although a thorough examination of late–twentieth-century media representations of strong women, does not address the paradoxical implication that it is the tough girls' very toughness — *i.e.*, their physical, intellectual, or emotional strength — that ultimately separates them from socially recognized forms of power, *i.e.*, empowerment.

While Inness focuses on cultural perceptions of toughness and the role gender plays within those perceptions, Elizabeth Hills, in "From 'Figurative Males' to Action Heroines: Further Thoughts on Active Women in the Cinema," attempts to deconstruct the "active male/passive female" binary that often accompanies psychoanalytic film analysis of strong female characters. In Hills's article, she asserts that this binary structure and any similar structures, since they render active female characters "phallic, unnatural or 'figuratively male,'" should be abandoned (39). In addition, Hills calls for theoretical constructions that allow for shifting contexts and emerging character types. While Hills's argument that action heroines should indeed be read as women (in a sense she is, in Inness's terms, proposing a new perspective on female toughness) is an important one, the terminology Hills uses to conclude her article — that action heroines should be perceived as "transformative, transgressive and alternative *women*" (49) — potentially sets up new and equally problematic binaries (transformative/static, transgressive/limited, and alternative/original). In addition, Hills does not address the source of, nor the development or use of, the power or empowerment that allows these characters to be active.

Dawn Heinecken, in her book *The Warrior Women of Television: A Feminist Cultural Analysis of the New Female Body in Popular Media*, also considers active female characters; she uses *La Femme Nikita*, *Buffy the Vampire Slayer*, and *Aeon Flux* (MTV, 1991–95) as case studies to argue that contemporary female action heroes on television present "contradictory" texts, *i.e.*, different perspectives yield different conclusions as to whether or not such texts indicate "progress" for feminism (151). Heinecken, although considering the cultural implications of female action heroes in terms of women's assumption of both power and public space, focuses on how the bodies of these female heroes differ from their male counterparts, specifically how "visual culture has begun to feature survival and transcendence of the female hero" (150). According to Heinecken, the vulnerable bodies represented by Nikita, Buffy, and Aeon Flux are more a consequence of shifting cultural perceptions about the body than how society perceives a female hero (156). While Heinecken does note that the "reconfigur[ation]" of the female body within these series creates space for "female power and physicality" (156), like Hills, she does not direct her analysis toward the origin or fulfillment of such power and ability.

In addition to the works mentioned above, there have been multiple other volumes in the last decade or more that consider the cultural implications of media depictions of powerful girls and women. Scholarship on *Buffy the Vampire Slayer* alone has yielded its own academic niche. "Buffy Studies" have produced works such as Rhonda V. Wilcox and David Lavery's edited collection *Fighting the Forces: What's at Stake in Buffy the Vampire Slayer*, James B. South's edited collection *Buffy the Vampire Slayer and Philosophy: Fear and Trembling in Sunnydale*, and Jana Riess's *What Would Buffy Do? The Vampire Slayer as Spiritual Guide*. Even though the series ended in 2003, Buffy Studies live on, although now often referred to as "Whedon Studies" to encompass *Buffy* creator Joss Whedon's other television, film, and online work, such as *Angel* (WB, 1999–2004), *Firefly* (FOX, 2002), *Serenity* (2005), *Dr. Horrible's Sing-Along Blog* (2008), and *Dollhouse* (FOX, 2009–10). More recent examples of Buffy/Whedon Studies include the Mary Kirby-Diaz edited volume *Buffy and Angel Conquer the Internet: Essays on Online Fandom*; the Jodie A. Kreider and Meghan K. Winchell edited volume *Buffy in the Classroom: Essays on Teaching with the Vampire Slayer*; and the Kendra Preston Leonard edited volume *Buffy, Ballads, and Bad Guys Who Sing: Music in the Worlds of Joss Whedon.*

Other edited volumes have included scholarship on a wider range of media offerings (not just *Buffy the Vampire Slayer*) while still examining the role of gender and power within late twentieth-century and early twenty-first-century culture. For example, *Fantasy Girls: Gender in the New Universe of Science Fiction and Fantasy Television*, edited by Elyce Rae Helford, contains essays that address how "the women of '90s speculative television articulate more suggestively than any other group of character types the cultural mood of '90s America" (7), while *Athena's Daughters: Television's New Women Warriors*, edited by Frances Early and Kathleen Kennedy, includes essays on *Xena: Warrior Princess*, *Buffy the Vampire Slayer*, *La Femme Nikita*, and *Star Trek: Voyager* (UPN, 1995–2001) that consider, similarly to Heinecken, "the sometimes contradictory meanings of the new woman warrior's appropriation of both violence and the male heroic narrative" (Early and Kennedy 10). Following *Athena's Daughters*, Inness, perhaps as a follow-up to *Tough Girls*, edited *Action Chicks: New Images of Tough Women in Popular Culture*, a compilation of essays about the female action hero in video games, film, comic books, action figures, and television, as well as about new representations of toughness in professional wrestling, television, and film.

More recently, single-authored texts have explored depictions of powerful and superpowerful female characters on television and beyond. Karin Beeler's *Seers, Witches, and Psychics on Screen: An Analysis of Women Visionary Characters in Recent Television and Film* analyzes the representation of contemporary Cassandra and Joan of Arc character types, as well as psychic detectives, in film and television from the 1990s. In addition, Jeffrey A. Brown's *Dangerous Curves: Action Heroines, Gender, Fetishism, and Popular Culture* discusses the pervasiveness of the action heroine in contemporary Western society, examining such topics as Pygmalion fantasies, cyborgs, revenge, postfeminism, and ethnicity as they are played out in recent films, television series, video games, and fiction, considering characters with powers (such as Buffy) and those without (such as Lara Croft of the *Tomb Raider* film series [2001, 2003]). Throughout this examination, Brown emphasizes the complex characterization of the action heroine, noting that such characters should not be read "as simply *either* good and empowering—*or* as bad and disempowering" (9); instead, he argues that the action heroine "mudd[ies] the waters of what we consider masculine and feminine, of desirable beauty and threatening sexuality, of subjectivity and objectivity, of powerful and powerless"

(10). While all of these works offer important contributions to the consideration of contemporary media representations of powerful girls and women, their specific focuses, in the case of Buffy Studies or genre-specific collections, or their broad subject matters, as with volumes that cross a number of media or character types, do not allow for a comprehensive contextualization of such representations within the specific medium in which they appear. Nor, as noted above, do such studies necessarily deconstruct the very notion of why these characters are (or are not) considered powerful in the first place.

Scope of Study

In contrast to the above works, this study solely analyzes representations of superpowerful — not just powerful — female characters on television. The specific focus on superpowered — not tough, active, or warrior — women was selected because the innate power of these characters within their respective narratives literally and/or symbolically conflicts with their limited empowerment; in other words, their power is not open for interpretation (as it may be with action heroines, for example), even if their empowerment is. Only the television incarnations of superpowered women are considered, even if such characters originated in or have been perpetuated through another medium. As television continues to be a pervasive medium, especially with the multiple viewing options afforded by contemporary technology, it offers the greatest potential to reach the largest audiences. Additionally, television's connection to women is a longstanding one; as Zeisler writes, "Television was, for most women, the first place they saw themselves represented" (9).

For the purposes of this study, "superpowered women on television" includes those female characters with supernatural or superhuman powers who are featured on U.S.-broadcast, regularly scheduled, scripted series television; the abilities of these characters include, but are not limited to, clairvoyance, psychic visions, telekinesis, extrasensory perception, telepathy, immortality, freezing time, molecular or electrical particle manipulation, super vision, super hearing, super strength, prophecy, astral projection, levitation, exceptional intelligence, and healing. Female characters who demonstrate or are described as having such powers are analyzed, regardless of age (no distinction is made between "girls" and "women"), humanity (thus non-human characters such as the mechanical protagonist of *My Life as a Teenage Robot* [Nickelodeon, 2003–09] is taken into account), and/or heroic classification (both superhero and non-superhero characters are incorporated).

Despite the often implicit connection of the supernatural or superhuman to a higher power, the majority of television series featuring superpowered women do not base their mythologies on a discernible set of religious practices or doctrine — most are amalgams. Therefore, no overall theological perspective is considered within this study. If a particular series explicitly references a theological perspective, then that perspective is taken into consideration when contextualizing its featured characters.

Furthermore, although ethnicity, class, and sexuality cannot be separated from gender when considering conditions of marginalization or discrimination, these other aspects of identity will not be addressed extensively, as nearly all representations of superpowered women have been white, middle-class heterosexuals. Max of *Dark Angel* (FOX, 2000–2002) and Willow of *Buffy the Vampire Slayer* are notable exceptions, as Max, a genetically enhanced young woman, is a poor Latina (at least judging from the character's and her portrayer's surnames—Guevara and Alba, respectively) and Willow, who is a witch, is a Jewish lesbian. However, Max's lack of finances match most of the other characters on her series, and her ethnicity is never directly addressed or even mentioned, as her superhuman abilities seem to trump all other aspects of her identity. Likewise, although Willow's Jewish heritage is mentioned on occasion and her sexuality is addressed openly in later seasons, she remains a supporting character, albeit an integral one; the series' title, of course, refers to the blonde, light-eyed, middle-class, heterosexual Buffy. While such a lack of diversity among superpowered women certainly is evidence of symbolic annihilation[7] or invisible stereotyping, an exploration of this lack would constitute a separate study.[8]

Finally, in regard to chronology, this study offers an in-depth analysis of superpowered women on television from 1996 to 2006, the period in which this character type experienced its greatest popularity. As background, the study also provides an overview of superpowered women from their origin in 1964, with the first episode of *Bewitched*, to the start of their golden/gilded age in 1996, with the first episode of *Sabrina, the Teenage Witch*. It also considers the direction these characters have taken in the post-gilded age (2006–2011), the era initiated by the final episode of *Charmed*. Analyses of superpowered women include comparisons to male superpowered characters to illustrate gender differences in the narratives and universes that govern these characters. Additionally, this study examines the parallels between superpowered women on television and their off-screen counterparts to examine the endurance of the superwoman as a metaphor in relation to cultural attitudes toward women and power.

The Superwoman Metaphor

Superpowered women on television serve as an important site of negotiation for determining the social and cultural acceptability of female power both on and off screen, as the representations of such characters both overtly challenge (through the characters' innate abilities) and subtly reinforce (through the characters' limited agency) hegemonic power structures. These characters warrant analysis because of the cultural conflict that they represent and the cultural indicator that they have become. In terms of conflict, superpowered women depict extraordinary power alongside restricted empowerment, a juxtaposition that provides the opportunity to deconstruct the concept of "empowerment" itself and its association with feminist rhetoric. As a cultural indicator, superpowered women have remained on television in one form or another for nearly fifty years, serving as pervasive metaphors for their real-life counterparts—women who hold powerful positions within the home, business, or government but are discouraged or prevented from developing higher levels of cultural influence.

While superheroes, in general, "represent the values of the society that produces [them]" (Fingeroth 17), the specific association between a fictional "superwoman" and actual women can be traced to the 1972 appearance of the comic-book Wonder Woman on the debut cover of *Ms.* magazine, forever linking that iconic superhero to second-wave feminism. More specifically, during this decade, the media icon of a successful career woman was the "Superwoman" (Faludi 76–77); the use of this icon suggests that women requiring superpowers to reach personal or professional goals within a patriarchal society was not a difficult concept for the media to sell to women at that time. In fact, Phyllis Chesler notes, in her article "The Amazon Legacy: An Interpretive Essay," that Wonder Woman is "grounded in reality," because "[the comic strip] clearly portrays the fact that women have to be better and stronger than men to be given a chance in a man's world." "Better and stronger" apparently were not enough, as the woman-as-superwoman metaphor took on negative connotations in the 1980s. Throughout the "Me Generation," the superwoman icon made for a convenient media scapegoat for the alleged failings of the feminist movement. As Susan Faludi writes in *Backlash: The Undeclared War Against American Women*, "Like graffiti artists, they [the media] defaced the two favorite poster girls of the '70s press—spray-painting a downturned mouth and shriveled ovaries on the Single Girl, and adding a wrinkled brow and ulcerated stomach to the Superwoman" (77). Despite the negative press, the superwoman did recover from these cosmetic and gastric assaults to be reinvented in the following decades.

During the 1990s and the aughts, new incarnations of the superwoman emerged that were, as with Wonder Woman in the 1970s, "grounded in reality." In particular, Buffy's struggle to maintain a social life while battling the supernatural forces of evil resonated with *Buffy the Vampire Slayer*'s audience. As a 27-year-old viewer explained, "You can take it [the show] out of the context of vampires and just think of it as all the usual bulls--[sic] women have to deal with" (qtd. in Rogers 60). Cartoonist Cathy Guisewite also associated "the usual bulls--" with the daily plight of women in her syndicated comic strip "Cathy." In Guisewite's 24 June 2002 cartoon, Cathy's friend Irving describes the pressure that "men are under today." He tells Cathy that men are "supposed to be tough business people, brilliant investors, nurturing parents, sensitive spouses, community leaders, fabulous athletes with abs of steel and great hair!!" He continues by saying that men are "expected to be like a ... a...." When Cathy attempts to finish his sentence with "Female!," he completes his thought with "Super hero! [sic]"—to which Cathy replies, "Same thing" (Guisewite). Advertisers, too, have banked on women thinking "same thing" when it comes to superwomen and actual women, especially actual women, *i.e.*, female consumers, with children, as noted by the conflation of superheroes and soccer moms in a 2003 Dodge Caravan print advertisement that declares "[s]ome superheroes use a phone booth. Moms have this [the Caravan]" or the use of the *Bewitched* theme song in a 2011 Electrolux television commercial that urges women to "be even more amazing" with Electrolux appliances. Representations of the "superwoman," then, are both rooted in and reflective of American women's realities and continue to be a cultural parallel worthy of examination.

Representation

This study's analysis of television's superpowered women focuses on close readings of the representations of this character type, *i.e.*, the visual depictions of and the narratives surrounding such characters and the possible meanings and messages audience members, most importantly female viewers, may intuit from them. Feminist scholars are concerned with representations, as such depictions influence cultural perceptions and performances of gender. As Joan W. Scott explains in "Deconstructing Equality-Versus-Difference: Or, the Uses of Poststructuralist Theory for Feminism," "[T]he meanings of gender become tied to many kinds of cultural representations, and these in turn establish terms by which relations between women and men are organized and understood" (380–81). Inness concurs by noting that popular culture representations of women, specifically those in television series, "deserve critical attention because they are helping to constitute how viewers understand both acceptable and unacceptable roles for both women and men" (*Tough Girls* 49). Consideration of media representations of women, then, falls within the feminist agenda, as these fictional representations potentially contribute to oppressive power structures in actual ways. Zeisler describes this connection between fictional representations and actual women's lives:

> There are feminist issues that seem, it's true, more immediately vital than whether TV or movie characters are reflecting the lives of real women. [...] But like the disintegrating line between high and low culture, the distinctions between political and pop have also all but disappeared. Pop culture informs our understanding of political issues that on first glance seem to have nothing to do with pop culture; it also makes us see how something meant as pure entertainment can have everything to do with politics [6–7].

For this reason, real-life parallels, as noted previously, are also included in this study's analysis. Therefore, the conflicts faced by the superpowered female characters under examination are compared to those conflicts faced by their off-screen counterparts — women who are, *e.g.*, working mothers, business executives, or politicians, as well as those women who aspire to hold powerful positions within or outside the home.

Whether viewers of television series featuring superpowered women believe that these extraordinarily abled protagonists are truly the same as they — the viewers — are, is of course, debatable. Karlyn, for one, argues that within third-wave feminism, popular culture is used as "a natural site of identity-formation and empowerment," and, moreover, that it is perceived as a "storehouse of images and narratives valuable less as a means of representing reality than as motifs available for contesting, rewriting and recoding." However, in opposition to Karlyn's contention, it is worth noting that the often-realistic themes of dis-empowerment found in popular culture, specifically in television series featuring superpowered women, must be consciously consumed to some degree before such themes can be opposed, revised, or reinscripted; just as parody cannot be humorous unless one is first familiar with the object of its imitation, television viewers must be familiar with the recurrent narratives of women's curtailed power before such narratives can become empowering. Since a truly oppositional decoding position is difficult — if not impossible — to achieve, messages of women's dis-empowerment and those messages' connections to reality, therefore, may continue to influence audience members' ideology and resulting behaviors regarding gender, albeit in often subtle ways. For female viewers, then, the superpowered woman on television carries connotations of cultural inequity and unfulfilled potential.

The subtlety with which television representations of superpowered women may affect viewers' perceptions and performance of gender is another reason why such characters have been chosen for analysis, since such an analysis allows for the recognition of the inscription of dominant ideologies upon these seemingly or potentially pro-feminist/empowering texts. As Judith Lorber writes in *Paradoxes of Gender*, "in order to dismantle the institution [of gender] you must first make it very visible" (10). The deconstruction of media images of strong female characters—such as the television images of superpowered women—provides one way to make oppressive gender inscriptions visible, potentially leading to the dismantling of such practices.

Theoretical Framework

Throughout this study, representations of superpowered women on television and comparisons to their male counterparts are deconstructed within the interdependent frameworks of hegemony and feminist theory. Hegemony, as proposed by Marxist scholar Antonio Gramsci, is the method by which dominant social groups acquire through "a process of 'intellectual and moral leadership'" the consent of subordinate social groups (Storey 13). More simply, hegemony may be seen as the way in which dominant power structures maintain dominance (Shoemaker and Reese 237). This quest for dominance on the part of those in power takes place on an ideological battleground. Gramsci emphasizes the part ideology plays within hegemony (237), and cultural theorist Roland Barthes describes ideology as the site for hegemonic struggles to restrict, fix, and produce connotations (Storey 6). Ideology is, therefore, not a static process; it "must continually absorb and incorporate disparate values" (Shoemaker and Reese 237). Likewise, hegemony, as a whole, remains a dynamic process. Although hegemony requires a high degree of consensus among subordinate groups, conflict still remains—and must remain—for hegemony to function (Storey 124), or, as cultural studies scholar Raymond Williams explains, hegemony "has continually to be renewed, recreated, defended, and modified" (Williams 112). The primary way that hegemony accomplishes its renewal, recreation, defense, and modification is through the dominant power structures' circulation of "commonsense" messages that advocate their right to rule (Collins 284). This commonsense aspect of hegemony illustrates the subtlety by which dominant groups maintain their influence—as their messages communicate to subordinate groups that deviating from the status quo would be illogical—and why a correlation between hegemony and feminist theory exists.

In regard to feminist theory, in the broadest sense, its principal goal is to expose and, therefore, ultimately eliminate power structures that limit women's agency. According to feminist scholars, feminist theory is a necessary component of feminism. Scott describes one of the primary reasons that feminism needs feminist theory: so that feminists "can analyze the workings of patriarchy in all its manifestations—ideological, institutional, organizational, [and] subjective" (378). As indicated in Scott's article title, "Deconstructing Equality-Versus-Difference: or, the Uses of Poststructuralist Theory for Feminism," she advocates a poststructuralist position within feminist theory; this position illustrates the complexity of both feminism and feminist theory. While all feminist scholars share the goal of expanding the degree of women's agency, as noted above, different forms of feminism (and therefore different forms of feminist theory) name different sources of power as the obstacle preventing the achievement of this goal. For poststructuralist feminists, such as Scott and Sandra Lee Bartky, the power that subordinates women is no longer institutionally based; instead, it is anonymous and widespread but no less effective in its oppression of women (Bartky 142). Other forms of feminism name a more institutionalized oppressor: radical feminists target patriarchy and advocate the creation of new social systems to replace it (Storey 135, Cirksena and Cuklanz 29); Marxist feminists impugn capitalism and argue for the eradication of class oppression, which will, in turn, eradicate gender oppression (Storey 135, Cirksena and Cuklanz 26); and liberal feminists denounce male prejudice and call for women's equality with men (Storey 135, Cirksena and Cuklanz 23).

As noted previously, hegemony and feminist theory are interdependent frameworks; their connection is twofold. First, the concept of hegemony informs feminist theory by offering a model that explains the construction and circulation of ideologies that contribute to the subordination of women. In other words, the hegemonic process relies on the "manipulation of ideas, images, symbols, and ideologies" to shape public consciousness (Collins 285) about gender. The manipulation of these ideas, images, symbols, and ideologies is based on those racial, class, and sex ideals privileged by dominant social groups, *i.e.*, white, middle-class men are presented more favorably than those who lack these idealized identity markers (Lorber, *Paradoxes* 33). Hegemony then explains the process by which gender subordination operates. In turn, feminist theory informs the concept of hegemony by exploring the manifestation of dominant power structures vis-à-vis gender (whether those power structures are defined as patriarchy, capitalism, or male prejudice). Feminist theory, in this regard, influences the study of hegemony in the same way that, according to Stuart Hall in "Cultural Studies and Its Theoretical Legacies," it did cultural studies—by underscoring the centrality of gender (and sexuality) to the nature/workings of power itself (104). Gender is therefore an integral component around which hegemonic power is formed and from which it is executed.

Consequently, hegemony and feminist theory, as applied to disability studies, psychoanalytic theory, panopticism/surveillance, and critical legal studies, closely align with the analysis of superpowered women on television. These mutually reinforcing frameworks address the nature and circulation of cultural power, including which individuals and/or institutions hold and recognize such power and which means are used to maintain and reinvent it. Pursuant to the concepts addressed by this combined framework, this study employs a thematic analysis that considers the nature and circulation of power within the fictional worlds of superpowered women, including how these characters gain their powers, who recognizes their powers as power, and which methods are used to contain and/or control their abilities.

Thematic Analysis

Although representative television texts featuring superpowered women may be identified, *e.g.*, critical and cult favorite *Buffy the Vampire Slayer*, a thematic — versus a case-study — approach was selected for this study because the viewers of one series of this type are likely to view others. Thus, audience members do not read superpowered women on television based solely on the audience members' knowledge of a single text; intertextuality influences their impressions of any given series. As Janice Radway explains in "Reception Study: Ethnography and the Problems of Dispersed Audiences and Nomadic Subjects," an actively engaged audience member "fashions narratives, stories, objects and practices from myriad bits and pieces of prior cultural production" (362). Therefore, viewers of such series must be considered "nomads" (or nomadic readers) to borrow the term Henry Jenkins uses — a term, he, in turn, borrows from the work of de Certeau (Jenkins 513); therefore, the connections between these series become equally — or perhaps more — important than the content of any individual series itself.

Such connections, in terms of superpowered women on television, stem from *Bewitched*, the series that, as noted previously, launched the first superpowered woman on television. *Bewitched*, then, also can be credited with establishing narratives that many later series with similar characters have followed. Just as *Entertainment Weekly* television critic Ken Tucker has recognized *I Love Lucy* (CBS, 1951–57) as "practically invent[ing] slapstick domestic comedy" ("Ask the Critic" 102), so, too, can *Bewitched* be recognized for inventing many of the conventions of series featuring superpowered women. Such conventions, or themes, include the labeling of superpowered women as abnormal when their powers are witnessed; the expectation that superpowered women exhibit a high degree of selflessness and only use their powers in the service of others; the constant surveillance of superpowered women by neighbors, friends, or more formal institutions; and the subjection of superpowered women to biased traditional and/or supernatural systems of authority. These conventions, or themes, are explored throughout this study.

Section and Chapter Divisions

1964–1996

Chapter 1, "Samantha as Archetype," describes how *Bewitched* and its protagonist, Samantha Stephens, emerged in the wake of Betty Friedan's *The Feminine Mystique*. While Friedan's book urged women to explore interests outside of the home, Samantha embraced domesticity — marriage to the non-magical, and according to Phoebe, repressive Darrin, which required her to limit the use of her powers. *Bewitched*'s introduction of the supernatural into an otherwise conventional suburban setting aligned it with numerous other "fantastic sitcoms" during the 1960s and early 1970s (Spigel 119–20), many of which, like *Bewitched*, connected the supernatural with the feminine. However, *Bewitched*'s longevity set it apart from these other series, as the story of Samantha and Darrin's happy, albeit magically complicated, marriage played out over eight seasons. Samantha's portrayer, Elizabeth Montgomery, likewise, experienced a happy marriage throughout the show's run, a fact that was covered extensively by the popular press, which emphasized that Montgomery shared Samantha's secret to happiness: devotion to a man. Despite the series' premise (a witch's willingness to set aside her powers for domestic bliss) and the press' characterization of its star's "true" purpose in life, media and cultural critics have recognized the subversive aspects of the series — a woman of great power disrupting the suburban idyll and challenging patriarchy, although perhaps in limited and covert ways. *Bewitched*, apparently, set a precedent for sending mixed messages regarding women and power, as series featuring superpowered women that followed in the 1970s, most prominently *Wonder Woman* and *The Bionic Woman*, offered the same frustrating blend of powerful women in restrictive settings and storylines. Superpowered women did not fare any better in the 1980s and early 1990s, as no iconic series emerged and protagonists during this time period were dominated by male characters, restricted to the domestic sphere, spied upon, tested unduly, conscripted for their abilities, and coerced into keeping their powers secret.

1996–2006

Chapter 2, "Misreading the Superpowerful Female Body," contains an analysis of the question of "what" versus "who" a superpowered woman is that often occurs when a male television character learns of or witnesses a demonstration of her abilities. This recurrent narrative was established in *Bewitched*'s premiere when Darrin utters "You're a what?" after Samantha's wedding-night revelation that she is not the girl he thought he had married, but, in fact, a witch ("I, Darrin, Take This Witch, Samantha"). As this narrative has developed in series featuring superpowered women, the male character, in the face of such female power, is in disbelief; he doubts *what* the superpowered woman *is*. As she is superpowerful, she cannot simply be labeled "woman"; therefore, she is deemed (and often feared as) a "freak"—despite her usually hyper-sexualized/feminized appearance. The fact that these characters were portrayed by conventionally attractive actresses with model-perfect bodies underscores this concept; all women with powerful bodies, even those who can pass as beauties, are actually freaks. This "enfreakment" (Thomson, *Freakery* 10) of superpowered women therefore resembles the experiences of female athletes, feminists, and other women who allegedly have strayed from traditional gender roles. The relegation of superpowered or actual women from subjects to objects via this enfreakment causes them to question their normalcy, fear revealing their true selves, and, at times, deny themselves personal fulfillment, thus encouraging these characters and their viewers to perform femininity in a culturally expected manner.

Next, Chapter 3, "Masquerade of Selflessness," explores the recurrent narrative of superpowered women facing near disaster when they attempt to evade their purposes, as their powers often demand that they help and protect those around them at all times. While Samantha does not have such a calling, she does attempt to put Darrin's—and later her children's—needs above her own; she rarely, if ever, pursues a personal agenda. For more contemporary superpowered women on television, their purposes are often clear. Despite these characters' heroic feats, though, they do not wear traditional superhero costumes; instead, they are masked by their responsibility. The absence of literal masking heightens these characters' performances of femininity. In fact, superpowered women enact a masquerade of selflessness to such a degree that they face repercussions for even temporarily privileging the personal. Furthermore, these characters' inability to take off their heroic personae is underscored by storylines in which physical masking results in danger to themselves and others. Superpowered women's guise of selflessness, then, results in a circumscribed use of their abilities, just as Samantha's witchcraft is limited to the improvement of the domestic sphere. In fact, the powers held by women in some gilded-age series are not extraordinary abilities in an active, physical sense, but instead the characters' willingness/ability to be selfless—to serve as conduits or instruments for some higher power. The prevalence of such scenarios in series that feature superpowered women suggests the rightness of women taking on such responsibility, perhaps then communicating to the series' predominantly female viewers that they, too, should enact their own masquerade of selflessness—albeit to a lesser degree (since they do not have to save the world, merely their homes and families). Like their superpowered counterparts on television, women experience a high degree of anxiety in their attempts to meet cultural expectations of selflessness, and those who do not fulfill their caring responsibilities to the degree that society demands, whether by choice (being a working parent) or by some force beyond their control (being mentally ill), are met with reproach.

Chapter 4, "Surveillance of Female Superpower," examines how superpowered women are often under the watchful eyes of friends, family members, the authorities, the press, and/or even spouses/lovers; surveillance, then, serves as one method to enforce the selflessness addressed in the previous chapter. On *Bewitched*, these watchful eyes most often belong to nosy neighbor Gladys Kravitz, who is certain that there is something unusual occurring within the Stephens's household; although, at times, such spying eyes belong to members of the Witches Council, who disapprove of Samantha's integration into the mortal world. Likewise, in more recent series featuring superpowered women, this surveillance may be conducted informally by neighbors, friends, and family members, or more formally by some type of institution. Regardless of the formality of the surveillance, this constant observation renders the powers of these characters less a cause for celebration than for inconvenience, paranoia, danger, and a mechanism by which they can be controlled. Such surveillance manifests itself in real women's lives in a similar fashion, as subjection to a male gaze or that of some other hegemonic power structure can include self-censorship, exposure to harassment, and/or a limiting of independence. This real-life surveillance can occur with pregnant women, as these women are, at all times, publicly scrutinized to ensure the privileging of their unborn children's needs above their own (Balsamo 110); with working women, as more female employees than male occupy non–closed-door workspaces (Spain 443); or with women in general, as cultural expectations for appearance and behavior are established by an invisible, yet omnipresent, male gaze (Bartky 140). The pervasiveness of the surveillance of women both on and off screen conveys to viewers that such a ubiquitous gaze is inevitable; hence, it should be accepted, since it cannot be avoided even in the fantastic worlds inhabited by superpowered women.

Then, Chapter 5, "Female Empowerment on Trial," considers how superpowered women are subject to both traditional and supernatural authorities that censor their autonomy. Such subjection is evident in *Bewitched*, as representatives from the Witches Council test Samantha's daughter Tabitha's powers and insist that said progeny attend witches' school ("Witches and Warlocks Are My Favorite Things"); the same Council later temporarily strips Samantha of her powers in an attempt to force her to leave mortal husband Darrin ("Samantha's Power Failure"). Similarly, in more contemporary series, the pronouncements of these authorities may include a restriction or removal of the superpowered women's powers. In addition, these characters may face public trials to reinforce social structures and/or to make superpowered women examples of those whose abilities must be dangerous since such abilities conflict with or challenge the powers that be. While men with such abilities initially may also be considered dangerous, their public trials generally result in their accusers' acceptance of their abilities. Furthermore, superpowered men may benefit from associations with traditional systems of law and order and may be able to manipulate these systems in ways not afforded their female counterparts.[9] Likewise, superpowered men rarely answer to sanctioning institutions the way that superpowered women do. What really is on trial then is superpowered women's ability to be fully recognized subjects; trials or other forms of subjection under the law serve as periodic repositionings of these characters from the active subjects they must be in order to function as protagonists to the more submissive—or at least passive—objects they must become to undergo these trials. These fictional trials of superpowered women recall the real-life trials of such powerful women as Martha Stewart, Oprah Winfrey, and Rosie O'Donnell. When these powerful and high-profile women stood trial for their alleged crimes (Stewart alone of the three faced criminal charges—the other two were civil cases), their worthiness as women to hold such power was standing trial as well. For viewers of superpowered women's fictional trials or coverage of celebrities' actual ones, the message is clear: the law as a cultural institution rarely recognizes women's authority; instead, it often serves as a mechanism to curtail that authority or question women's right to hold such influence in the first place.

2006–2011

Chapter 6, "Sacrifice and Sanctuary," explores the continued presence of superpowered women on television following the gilded age. While numerous superpowered women made their television debut during this time period, they were often members of mixed-sex superpowered ensembles rather than solo acts or were outnumbered by superpowered men. These more contemporary superpowered women face constraints similar to their predecessors. They, too, are called freaks, expected to be selfless, put under surveillance, and judged or tested unfairly. In addition, this more recent era also introduced a new/old theme for superpowered women—that of seeking sanctuary. These sanctuaries often connect superpowered women to a re-imagined domestic sphere, as they serve as symbols of home and family, even if those homes and families are not traditional ones. This emergent theme in series featuring superpowered women paralleled the real-life trend of a "new domesticity" (Stiehm, "New Domesticity") that includes women embracing household activities. Also new to this more contemporary era is superpowered women's tendency to "choose" their fates, especially choosing to be self-sacrificing. This recurring rhetoric of choice is actually rhetoric of false choice, as the choices available to superpowered women are limited and/or trivial. Therefore, this new era, while seemingly progressive, failed to present empowered female characters, just as the gilded age had.

Finally, the conclusion addresses the significance of contemporary series featuring superpowered women, considering why these series are appealing to their female viewers despite limitations placed on the protagonists' empowerment. The constrictions placed on the abilities of superpowered women can be traced to the origin of this character on *Bewitched* in 1964. An overview of the television appearances of this character type from its origin to 2011 indicates that the popularity and presentation of superpowered women parallel the gains and setbacks of the feminist movement. The most recent series featuring superpowered women even have much in common with their 1960s predecessors, as the series from that decade and many from this one focus on the consequences of introducing an element of the supernatural, *i.e.*, a superpowered woman, into an otherwise realistic and domestic setting. With all television series featuring superpowered women, both past and present, the paradoxical nature of these iconic characters — female characters who possess tremendous power while simultaneously experiencing limitations on that power — calls into question the use of the term "empowerment" within feminist rhetoric, since such a term implies that power must be granted or sanctioned rather than held or embodied, as it is with superpowered women.[10] The nearly five decades of television's superpowered women therefore indicate that women's empowerment cannot be imagined even in series that contain elements of the fantastic, thus reinforcing the status quo for female television viewers, rather than serving as empowering texts.

The marginalization of superpowered women — and the equating of constrained abilities with the feminine — offers viewers a subtle reinforcement of hegemonic power structures — it is a backhanded bestowal of power. Female empowerment, then, cannot be represented fully or even imagined, as even the most innately powered women depicted on television must concern themselves with being called freaks, face reproach for even temporarily privileging the personal, elude formal and informal surveillance, undergo trials not afforded their male counterparts, and continue to be associated with the domestic sphere (although a nontraditional one). So, to paraphrase Phoebe's summary of *Bewitched*'s Darrin's repression of Samantha's powers ("Lost and Bound"), is this the way it has to be?

CHAPTER 1

Samantha as Archetype

The problem lay buried, unspoken, for many years in the minds of American women. It was a strange stirring, a sense of dissatisfaction, a yearning that women suffered in the middle of the twentieth century in the United States. Each suburban wife struggled with it alone. As she made the beds, shopped for groceries, matched slipcover material, ate peanut butter sandwiches with her children, chauffeured Cub Scouts and Brownies, lay beside her husband at night—she was afraid to ask even of herself the silent question—"Is this all?"—Friedan 15

SAMANTHA: I happen to think that cooking on a stove is more fun than using witchcraft. I also enjoy taking care of my husband and my child in the everyday, mortal way. If I didn't, I wouldn't be here.—*Bewitched*, "The No-Harm Charm"

Here was a housewife [Samantha] with logical and creative ideas about how to make the world better, and with an ability to act on those ideas and get them a fair hearing, even if she had to do so through her bumbling surrogate, Darrin.—Douglas 131

The Fantastic Sitcom

In September 1964, in the wake of Betty Friedan's *The Feminine Mystique* (1963), which urged suburban housewives to "no longer ignore that voice within [...] that says: 'I want something more than my husband and my children and my home'" (32), ABC debuted *Bewitched*, a sitcom, as noted previously, about a woman, Samantha, who already has that "something more" (witchcraft) but is willing to relinquish her "something" for the assurance of husband (advertising-executive Darrin) and home (in suburban Westport, Connecticut).

With *Bewitched*, production company Screen Gems offered viewers a twist—or, in this case, a "twitch," as Samantha makes magic happen with a twitch of her nose—on the traditional "boy-meets-girl, boy-marries-girl" plotline. In *Bewitched*, Darrin does indeed meet and marry the girl, but learns, from Samantha's confession on their wedding night (post-vows/pre-consummation), that the girl happens to be "a real-live, house-haunting, broom-riding, cauldron-stirring, card-carrying witch" ("I, Darrin, Take This Witch, Samantha"). After recovering from his initial shock, Darrin declares his love for Samantha; however, he stipulates that for them to stay together Samantha must no longer use witchcraft and become a "normal" housewife. Samantha happily complies:

> DARRIN: I mean you're going to have to learn to be a suburban housewife.
> SAMANTHA: I'll learn. You'll see. I'll learn.
> DARRIN: Now, you'll have to learn to cook. And keep house. And go to my mother's house for dinner every Friday night.
> SAMANTHA: Darling, it sounds wonderful. And soon we'll be a normal, happy couple with no problems. Just like everybody else ["I, Darrin, Take This Witch, Samantha"].

Despite this first-episode promise to forego her powers for domestic harmony, Mrs. Darrin Stephens finds many an occasion to practice her magical abilities. In her efforts to fulfill the second half of her promise, Samantha often disregards the first half and resorts to witchcraft to be a more efficient homemaker and to assist Darrin in his various professional endeavors; such help generally leads to further complications in Darrin's life, thus more magic is required to resolve the increasingly convoluted situations found in this comedy. Darrin is so adamant about the absence of witchcraft in their lives that Samantha's magical maneuvering is often conducted without Darrin's knowledge (at least initially).

Bewitched's supernatural variation on the situation comedy proved to be a successful invention on the genre, as the "fantastic sitcom," according to Lynn Spigel in *Welcome to the Dreamhouse: Popular Media and Postwar Suburbs*, began replacing, around the time of *Bewitched*'s debut, "classic family sitcoms" (62–63, 118–19), such as *Leave It to Beaver* (ABC and CBS, 1957–63) and *Father Knows Best* (ABC, CBS, and NBC, 1954–63). *Bewitched* joined or preceded on the airwaves such fantastic sitcoms as *Mr. Ed* and *My Favorite Martian*, as noted in the Introduction, as well as *My Living Doll*, *The Munsters* (CBS, 1964–66), *The Addams Family* (ABC, 1964–66), *I Dream of Jeannie*, *My Mother the Car* (NBC, 1965–66), *The Flying Nun* (ABC, 1967–70), and *The Girl with Something Extra* (NBC, 1973–74). While many of the fantastic sitcoms contained male characters with a connection to the supernatural, such as the martian Martin from *My Favorite Martian* or the equine title character of *Mr. Ed*, as referenced previously, Spigel notes that often these sitcoms equated their alien elements with the decidedly female — "Jeannies, witches, and sexy robots" (125) or, in the case of *My Mother the Car*, a 1928 Porter automobile.

Therefore, during *Bewitched*'s run (and shortly after), the television airwaves included not only suburban housewife witch Samantha, but also *My Living Doll*'s sexy and fully programmable female robot, *I Dream of Jeannie*'s wish-granting and harem-pants-clad genie, *My Mother the Car*'s distinctly feminine and communicative automobile, *The Flying Nun*'s novitiate aviatrix who piloted her habit rather than an aircraft, and *The Girl with Something Extra*'s mind-reading newlywed (who, like Samantha, made a wedding-night confession about her ability) (Brooks and Marsh 538). While the majority of these series were short-lived, lasting one to three seasons (or five in the case of *I Dream of Jeannie*), *Bewitched* had greater longevity, airing eight seasons (1964–72). Viewers tuned in week after week to see Samantha twitch her nose to make objects appear or disappear, transport herself from location to location, or instantly complete household chores without the risk of dish-pan hands or dirt under her fingernails. Samantha primarily employed her magical powers with the intention of bettering the lot of the man in her life; despite the fact that Samantha could have twitched Darrin away if she so desired, this superpowered woman did her best to use her abilities according to the regulations set forth by this male authority figure in her life — they were "a normal, happy couple."

The Happy Housewife (Super)Heroine[1]

Samantha and Darrin's not-so-normal, but happy, story of couple-dom unfolded over 254 episodes, and, despite revolving lead-ins over the years that ranged from *My Three Sons* (ABC and CBS, 1960–72) to *The Flying Nun* to *That Girl* (ABC, 1966–71), *Bewitched* became ABC's "biggest hit" up to that time (Brooks and Marsh 134, 1587, 1590, 1592). In fact, *Bewitched* reached as high as number two in the ratings for its first season and remained in the top twenty-five for the next five seasons (1684–85). *Bewitched*'s ratings popularity translated into significant media coverage for the series, much of which focused on Samantha's portrayer's, Elizabeth (Liz) Montgomery's, relationship to husband William (Bill) Asher, a *Bewitched* producer/director, and that real-life love story's parallels to the series' appeal — that of a woman finding happiness through devotion to a man.

Magazine articles about Montgomery during *Bewitched*'s original run often read like a fairytale, complete with the requisite happy ending. Montgomery's high-profile childhood was generally mentioned (she was the daughter of actor Robert Montgomery), as were her two previous marriages (to socialite Freddie Cammann and actor Gig Young). According to these articles, Liz had found true love at last with Bill. By many accounts, the "Ashers" had an ideal marriage. A 1964 *TV Guide* article, "Double, Double Toil and Trouble," mentioned the fondness the Ashers had for "humming along to Broadway musical scores on the phonograph" (Lewis 22–23), while a 1965 *Saturday Evening Post* article, "Samantha Gets Her Way," described the Ashers' weekends of attending football games, riding bikes, shopping for antiques, and taking turns cooking beef Stroganoff (Hyams 32). By 1967, a *TV Guide* article titled "Rough, Tough, and Delightful" compared the Ashers to the Kennedys and described them as "two people in love" who "after nearly four years of marriage, and a siege of togetherness unequaled since the last Siamese twins [...] seem to *like* each other" (Hano 20).

As much of that "siege of togetherness" occurred on the *Bewitched* set, the press coverage also focused on the Ashers' work-place relationship, which was described in equally glowing terms to their home life. Asher was characterized by *TV Guide* as a "sympathetic morale booster" for Montgomery during rehearsal and production, with the couple blowing kisses to one another on set and Asher whistling "to assess his wife's charms from a distance" (Lewis 22). During long days on the set, Montgomery, according to a 1969 *Good Housekeeping* article, "The Secret Magic of Elizabeth Montgomery," "invariably f[ound] herself bolstered by the nearness of Bill" (Wilkie 71). *TV Guide* even quoted Montgomery as saying, "The only problems we [she and Asher] have are when we're not together" (Lewis 23).

Based on these articles, the Ashers' togetherness not only brought happiness to Montgomery's life but eclipsed all other aspects of that life. As a 1965 *Look* magazine article titled "Home-Model Witch" reported, "Marriage to director Bill Asher, her third, and their child, her first, seem almost the only real parts of Liz's life. Everything else — the series, her personal success, old friends and the love and loyalty of 39 million viewers — is slightly out of focus" (79). Likewise, *Good Housekeeping* quoted Montgomery as saying "Bill is really ... well ... my life. [...] Or something" (Wilkie 73).

The Ashers' marriage, at home or on set, and Montgomery's prioritization of that marriage, according to the press coverage, resembled the relationship and spousal roles of the fictional Darrin and Samantha Stephens. For example, *Look* noted that Montgomery once proudly explained, "There's one thing that makes Samantha easy to play. [...] She's as much in love with Darrin as I am with Bill" ("Home-Model Witch" 79), while *Good Housekeeping* quoted Asher as stating, "There's a parallel between the Stephens' marriage and ours. In other words, it's a love story" (Wilkie 56). Based on such coverage, the Ashers' real-life love story was clearly defined along traditional gender lines.

Montgomery, the press attested, happily assumed the role of housewife and mother just as Samantha did. Such coverage was careful to describe Montgomery's domestic duties. *The Saturday Evening Post* reported that she woke at 5:30 A.M., dressed in a terry-cloth housecoat, and prepared orange juice and coffee for Asher (who breakfasted in bed) before leaving for the studio; in other words, Montgomery, "like most housewives," had "a daily routine that would hospitalize a husband" (Hyams 32). *Look* magazine noted the Montgomery "resent[ed]" this difficult daily routine (that included studio work), as it cut into her family time ("Home-Model Witch" 79), while a 1965 *TV Radio Mirror* article, "You Know Her as Witch ... Now Meet Her as a Woman," recounted that if Montgomery were pressed to choose between family and career, she "would rather be a hit as wife and mother," just as her alter ego would "prefer lighting a fire in her man's heart to cooking up a brew to enchant the rest of the world" (Field 42). This article also cited Montgomery's opinion that any woman would choose "home and family over career"; those women that "choose a life of competition with men in the market-place," according to Montgomery, do so because of extreme circumstances, like an illness in the family or some "inner drive for success that's caused by a childhood of frustration" (Field 42–43).

Montgomery's philosophy on the joys of marriage and family also included recognition of Asher as patriarch; just as the press coverage equated Montgomery with housewife Samantha, so, too, did it equate Asher with familial voice of authority Darrin. *The Saturday Evening Post* described Asher as Montgomery's "prize"—"a husband with a mind of his own who can stand just as tall as her father" (Hyams 32), while *TV Guide* noted that "for a reasonably headstrong girl, she [Montgomery] defers to her husband in nearly all matters" (Hano 21). This article continued to explain that Montgomery's "deference to her husband" constituted a "return to the double standard," as Montgomery noted that if she were asked to travel for a publicity trip and Asher could not accompany her, then she would not go. The same, however, would not hold true in reverse; according to Montgomery, "It's all right for the man to go off by himself. The man is head of the family" (21).

Such descriptions of the Ashers' strict separation of gender roles within their marriage corresponded to descriptions of *Bewitched*'s "true" premise and appeal to viewers. According to Asher, as noted by *Good Housekeeping*, the "basic appeal" of *Bewitched*, "besides Elizabeth [...] is the marriage—real and warm and good" (Wilkie 56). *TV Guide* attributed a more in-depth explanation of the series' premise to Asher:

> The show [...] portrays a mixed marriage that overcomes by love the enormous obstacles in its path. Samantha, in her new role as housewife, represents the true values in life. Material gains mean nothing to her. She can have anything she wants

through witchcraft, yet she'd rather scrub the kitchen floor on her hands and knees for the man she loves. It is emotional satisfaction she craves [Hano 22].

The Ashers' opinion of the show seemed to be shared by others, as producer Danny Arnold was quoted in a 1965 *TV Guide* article about Dick York (who originally portrayed Darrin), "He's Almost Invisible in the Glare of Success": "People are sympathetic to the witch solely because of her relation to him [Darrin]. A witch who is interested in being a housewife to an American male is interesting. If she just went around being a witch, nobody would care. He supplies the motive for everything she does" (Efron 20). Therefore, press coverage of *Bewitched*/Montgomery from 1964 to 1972 described the actress and her supernatural alter ego as deriving their raison d'être from the man in their lives, with little discussion of how their talents/powers were (or could be) applied outside of the domestic sphere.

Subversion in the Suburbs?

Despite this less-than-empowering presentation of *Bewitched*'s protagonist and her portrayer during the show's initial run, the series' enduring popularity (it became nationally syndicated in 1973, most notably airing on Nick at Nite beginning in 1989 [Pilato 106] and later joining the TV Land lineup) coupled with its superpowered heroine has garnered positive critical attention in recent years. More specifically, media and cultural scholars suggest that the sitcom presented a satirical perspective on suburbia and actually challenged patriarchy, thus reflecting the then-emergent second wave of feminism. As Steve Cox writes in "Strictly Taboo," a chapter devoted to *Bewitched* within his tribute book to *Bewitched*'s "sister" show, *I Dream of Jeannie*, *Bewitched* is "now considered by many critics and popular culture historians a landmark for women" (269). For some critics, *Bewitched* was a "landmark for women" because of its break from — or at least its reconsideration of — the traditional domestic-based sitcom. For other critics, the show was progressive because Samantha had the ability to exert influence both within and outside of the home and because she *chose* her role as housewife (and later as mother).

As a fantastic sitcom, *Bewitched*'s premise includes supernatural divergence from the domestic comedies that preceded it (and/or overlapped with its time frame), a divergence that has been interpreted as a satire of the suburban lifestyle idealized in the 1950s. Spigel argues that the introduction of Samantha's witchcraft into the domestic setting "problematized" that otherwise idyllic environment: "Samantha is a witch, and her supernatural powers recast the narrative situation so that the conventional becomes strange. [...]

Rather than portraying the future, the fantastic sitcoms presented critical views of contemporary suburban life by using tropes of science fiction to make the familial strange" (120, 122). This juxtaposition of the exotic with the familiar, according to Spigel, led viewers to "question the 'naturalness' of middle-class existence" and reconsider their acceptance of/compliance with the gender, class, and racial norms that were integral to suburban life (123). For Spigel, then, the very presence of a superpowered woman in suburbia subverted traditional gender, and other social, roles.

Samantha's move to the suburbs also has been read as an early televised affront to patriarchy. As David Allen Case notes in "Domesticating the Enemy: *Bewitched* and the Seventies Sitcom," "The very real threats to patriarchy emerging between 1964 and 1972 [in *Bewitched*] are presented in the guise of forces invading the suburban family from a supernatural (and, unavoidably, theological) world of apparitions and disappearances—forces brought to the marriage by the wife" (197). Since the central female character instigates change in the suburban landscape, Case argues that this is a display of power "beyond the control of The American Father who had Once Known Best (here, the feckless Darrin Stephens)" (197). According to Case, Samantha's powers indicated a questioning, if not an erosion, of the patriarchal family structure.

Similarly, in *Where the Girls Are: Growing Up Female with the Mass Media*, Susan J. Douglas contends that *Bewitched*'s fantastic scenario provided female viewers with a temporary escape from their male-dominated real lives. Douglas asserts that instead of Samantha confronting patriarchy on a weekly basis, it is Darrin who confronts an "endearing yet constantly troublesome matriarchy," as the magical powers held by his wife, mother-in-law, and other in-law witches "constantly threatened his professional status and his authority as head of the household" (127). Therefore, Douglas describes *Bewitched*'s premise as a "woman's dream" (127), one which Douglas and others have suggested includes Samantha as a female viewer's stand-in for influence outside of the home.

While women in the 1960s and 1970s were entering or re-entering the workforce as the feminist movement gained momentum, Samantha remained a "suburban housewife" ("I, Darrin, Take This Witch, Samantha") and—eventually—a mother (daughter Tabitha arrived in season two and son Adam in season six). However, according to Helford, *Bewitched*'s and *I Dream of Jeannie*'s protagonists metaphorically represented female viewers' yearning for fulfillment beyond the home. She writes, "Neither *Bewitched*'s Samantha nor *I Dream of Jeannine*'s Jeannie work outside the home, but both can be read as symbolic articulations of women's (at least white, middle-class women's) aspirations for respect in roles other than wife and mother" (2).

Zeisler, in contrast, finds the "increasingly outrageous premises" of such shows as *Bewitched* and *Jeannie* "way-too-obvious metaphors for womanly rebellion" (40), although Steven Stark concurs with Helford. In *Glued to the Set: The 60 Television Shows and Events That Made Us Who We Are Today*, Stark asserts that "the *real* theme of both shows [*Bewitched* and *I Dream of Jeannie*]" was "females testing the boundaries" (118).

One such boundary that was "tested" was Samantha's opportunity to *choose* her role as housewife. While this choice in and of itself did not seem to advance women's causes, John Bryant argues, in "Situation Comedy of the Sixties: The Evolution of a Popular Genre," that such a choice did indicate an improvement in women's representation on television: "Although her submission [to male authority] is dictated by the comedy formula, Samantha's ability to choose this safe restriction of her powers places her a small but important evolutionary step above earlier situation comedy heroines" (136). Case, too, cites Samantha's options, specifically those presented to her by her highly liberated mother, Endora, as significant for female viewers. As Case notes, Endora often tries to entice Samantha to leave the house for a trip to Paris or some other glamorous locale. Although Samantha often declines, Case argues that "Endora is also pleading with the viewers: for once, leave your vacuum behind and see the World [sic]" (198). Samantha's world, however, remains somewhat restricted; the young and fashionable Samantha generally sticks close to the presumed comforts of suburban Westport, while the older, garishly attired Endora frequents the four corners of the world.

Although scholarship on *Bewitched* recognizes its forward-thinking nature in terms of gender, it also acknowledges that this progression was rather limited and often surreptitious. For example, Bryant describes *Bewitched*, *I Dream of Jeannie*, and *The Flying Nun* as "early, covert portraits of 'liberated' women" (134), and Spigel notes that Samantha's use of her powers to do *housework* "became opportunities for displays of women's liberation" (63). Critical analyses of *Bewitched* have also referred to Samantha's appearance and manner as perhaps diluting the liberating elements of the show. As Douglas points out, "Young, slim, blond, and beautiful, with practical, intelligent ideas about what needed to be done in her community, yet a witch, Samantha stood at the intersection between middle-class definitions of the ideal young wife and rebelliousness against those definitions" (128). Similarly, Spigel indicates that Samantha's housewife guise probably assuaged the audience's anxieties about shifting family, social, and professional roles for women at that time (129). Despite such caveats about how progressive *Bewitched* was, Spigel still asserts that the series demonstrated to viewers that female power could not be completely contained (129).

On *Bewitched*, Samantha's mother, Endora (center), begins interfering in Samantha and Darrin's relationship on their wedding night. Endora laments Samantha's union with the non-magical Darrin (or "Durwood," as Endora often calls him), thinking her daughter has married beneath her (ABC/Photofest).

And Bewitched Begat...[2]

Following *Bewitched*, ABC attempted to duplicate *Bewitched*'s success with *Tabitha* (1977–78), a spin-off featuring Samantha and Darrin's magically inclined daughter, as well as Tabitha's brother, Adam, and Aunt Minerva (Brooks and Marsh 1351). The popularity of the fantastic sitcom, though, had waned, as only twelve episodes of *Tabitha* aired. During the latter half of the 1970s, the superpowered woman on television found more success outside the domestic sphere, as she now fought evil as a bona fide hero. Although some characters, such as *Electra-Woman and Dynagirl*[3] (ABC, 1976–77), failed to last more than a season, others achieved moderate success. *The Secrets of Isis*[4] (CBS, 1975–78), a live-action Saturday-morning series, chronicled the adventures of "dual person" Andrea Thomas, a bespectacled science teacher who can harness the powers of the "animals and the elements" through a 3000-year-old amulet to become the goddess Isis, "dedicated foe of evil, defender of the weak, champion of truth and justice" ("The Lights of Mystery Mountain"). Andrea's closest friends, colleague Rick and student Cindy, of course, do not realize Andrea is superhero Isis. After Isis saves the day in the series premiere, Rick, with predictable 1970s machismo, tells Andrea, "It's probably just as well [that she was not present during Isis's heroics]. There was a lot going on, and the excitement might have gotten to you"; Andrea replies, "You're right, Rick. At times like that, it's well that a woman isn't there to get in the way" ("The Lights of Mystery Mountain"). Andrea/Isis continued "to get in the way," fighting injustice and introducing younger viewers to a superpowered woman who employed her powers outside the home. However, most of these adventures revolved around Andrea/Isis helping Rick or her students in some way; in other words, she most often used her powers to assist her surrogate family, not unlike Samantha's magical support of her traditional brood.

While Isis kept Saturday mornings safe from injustice, *The Bionic Woman* and *Wonder Woman*[5] featured their protagonists, cyborg Jaime Sommers and Amazonian princess Diana, aka Wonder Woman, fighting prime-time crime (and, in the case of Wonder Woman's first season, the Nazis) in hand-to-hand, or, more specifically, hand-to-bionic arm and hand-to-magical bracelets combat. These superpowered women were seeing the world — and using their powers — even further from home, ostensibly indicating a giant step forward in the evolution of television's superpowered women. Unfortunately for Jaime, Diana, and their female audience members, the outside world presented as many obstacles to their cultural empowerment as marriage and homemaking did for Samantha. In fact, Jaime is obligated to serve the Office of Scientific Investigation (OSI), the government agency that performed the surgery that equipped her with a bionic ear, arm, and legs, thus saving her life following a sky-diving accident (*The Six Million Dollar Man*, "The Bionic Woman, Part 2"), and Diana, after leaving her native Paradise Island and arriving in the United States, is exploited by a promoter who has Diana (in her Wonder Woman guise) display her Amazonian abilities for paying crowds, although Diana ultimately turns the tables on him when he tries to flee with her portion of the proceeds (*The New Original Wonder Woman*).

Although the Bionic Woman exercised more agency than Samantha or Jeannie, such agency was not without restrictions. As Inness notes in *Tough Girls*, *The Bionic Woman* depicted its protagonist with a high degree of self-sufficiency, at least in comparison to those characters featured by that series' contemporaries, such as the titular trio of *Charlie's Angels* (ABC, 1976–81) (45), while Tricia Jenkins, in "Nationalism and Gender: The 1970s, *The Six Million Dollar Man*, and *The Bionic Woman*," contends that "patriarchal supervision and the use of technology controlled and designed by men" are fundamental components of both *Charlie's Angels* and *The Bionic Woman* (103). Inness, however, aligns more closely with Jenkins when she describes how Jaime's tough and independent persona was softened in a number of ways (45–48); for example, Jaime is a successful secret agent on the weekends, but her weekday job is schoolteacher, a more "socially acceptable" (46) profession for a woman (although she finds occasion to employ her bionic abilities in the classroom at times [*The Six Million Dollar Man*, "Welcome Home Jaime"]), and her weekend missions often include undercover work that position her in traditional roles for women, such as nun, governess, and beauty contestant (Inness 47). Furthermore, as Douglas points out, secret agent Jaime still took her orders from a man, Oscar Goldman, and her best friend was a dog, albeit a bionic one (218). Oscar was not the only man in Jaime's life who guided her outcomes; in fact, it was boyfriend Steve Austin, the protagonist of *The Six Million Dollar Man* (ABC, 1974–78), who was responsible for Jaime's bionic status in the first place.

Prior to the debut of *The Bionic Woman*, the character of Jaime Sommers appeared in five episodes (two in season two and three in season three) of *The Six Million Dollar Man*; Steve's female counterpart was added to boost ratings (Jenkins 93) and eventually became popular enough for a spin-off. Jaime and Steve had grown up together in Ojai, California; in fact, Steve's mother and step-father became Jamie's legal guardians when her parents died during her teen years ("Welcome Home, Jaime"). When Steve and Jaime both return to Ojai for a visit — he as an acclaimed former astronaut, and she as a "lady tennis pro," as Steve refers to her — they renew their friendship and begin a romantic relationship (as depicted in a montage set to the musical stylings of Lee Majors, Steve's portrayer, singing "Sweet Jaime, I Love You") ("The Bionic Woman, Part 1"). Their idyllic love story takes a tragic turn when a skydiving date ends with Jaime taking a terrible fall due to a malfunctioning parachute. As a semi-conscious and dying Jaime weakly tells Steve, "It's over," he says he might have "a way" and asks if she trusts him; she nods. Steve then convinces Oscar to approve the surgery, assuring Oscar that Jaime will be a worthy OSI agent, that her tennis pro cover will be useful. When Jaime regains consciousness following the surgery, she is at first angry with Steve and is self-loathing: "What did you let them do to me?"; and "I don't want to be a freak. [...] Why didn't you just let me die?" ("The Bionic Woman, Part I"). After Steve demonstrates his bionic abilities, Jaime eventually comes to accept hers— she is a cyborg (although that term is not used in the series). According to Jenkins, Jaime's identity as a cyborg could have allowed the series to challenge, as radical feminists do, the essentialist notion that women's bodies determine their social roles; the series fell short on this count, though, as Jaime was depicted as decidedly gendered (104–5), despite her superhuman strength, speed, and hearing. In fact, Kenny Johnson, *The Bionic Woman*'s director, writer, and executive producer, acknowledged that Jaime's superpowers were downplayed purposely so as not to alienate male viewers: "We wanted to create a woman who was obviously physically powerful and yet not threatening to some guy who might want to sit down and have a cup of tea with her.... So we carefully crafted it so that she never actually hit anybody. She would pull a rug out from under them or cause something to fall on them..." (qtd. in Stowe qtd. in Jenkins 106).

While, extratextually, male viewers could safely contemplate tea dates with Jaime, intratextually, Steve proposes more than shared beverages: following Jaime's bionic surgery, Steve and Jaime become engaged. All seems well until Jaime's body starts rejecting the bionics, and she seemingly dies on the operating table ("The Bionic Woman, Part 2"). It was *The Six Million Dollar Man*'s creators' original intent to kill off Jaime via this episode; however, more than 200,000 letters to ABC from fans protesting the character's death made them change their minds (Jenkins 94). Thus, the OSI team is able to resuscitate Jamie (a fact that the team does not initially share with Steve), although the back-from-the dead Jaime has amnesia until yet another risky surgery restores her memory. Following that surgery, she returns to Ojai, settles into an apartment on Steve's parents' property, begins teaching middle school, and talks to Steve about starting over. When Oscar tells Jaime that she has been through enough and no longer needs to work for the OSI, Jaime tells him that he should contact her for a mission soon ("Welcome Home, Jaime"). Jenkins explains that Jaime's dutiful patriarchy, equal to Steve's in *The Six Million Dollar Man*, reflected U.S. Cold War mentality, as the two bionic characters modeled proper beliefs and behaviors for American citizens. Furthermore, Jenkins argues that "*The Bionic Woman* negotiated radical and liberal feminism through the use of a cybernetic-spy that literally possessed the ability to overthrow patriarchal institutions but instead adhered to dominant concepts of femininity in order to project a desirable image of American capitalism during the Cold War" (Jenkins 97). Thus, *The Bionic Woman*, while indicating a few quasi-feminist steps forward from *Bewitched*, failed to fulfill its potential as a truly resistant text, as Jaime's purpose — and very identity — are circumscribed by individual males, like Oscar and Steve, and patriarchal institutions, like the OSI, not to mention American capitalism.

Although Wonder Woman's orders did not come from a man, her purpose in life, like Jaime's, did. Amazonian princess Diana discovers an injured man on the shores of her Paradise Island home (an uncharted, all-woman idyll near the "Devil's Triangle"); the man, Major Steve Trevor, had parachuted to the Amazons' island after his plane was shot down by the Nazis (*The New Original Wonder Woman*). Zeisler contends that Diana's almost-immediate romantic interest in Major Trevor mitigated any unease the audience might have had "about the whole Amazon thing" (79). Motivated by her feelings for Steve, Diana wins the honor of escorting the Major back to the United States by prevailing in an athletic tournament designed by her mother, even though her mother has forbidden her to compete, as the Queen is not willing to risk her daughter (leaving Paradise Island means leaving immortality behind) for the sake of a "savage" (read: man) (*The New Original Wonder Woman*). Once in the United States, Wonder Woman employs her nearly limitless abilities, including mimicking voices, lifting cars, and surviving gunshots at point-blank range (her bracelets are as practical as they are fashionable), for the purpose of serving and protecting both Steve and her newly adopted country — an allegiance evidenced by her costume, which Douglas terms "Old Glory short shorts" (218),[6] Zeisler calls "male gaze-tastic" (80), and a more recent superpowered woman (George from *Dead Like Me* [Showtime, 2003–04]) called "hooker boots and a swimsuit" ("Last Call"). When not saving Steve or the country dressed in said "short shorts" (as the theme song notes, "in your satin tights/fighting for your rights") and eagle-emblazoned bustier (one male character in the pilot remarked to Wonder Woman that "Betty Grable looks like a boy compared to you" [*The New Original Wonder Woman*]), Diana serves as Steve's secretary. The Major, however, knows nothing of his assistant's alter ego (Diana wears glasses and her hair in a bun, while Wonder Woman does not) or her association with Paradise Island (the Major's eyes were bandaged during his stay with the Amazons, and he only briefly gained consciousness on the trip back to the United States) (*The New Original Wonder Woman*).

As both Inness and Douglas contend, Diana's double duty as secretary and savior left no time — and apparently no motivation — for the pursuit of her own interests (Inness, *Tough Girls* 47; Douglas 217). Thus, Wonder Woman has not captured viewers' imaginations in perhaps the same way that Superman (in his many incarnations has); Fingeroth sums up Wonder Woman's comic-book and television persona as "pleasant but not really all that interesting" (88), and Carrie, the extraordinary protagonist of a more recent series (*Unforgettable*, CBS, 2011–   ), notes of Wonder Woman, "I mean I always thought she was kind of boring" ("Heroes"). To be fair, though, Wonder Woman does attempt to educate (female) Nazis about the value of women in at least superficially feminist rhetoric: "[A]ny civilization that doesn't recognize the value of the female is doomed to destruction. Women are the wave of the future, and sisterhood is stronger than anything" (*The New Original Wonder Woman*) and "Perhaps now you'll appreciate it [democracy] and learn from your unwomanly mistakes" ("Wonder Woman Meets Baroness Von Gunther"). Wonder Women, of course, avoids "unwomanly mistakes," in both her mild-mannered secretary and costumed superhero guises; she is powerful, but remains beautiful and feminine (Zeisler 79).

So, like Jaime Sommers, Wonder Woman exhibited a degree of female—if not feminist—power previously unseen on television, but the characterization of the Amazon princess offered little improvement from the previous decade in regard to women's empowerment. As Douglas writes of *Wonder Woman*, "As in 1964, female power was still a secret power, kept under wraps, never discussed, used only in emergencies, never used for self-advancement," although it was not confined to the domestic sphere (218). Zeisler, in contrast, recognizes that, despite changes to the series in season two that disregarded Diana's "Amazon roots" and further underscored Wonder Woman as a sex symbol, viewers still recognized the character as a "beautiful superhero who happened to be female"; therefore, the character represented a "step forward in a decade when every step counted" (80). The feminist potential evident—although not exercised—in the fantastic sitcoms of the 1960s had, at worst, stagnated or, at best, inched ahead in the superhero series of the 1970s, perhaps reflecting anxiety over women and power generated by second-wave feminism. As real-life women fought to increase women's presence in traditionally male-dominated professions, expand women's legal rights, and strengthen women's political representation (Lorber, *Gender Inequality* 3) during the "Disco Decade," series featuring superpowered women failed to reflect such gains in equality, even via their fantastic premises.

Wonder Woman's costume, a gift from her mother, the Amazon queen, often draws more attention than the superheroine's incredible abilities, which include deflecting gunshots with her bracelets (ABC/Photofest).

Bionic Backlash?

Following the cancellation of *The Bionic Woman* in 1978 and *Wonder Woman* in 1979, the superpowered woman remained on television, but in a far less prominent way. During the 1980s, the adult version of this character type found little exposure or success on network television. Early in the "Me Decade," the hour-long drama *Tucker's Witch* (CBS, 1982–83) featured a magical woman named Amanda with unreliable powers as part of a husband-and-wife private-detective team (Muir 592). The series, which offered a supernatural, dramatic take on *Mr. & Mrs. North* (CBS and NBC, 1952–54), survived only one partial, hiatus-filled season (Brooks and Marsh 1429), and, as with *Bewitched* and *I Dream of Jeannie*, its title indicated that a masculine perspective prevailed. Following *Tucker's Witch*, *Jennifer Slept Here* (NBC, 1983–84) did not center around a masculine perspective, per se, but it did center around a superpowered woman employing her powers for a man's—or in this case, a teenage boy's—benefit. *Jennifer Slept Here*, a sitcom in the tradition of *Topper* (Brooks and Marsh 695), featured the ghost of Jennifer Farrell, the "world's most famous movie star." Jennifer haunts the transplanted New York family who now lives in her former California home. Teenage Joey is the only member of the family who can see and hear Jennifer, whose undead existence and resulting abilities (walking through walls, appearing, and disappearing) are dedicated to helping Joey adjust to his new home, much to his chagrin, since Jennifer becomes his constant companion ("Pilot"). As indicated by these series, representation of superpowered women on television in the early 1980s did not build upon the slight gains in female empowerment depicted by *The Bionic Woman* and *Wonder Woman* (although such gains were, of course, debatable); instead the potential for empowerment was replaced by the cutesiness of *Tucker's Witch* and the broad one-liners of *Jennifer Slept Here*.

The three other short-lived network series featuring superpowered female protagonists that rounded out the decade, *Something Is Out There* (NBC, 1988), *Nearly Departed* (NBC, 1989), and *Free Spirit* (ABC, 1989–90),[7] also failed to build on the potential of the previous decade. *Something Is Out There*, an hour-long science-fiction show based on a mini-series, paired a street-smart male detective named Jack with a mind-reading, laser-gun-toting, and jumpsuit-wearing alien named Ta'ra (Brooks and March 1269); although Ta'ra is the more powerful member of the duo, Jack provides the series opening narration and serves as Ta'ra's guide to all things Earth-related, including knock-knock jokes, throughout their crime-fighting adventures ("Gladiator"), making it more a fish-out-of-water tale than an exploration of female power. Sitcom *Nearly Departed* offered viewers a variation of *Jennifer*

Slept Here, with husband-and-wife ghosts (Grant and Claire Pritchard) haunting the family that moves into the couple's former home; the male ghost, however, has the more prominent role, as he can make contact with one of the family members (and was portrayed by Eric Idle of *Monty Python* fame) (Brooks and Marsh 966). While alien Ta'ra and ghosts Jennifer and Claire indicated a departure from the types of superpowered women on television in the 1960s and 1970s, *Free Spirit* returned to "classic" fantastic sitcom terrain, featuring a witch, who was, once again, consigned to the suburbs, this time as a nanny/housekeeper to a typical American family (Muir 596). The family's youngest child, Gene, wishes that someone would have time for him (as his divorced father, Thomas, and two teenage siblings, Robb and Jessie, often overlook him), and witch Winnie Goodwinn appears, explaining that every 100 years or so witches have to do community service. The unconventional Winnie, the titular "Free Spirit," pretends to have answered the ad Thomas placed for a housekeeper, and she soon falls in love with the kids and, perhaps, their father; thus, she decides to stay to "cook, clean, and keep up with the kids," although she does so via magical means whenever she can get away with it ("Pilot"). Winnie was, for all intents and purposes, the younger, babysitter version of *Bewitched*'s Samantha Stephens.

Neither *Free Spirit* nor the other 1980s network series lasted for more than a season, although syndicated series featuring superpowered girls or teens fared slightly better,[8] as both *Small Wonder* and *Out of This World* ran for four seasons. Sitcom *Small Wonder* presented the escapades of child robot "Vicki"; Vicki is really an experimental "VICI — Voice Input Child Identicon"—created by electronics expert Ted Lawson. Ted introduces Vicki to his wife, Joan, and son, Jamie, working on Vicki at home while he perfects her programming; Ted warns Joan and Jamie that they must keep Vicki a secret from nosy neighbors the Brindles (Brindle patriarch Brandon is a coworker of Ted's). Joan notes that adding Vicki to their family is "suddenly like having another child in the house," while Ted quips, "Only this time I gave birth" ("Vicki's Homecoming"). Jamie is delighted with the voice-activated robot, who, along with having mechanical super strength, has been programmed to know and do what a 10-year-old would; Jamie commands Vicki to carry out his household chores, and, when her literal processing of those commands causes trouble, he stores her in his toy cabinet ("Vicki's Homecoming"). Although Ted wonders if a robot raised as a child will be able to program itself and have real emotions ("The Neighbors"), Vicki remains programmable and is used at the convenience of her adoptive human family.

Overlapping with *Small Wonder* was *Out of This World*. *Out of This World* opens on the eve of Evie Garland's thirteenth birthday, with her mother,

Donna, asking if Evie has noticed any "powerful changes," like being able to see through walls, float in the air, make herself invisible, or "deep fry plastic" ("Evie's Thirteenth Birthday"). During Evie's birthday party the next day, she learns why her mother was asking such odd questions. After an inexplicable urge to put her index fingers together, Evie learns that she can freeze time (through another inexplicable urge, she learns she can unfreeze time by putting her palms together). Evie's mother is then forced to confess that Evie's absent father, Troy, is an alien from the planet Antareus (and not a spy like Donna had previously told Evie). Years ago, Troy had come to earth on a mission, fell in love with Donna, married her, and "blended life forms"; Evie, distressed by the news of her parentage, calls herself a "freak" and a "beast." Donna reassures Evie that her

Ted Larson's creation, robot child Vicki (the titular *Small Wonder*, right), becomes the fourth member of his family (along with son Jamie and wife Joan), although Vicki's penchant for following commands literally often causes chaos and draws the spying eyes of precocious neighbor Harriet Brindle (left) (20th Century–Fox/Photofest).

father is a wonderful — and handsome — man, and presents Evie with the gift Troy left for Evie for this occasion: a cube through which she can communicate with her father. Troy explains that on Antareus, thirteen is the age of maturity, and Evie now possess "the power to hold time in [her] hands"; if she uses that power wisely she will gain others ("Evie's Thirteenth Birthday"). By episode two, however, Evie learns that her power cannot be used whenever she wants. When she asks, "What good is having a power if you can't have fun with it," her mother responds, "It's for important things, not practical jokes," and her father withholds her power at a critical moment (when she is trying to cheat on a timed math test) as punishment for Evie's previous use of said power to win a spelling challenge and a softball game. Evie's father explains that any time she misuses her power, he can see it; her response is

"You're like one of those surveillance cameras at the bank" ("Playing with the Power"). Such surveillance prevents Evie from fully embracing her ability, since her more powerful father, if he deems her transgressions serious enough, can strip her of that ability.

The lack of network ratings success for series featuring superpowered women during the "Me Decade" echoed the backlash to the feminist movement prevalent in Reagan-era America; this veritable demotion of the superpowered woman was not surprising, since, as noted in the Introduction, the feminist superwoman icon of the 1970s became the symbol for failed feminism in the decade that followed (Faludi 77). Whether on short-lived network series or longer-lived syndicated ones, television's superpowered women in the 1980s, while perhaps not symbols of failed feminism, were derivative and even less empowered to use their abilities than their predecessors. These extraordinary women and girls were subjugated to the men in their lives, confined to the domestic sphere (literally in the case of Vicki's toy closet), and spied upon by overly curious neighbors and overly protective (if absentee) fathers.

Eclectic, Not Empowered

While the 1970s are nicknamed the "Disco Decade" and the 1980s the "Me Decade," the 1990s are not as easily characterized, as that decade brought with it the end of the Cold War, the start of the first Gulf War, the establishment of the World Wide Web, the rise of boy bands, and the devastation wrought by Hurricane Andrew, among other cultural milestones (or millstones, as the case may have been). Regarding this eclectic era, poet and critic Tom Paulin argued that "[n]ineties culture is about stress, solipsism and anxiety. If the 1980s was the 'me' decade, the 1990s has been the 'me, me' decade" (qtd. in "The 1990s in Review"). Television during the early 1990s reflected the eclectic nature of the decade, offering an array of superpowered female characters who ranged from angels to tattooed teenage alien fighters that certainly faced their share of stress and anxiety but were discouraged from adopting the solipsistic attitude of the day, as their powers were not fully realized or required them to know and consider others before themselves.

Television's first series with a superpowered woman in the "me, me" decade, *Mann & Machine* (NBC, 1992), had more than a few similarities to *Something Is Out There*, including a less-than-a-full-season run. This futuristic series featured a homicide detective named Bobby Mann and his partner, Eve, a new form of artificial intelligence that is capable of "learn[ing] to be human." Once again the world-weary male detective must guide his highly intelligent and powerful (Eve describes herself as "the brains and the muscle") but naïve-to-human-behavior female associate; Eve is intellectually advanced but has the emotional complexity of a seven-year-old and daydreams about "being human" ("Prototype"), thus rendering her an example of potential more so than empowerment. *Mann & Machine* was followed, two years later, by two series featuring angels: one successful and one not. *Touched by an Angel*, a long-running mainstay for CBS, focused on an apprentice angel named Monica, who, along with her supervisor, the angel Tess, travel across the United States to assist those in need; beginning in the second season, the male Angel of Death, Andrew, joins Monica and Tess on their journeys. Andrew serves "as a liaison from heaven" who has the ability to tell his female colleagues when it is or is not "someone's 'time.'" Monica and Tess, it appears, only have the power to assist others, as they employ "their common sense, concern, and the occasional minor miracle to help people improve themselves" (Brooks and Marsh 1414). *Heaven Help Us* (Syndicated, 1994) offered a similar, although racier and comedic premise; newlyweds Doug and Lexy perish in a plane crash on their way to their honeymoon (the two attempted to join the mile-high club while in a private plane). To earn their place in heaven, the couple has to help others, influencing them via "a sort of emotional osmosis" (Brooks and Marsh 598), surely the most passive ability ever held by a super-powered character — female or male — on television.

The superpowered women that emerged via half-hour kids- and teen-oriented fare in the early to mid–1990s had more active powers than their heavenly predecessors, but the way they gained their powers and/or the expectations or consequences that came with them were problematic. In *Mighty Morphin Power Rangers*[9] (FOX, 1993–95), a co-ed team of five teenagers is recruited by Zordon, an "interdimensional being," to battle intergalactic evil; each teen is granted the ability to call on the powers of a dinosaur to transform herself/himself (hence, "morphin") into a Power Ranger with exceptional fighting abilities (and a color-coded, helmeted costume that looks equally alien and equestrian). With such great powers, though, of course, comes great responsibility. Zordon explains that the Rangers may never use their powers for personal gain and they must keep their superpowered identities a secret ("Day of the Dumpster"). The similarly premised *Tattooed Teenage Alien Fighters from Beverly Hills* (USA, 1994–95) premiered a year later; in this *Power Rangers* "rip-off" (Brooks and Marsh 1360), a co-ed team of four teenagers is recruited to be Galactic Sentinels in a fight against evil aliens but sworn to keep their Sentinel identities a secret ("In the Beginning"). Likewise, the title character of *The Secret World of Alex Mack* (Nickelodeon, 1994–98) has to keep her abilities under wrap. On tomboy Alex's first and not-so-successful day of junior high (she feels she is "sinking" and laments that she is "such a geek"), she gains extraordinary abilities—such as being able to liquefy—after being exposed, via a truck crash, to "a barrel of gold stuff," otherwise known as GC161, a top-secret and, presumably, dangerous chemical. The truck driver, an employee of the company that created the chemical, realizes that there was a witness to the crash, and he and another employee search door to door to find that witness. Alex, with her sister's help and her GC161-fuled abilities, is able to evade identification, but lives in fear of becoming a guinea pig ("The Accident"). Although Alex fears exposure, she does embrace the fact that she is "not so average anymore" ("Hoop War"). Like Alex, there is nothing average about Lisa of *Weird Science* (USA, 1994–98). Lisa, a "PC genie," was created by teenage nerds Gary and Wyatt in their quest to learn about women. While Lisa has the ability to grant their every wish, she chooses not to and, at times, withholds her powers to teach them a lesson ("She's Alive"), demonstrating a degree of empowerment. However, Lisa owes her very existence to Gary and Wyatt and maintains a connection to them (she explains that she's a part of both of them ["She's Alive"]) that limits the use of her abilities. As in the 1980s, early 1990s series[10] featuring superpowered women did not introduce viewers to female characters with a high degree of empowerment; instead, the early 90s incarnations of these characters, like their predecessors, have to prove themselves to male authority figures, use their powers in the service of others (although well beyond the domestic sphere), and fear repercussions if their powers are revealed.

Entering the Gilded Age

From the mid–1990s to 2006, coinciding with the girl power movement associated with third-wave feminism, television series featuring superpowered women (and/or featuring ensembles with both superpowered women and men) could be found across the dial (network, cable, and premium channels) and across a number of styles (animation and live action), genres (situation comedy, science fiction, fantasy, adventure, and drama), and target audiences (children, adolescents, and adults), including *Sabrina, the Teenage Witch*, *Profiler* (NBC, 1996–2000), *3rd Rock from the Sun* (NBC, 1996–2001), *Leaving L.A.* (ABC, 1997), *Buffy the Vampire Slayer*, *Animorphs* (Nickelodeon, 1998–99), *Highlander: The Raven* (Syndicated, 1998–99), *The Wild Thornberrys* (Nickelodeon, 1998–2004), *The Powerpuff Girls* (Cartoon Network, 1998–2005), *Charmed, Roswell, The Others* (NBC, 2000), *Sheena* (Syndicated, 2000–01), *Dark Angel, Dead Last* (WB, 2001), *Witchblade*,[11] *Wolf Lake* (CBS and UPN, 2001–02), *Mutant X* (Syndicated, 2001–04), *Justice League Unlimited*[12] (Cartoon Network, 2001–06), *The Fairly OddParents* (Nickelodeon, 2001–), *Fire-*

fly, *Birds of Prey* (WB, 2002–03), *Dead Like Me*, *Tru Calling*, *That's So Raven* (Disney, 2003–07), *My Life as a Teenage Robot*, *Missing*[13] (Lifetime, 2003–06), *Joan of Arcadia*, *Wonderfalls* (FOX, 2004), *Point Pleasant* (FOX, 2005), *Medium*, and *Ghost Whisperer*. In addition to these series with title or featured female characters clearly embodied with supernatural or superhuman powers, series such as *Xena: Warrior Princess*, *Black Scorpion* (Sci-Fi, 2001), and *Alias* (ABC, 2001–06) also focused on physically impressive female characters who may have connections to the supernatural (*e.g.*, Sydney on *Alias* is the "Chosen One" referred to in a fifteenth-century prophecy)[14] or who encounter evil gods (as Xena does) or supervillains (as the Black Scorpion does) on a regular basis. These superpowered, female-centered series achieved varying degrees of success—for every multiple-season *Buffy the Vampire Slayer* (seven seasons), there were several single-season (or less-than-a-season) *Wonderfalls* (four episodes), and for every critically praised *Medium*, there were several critically panned *Birds of Prey*s; regardless, additional series were developed and aired. Beginning with *Sabrina, the Teenage Witch* in 1996 and concluding with the final episode of *Charmed* in 2006, superpowered woman after superpowered woman appeared on television, marking what should have been a golden age for this character type, but, instead became a gilded age, as these superpowered women channeled their foremother, *Bewitched*'s Samantha, exemplifying incredible power but limited empowerment. Thus, series that premiered between 1996 and 2006 followed the thematic patterns set by *Bewitched*: superpowered women were deemed freaks, held to a higher degree of selflessness than their male counterparts, kept under constant surveillance, and subjected to biased systems of authority.

CHAPTER 2

Misreading the Superpowerful Female Body

DINAH: I was a freak, and everybody knew it.—*Birds of Prey*, "Prey for the Hunter"

BUFFY: I guess I can't fight it. I'm a freak.—*Buffy the Vampire Slayer*, "What's My Line? Part 2"

BOY: Are you a freak?
YOUNG GWEN: I don't know.
BOY: Guess you don't look like one.
YOUNG GWEN: Thanks.—*Angel*, "Ground State"

"What the hell are you?"

In "Prey for the Hunter," the third episode of *Birds of Prey*, Helena, a half-human/half-metahuman, grouses to Barbara, her partner in crime fighting, that her—Helena's—superpowered efforts to rid the city of New Gotham of its non–law-abiding element prevent her from being like "other girls." Despite the fact that Helena, who uses the name "Huntress" while in superhero mode, is definitely not like other girls, as she possesses superior speed, strength, and jumping and fighting abilities (not to mention uncommon beauty), her musing about "trying [normality] on for size" indicates a privileging of her human heritage and a reluctance to identify too closely with her metahuman roots. While Barbara comments that such yearning for normalcy "doesn't sound like" Helena, viewers can link such insecurities to Helena's unspoken (at this point in the series) romantic interest in Jesse Reese, a New Gotham police detective.

While Reese finds Helena mysterious and is curious about her unusual abilities, he has concluded from their crossed paths and collaboration on previous cases that she is "no criminal." However, when a case arises that involves metahumans seemingly killed by their own powers, Reese's curiosity converts to suspicion and intolerance — due, in part, to the influence of his new partner, Morton, a closeted metahuman viewers learn is responsible for the killings. Morton confirms for Reese that metahumans indeed exist, citing as evidence his numerous past dealings with such "creatures"; in fact, Morton scoffs at the politically correct term "metahuman" when he claims "the real word for what they are is 'dangerous.'" Thus confronted with Morton's perspective, Reese, in turn, confronts Helena:

> REESE: It's true, isn't it? You're one of those meta-things, aren't you?
> HELENA: Things? You think I'm a thing?
> REESE: I don't know. Why don't you just tell me? What the hell are you? I mean you damn sure aren't normal.

Hurt and angry, Helena disappears when Reese's back is turned ("Prey for the Hunter").

Although Helena's passive-aggressive response is unusual for superpowered women on television during the 1996–2006 gilded era, since such characters generally reflect their postmodern origins by facing their opposition with popular-culture laden sarcasm or affected indifference, the confrontation that provoked Helena's disappearing act is all too familiar for this character type. Similar exchanges to this one between Helena and Reese also can be found on *Buffy the Vampire Slayer*, when Buffy's boyfriend, Riley, asks the Slayer "What are you?" after he observes her impressive dispatch of a group of demons (her response is "Capricorn on the cusp of Aquarius" ["Doomed"]); on *Angel*, when the titular vampire asks a thief named Gwen "What ... are you?" after he sees her manipulate electrical particles to disable a security system (her response is "I'm a freak" ["Ground State"]); on *Charmed*, when a criminal named Wike asks witch Piper "What are you?" after she blows up a hat he is holding with the wave of a hand (her response is to answer a subsequent question ["Trial by Magic"]); and on *Witchblade* (the telefilm that launched the series), when a murderer named Gallo asks homicide detective Sara "What the hell are you?" (and calls her a "freak") after he sees her fully powered by the witchblade (her response is "Justice" [*Witchblade*]). As demonstrated by these scenes, television series or episodes that featured female characters with supernatural or superhuman abilities from 1996 to 2006 often contained narratives in which a male character who witnesses a display of such extraordinary female power expresses his incredulity — often mingled with suspicion and intolerance, like Reese — with a "*What* are you?" In the face of such female power, the male character is in disbelief; he doubts *what* the superpowered woman *is*. As she is superpowerful, she cannot simply be labeled "woman." Therefore, she is deemed, and often feared as, a "freak"—despite her usually hyper-sexualized/feminized appearance—and subjected to all the negative repercussions associated with such a marginalizing term.

The relegation of superpowered women from subjects ("who"s) to objects ("what"s) limits their agency, a demotion demonstrated when Helena later tells Reese: "When we first met you asked me who I was. But last night you asked me what I was" ("Prey for the Hunter"). Disregarding superpowered women as individuals and regarding them as things, then, causes these characters to circumscribe the use of their abilities in an attempt to avoid or lessen the effects of this stigmatization. Furthermore, in anticipation of or in response to such stigmatization, these extraordinary women question their normalcy, reveal their true selves only reluctantly, and, at times, deny themselves personal fulfillment—all to a greater degree than their male counterparts do. The fact that these extraordinary female characters were portrayed by conventionally attractive actresses with model-perfect bodies underscores the inevitability of this marginalization for physically strong women; all women with powerful—or superpowerful—bodies, even those who initially can pass as beauties, are actually freaks. Thus, for television's superpowered women from 1996 to 2006, the enactment of traditional femininity is a longed-for, yet unobtainable privilege; subsequently, female viewers of series featuring these extraordinary characters receive the message that they, too, should long for only culturally acceptable gender presentations.

The Freak Tradition

The appellation "freak," even when applied to a beautiful—and superpowered—woman, recalls the tradition of displaying allegedly abnormal individuals for consumption by a voyeuristic public that was popular in the United States in the nineteenth and early twentieth centuries. From approximately 1840 to 1940, these living exhibits were transformed from acts in traveling sideshows to more institutionalized amusements. Hence, those with what were considered physical deformities—"little people," "giants," "human skeletons," "armless and legless wonders," "fat people," "Siamese twins," et al.—could now be viewed in mainstream settings, such as when P.T. Barnum showcased his "human curiosities" at the American Museum in New York City in the 1840s (Bogdan 23–24).

In addition to those human curiosities whose physical appearances made them readily identifiable as "Other," and, therefore, freak, there were also those whose freakishness stemmed from their physical abilities, rather than (what were considered) disabilities, such as "the strong man." For those called

"Strong Man" or "Lady-Hercules," their superior strength could not, with certainty, be recognized at birth, nor could it be deemed "forever unchangeable" (Fiedler 122, 124). Therefore, according to Leslie Fiedler in *Freaks: Myths and Images of the Secret Self*, "The abnormally strong [...] cannot really be classified with other 'Freaks' since they are able, if so inclined, to pass in the world of normals" (122). Despite these seemingly normal freaks' ability to pass, they aroused the interest of and evoked reactions from spectators in ways similar to their so-called physically deformed counterparts.

Regardless of the classifications of freaks present, it was human curiosity, as Barnum's label indicates, that enticed spectators to purchase admission to exhibits; once there, however, the spectators often found their curiosity matched with revulsion. As Elizabeth Grosz describes in "Intolerable Ambiguity: Freaks as/at the Limit," "The freak is thus neither unusually gifted nor unusually disadvantaged. He or she is not an object of *simple* admiration or pity, but is a being who is considered simultaneously and compulsively fascinating and repulsive, enticing and sickening" (56). This sense of ambiguity that freaks elicit from their onlookers results from the freaks' challenge to the normal body. Freaks both define — through what they are not — and question — through what they are — what constitutes a socially acceptable body, or what Rosemarie Garland Thomson calls "the canonical body" ("The Beauty" 465). According to Thomson, "The unexpected body fires rich, if anxious, narratives and practices that probe the contours and boundaries of what we take to be human" (*Freakery* 1). When an individual falls outside of "what we take to be human" in appearance, physiology, and/or abilities — when that individual is no longer considered a *who* but a *what* — she/he is classified freak.

Although scholarship on freakery, as it stems from disability studies, addresses the marginalization of both men and women who physically deviate from the canonical body, such deviations historically have been associated more closely with women's bodies. As Simone de Beauvoir perhaps noted most famously in *The Second Sex*, "A man is in the right in being a man; it is the woman who is in the wrong" (33). While de Beauvoir is referring not just to men's and women's physical bodies but to societal perceptions of the essentiality or importance of each sex, women's state of being in the wrong — or their "otherness," as de Beauvoir also terms it (37) — is often inscribed culturally on their bodies. Women's bodies, then, are a de facto indication of their difference. Therefore, when a woman — on screen or off — demonstrates physical traits or abilities that set her apart not just from men but from other women (the other Others), she is marked doubly as "wrong." Television's superpowered women from 1996 to 2006 thereby serve as exaggerated examples of this double marking, as their extraordinary physical differences are labeled pejoratively as liabilities or even disabilities. For superpowered women on television during this time period — and their real-life counterparts, most specifically female athletes — the parameters for a culturally acceptable body were narrow and inelastic.

When the Beauty Is a Freak

The superpowered woman of this time period, therefore, represents an archetypal paradox: she is both beauty and freak. Just as *Bewitched*'s Samantha carries out household tasks via a twitch of her nose while attired and coiffed in 1960s and 1970s styles, so, too, do Helena, Buffy, Gwen, Piper, and Sara use their respective powers to fight crime, avert an apocalypse, commit larceny, or save innocents while clad in 1990s or early 2000s form-fitting or revealing fashions — all without mussing their shiny, salon-styled hair. While "the beauty" and "the freak" logically would be opposing borders in regard to the canonical body, these icons actually serve similar functions vis-à-vis their spectators. As Thomson writes, while the beauty "traffics in the ideal" and the freak "in the anomalous" ("The Beauty" 459), both become "hyper-legible texts from which the onlookers can pay to read their own desires, anxieties, and destinies" (465). While Reese, Riley, Angel, Wike, and Gallo do not have to pay to read Helena, Buffy, Gwen, Piper, and Sara, the male characters' reactions to these female characters' displays of power certainly communicate male anxiety: How can a beautiful woman possess extraordinary physical power?

Superpowered female television characters from the gilded age — and, consequently, the actresses who portrayed them, many of whom have modeling experience — have often been described as not only beautiful, but stunningly so. One reviewer described Helena as "a statuesque looker" (Gliatto), while *Birds of Prey* cast member Shemar Moore (Reese) noted that "God smiled on" Helena's portrayer, Ashley Scott ("Great Scott"). Similarly, a reviewer of the *Witchblade* pilot characterized Sara (and, one would assume, her portrayer, Yancy Butler) as "gorgeous" and "buff" (Oxman 6). The character of Buffy (and, subsequently, her portrayer, Sarah Michelle Gellar), though, perhaps best exemplifies the hyper-sexualized/feminized appearance of the superpowered woman. As Fudge writes in "The Buffy Effect: Or, A Tale of Cleavage and Marketing," "Her [Buffy's] ever-present tank tops showcase her rack quite efficiently. [...] Her makeup is impeccable, her eyebrows well-groomed. She's a girl's girl. [...] She may have returned from a night of heavy slaying, but her frosted hair is still in its pigtails, her sparkly makeup intact." While other superpowered women may be "girls' girls" to a lesser

On *Birds of Prey*, Helena and Reese share an attraction, but Reese struggles to overcome his prejudice against Helena's metahuman heritage (WB Television/Photofest).

degree than Buffy, they, nevertheless, are still perceived as beautiful by the other characters (and the audience alike).

The outwardly feminine appearance of superpowered women is enhanced by the signifiers the characters wear to accentuate their beauty/sexuality, such as long hair and expertly applied cosmetics. Thomson explains that such traditionally feminine trappings usually heighten a male spectator's sense of masculinity: "Through hyperbolized sexual role performances, the figure of the beauty offers to make her viewers into men" ("The Beauty" 470). When combined with the strength of the superpowered woman, though, these markers of femininity actually threaten a male character's masculinity, as these women are potentially — or obviously — more physically powerful than he is. This threat to masculinity is intensified by the superpowered woman's ability, like the strong man of the freak show, successfully to pass as normal; these characters appear conventionally beautiful — much like female athletes, they have thin bodies with well-sculpted, but not bulging, muscles. The superpowered woman on television, then, is a veiled — versus an obvious — threat to the masculine. As her beauty initially cloaks her extraordinary power, such power comes as a shock when beheld by male characters; thus, she elicits a "What the hell are you?" (or the more family-hour friendly "What are you?").

For these male characters, their demeaning interrogative is often prefaced with at least a moment of disbelief—or perhaps amazement—at the displays of female power/ability they witness. This disbelief is evident when Angel stammers "Wha-at?" before formulating the more complete but no less stammered "What ... are you?" ("Ground State"), when Wike precedes his "What are you?" with "[W]hat the hell?!?" ("Trial by Magic"), and when Reese incredulously asks, "How high was that?" after watching Helena jump from a rooftop ("Prey for the Hunter"). For superpowered women, it is not only physical strength and agility that can arouse disbelief, but sexual prowess as well. On *Roswell*, Jesse becomes suspicious that his wife, Isabel, has special abilities. When he confronts her about these suspicions, Isabel, who, unbeknownst to Jesse, is an alien, asks what prompted his questions. Jesse's answer is: "[O]ur sex life. Not that I'm complaining. Sex with you is almost hallucinogenic, like I'm on acid or something. [...] I love it ... [but] it's definitely weird" ("I Married an Alien"). Any extraordinary female power, then, physical, psychic, or sexual, can provoke disbelief or amazement in a male character. This disbelief or amazement soon turns to unease, though, as hesitation and head-shaking give way to accusation: "Wha-at" is followed by "What are you?"—or in Jesse's case "[D]o you have some kind of psychic ability?" ("I Married an Alien"). In other words, since the extraordinary cannot be reconciled with the ordinary, the astonishment it evokes soon leads to condemnation. Thomson describes this trajectory of "freak discourse" as "wonder becom[ing] error" (*Freakery* 3).

The error made by superpowered women, or actual women with spectacular physical abilities, then, is one of transgressing traditional gender boundaries, or more specifically, possessing super strength and abilities. According to Shirley Castelnuovo and Sharon R. Guthrie in *Feminism and the Female Body: Liberating the Amazon Within*, women in Western society have traditionally been associated with "inferior, irrational bod[ies]"; consequently, "physical development among women, accompanied by an empowered consciousness, has generally been viewed [...] as dangerous and subversive. [...] The message seems to be that physically strong women should be feared" (31, 36). This fear of superpowered women stems, at least in part, from the cultural association of feminine abilities with unrestrained power. As Scott Bukatman, drawing from the work of Grant Morrison, explains in "X-Bodies (The Torment of the Mutant Superhero)," the 1950–60s DC Comics's trend of depicting "invincible" characters such as Superman with temporarily uncontrollable powers is known as "feminizing" them (114). In addition, characters like the X-Men's Cyclops, who has, theoretically, a world-ending power ("optic blasts" shoot from his eyes, thus they must be shielded), in Bukatman's terms, "evok[e] such figures of the monstrous feminine as

Medusa and Pandora's Box" (115). Superpowered female — or feminine — power, then, is automatically considered not only dangerously unstable but even monstrous; it is ability with the inherent potential for destruction.

The fear of superpowered women is further multiplied by the fact that their powers are natural and not developed, whether these women are metahumans, Slayers, self-described freaks, witches, or wielders of ancient power. Although Helena, Buffy, Gwen, Piper, and Sara may train or practice to hone their instincts and refine control of their powers, these powers are innate. As mentioned previously, Helena is half metahuman and half human; likewise, Buffy was "born with the strength and skill to hunt the vampires, to stop the spread of evil" ("Welcome to the Hellmouth"); Gwen presumably has had her electrical powers since birth (the character is introduced as a child via flashback); Piper, a witch, inherits her powers from her female ancestors; and Sara, although powered by the witchblade, was predestined to be its bearer for her generation (previous wielders include Joan of Arc).

As superpowered women embody their transgression through their innate powers, they violate conventional constructions of gender or sexual identity. Whereas natural strength — or even super strength — in men is celebrated (witness the adulatory description of Superman's musculature by the narrator of *The Adventures of Superman*—"More powerful than a locomotive!" ["The Mind Machine"] — or the opening-credits reference to the "computerized" Jake of *Jake 2.0* as "the ultimate human upgrade" ["The Spy Who Really Liked Me"]), such physicality in women is deemed freakish. In this regard, superpowers for men are perceived as the exaggeration of desired traits, while for women, superpowers are perceived as the assumption of transgressive ones. Castelnuovo and Guthrie, referencing the work of Michel Foucault, note that "one's 'true' sexual identity, feminine or masculine, is the primary way that individuals in Western societies define themselves" (50). Since physical strength has traditionally been associated with the truly masculine, the naturally powerful — even more so the supernaturally powerful — woman, by her very existence, questions the fixity and mutual exclusivity of gender categories. The superpowered woman, then, like other freaks, "exist[s] outside and in defiance of the structure of binary oppositions that govern our basic concepts and modes of self-definition" (Grosz 57). Male characters who witness displays of female powers are, therefore, glimpsing the "impossible middle ground between the oppositions dividing [...] one sex from the other" (Grosz 57). Off-screen women during this time period, such as athletic prodigies, elicited similar responses, as these physically gifted women possess stereotypically masculine abilities.

Unlike the human, albeit remarkable, abilities of their real-life counterparts, though, the supernatural/superhuman nature of the superpowered woman's abilities heighten this confusion regarding gender binaries. As David Greven notes in "Throwing Down the Gauntlet: Defiant Women, Decadent Men, Objects of Power, and *Witchblade*," "Neither quite male nor female, hero nor heroine, animal nor human, immortal nor mortal, the tough woman of the action heroine genre boldly resists a network of categorizing programs, remaining intransigently unclassifiable" (125). While superpowered male characters may also defy categorization, at least in terms of their humanity or mortality, such characters are more culturally acceptable. According to Bukatman, referring to the work of anthropologist Mary Douglas, "marginal beings," such as comic-book mutant superheroes, are either "reincorporate[ed]" into society or "brand[ed ...] as taboo" (116). In the case of the aforementioned Superman and Jake, reincorporation occurs; Superman is Metropolis's resident hero, and Jake proves integral to and gains influence within an NSA special operations team. However, for their female counterparts, reincorporation does not seem to be an option; they largely remain marginalized. Superpowered women automatically, by their very existence, are branded, if not taboo, then freaks. For female viewers of gilded-era series featuring these characters, extraordinary power for women, then, was not depicted as desirable.

The Freak Stigma

Gender transgression has long been a staple of sideshows, as "bearded ladies" were often exhibited (Bogdan 31); however, those women could not conceal their freakishness. In contrast, superpowered women on television not only successfully conceal their powers through their hyper-sexualized/ feminized appearances, as noted previously, but often they must do so as an act of self-preservation, or, in Samantha's case on *Bewitched*, as an act of marital preservation. As Mary Russo explains, in "Female Grotesques: Carnival and Theory," regarding the public display of women's bodies: "In other words, in the everyday indicative world, women and their bodies, certain bodies, in certain public framings, in certain public spaces, are always already transgressive — dangerous, and in danger" (323). While Russo is referring to women's fear of making "spectacles out of themselves" in anticipation of social repercussions even in carnivalesque settings (322), this type of self-preservation via the hiding of the body's culturally unexpected abilities or unacceptable appearances may be necessary for any and all women in particular circumstances, whether it be superpowered women attempting to hide their abilities on scripted series or women seeking cosmetic surgery on reality television shows. While women on reality shows may be revealing their (often

2. Misreading the Superpowerful Female Body   53

self-perceived) physical flaws to the embarrassment of themselves or their families, when superpowered women reveal their abilities, there may be graver results, as they may be physically endangering themselves or those with whom they are close. For example, on *Charmed*, Piper becomes angry with her half-sister, Paige, for sharing the family secret with her — Paige's — friend, Glen; Piper's anger stems from the loss of her sister Prue, whose death resulted, in part, from the media's discovery that Prue was a witch. When Glen jokes that he "better call off the tabloids," Paige defends him, much to Piper's disgust:

> PAIGE: He [Glen] just thought he was being funny. Nobody got hurt.
> PIPER: Maybe you'd feel a little bit differently if you lost a sister [Paige and Prue never met] ["Trial by Magic"].

Similarly, on *Roswell*, when Isabel is shot after a failed attempt to rescue her brother, Max, (whose life was in danger because his own alien powers had been discovered), her friend Michael, also an alien, must tell Jesse Isabel's secret so Jesse does not take her to a hospital (where even more people will discover she is not human). After Isabel recovers, she tries to explain her dishonesty to Jesse by telling him "lying about who I am is a given" ("Chant Down Babylon"). Superpowered women, therefore, often must guard their secret for fear of harm to themselves or to their loved ones.

Some superpowered men also may conceal their powers out of concern for their own safety or the safety of others, such as Jake from *Jake 2.0* (who was a mild-mannered systems analyst before the NSA laboratory accident that caused his upgrade) and the aforementioned teenage aliens Max and Michael from *Roswell*. Likewise, the teenage Clark Kent on *Smallville*, who has developing — and often unstable and hormonally linked — powers, is hesitant to reveal the superpowered aspect of his identity; he even discontinues his courtship of his first love, Lana Lang, at one point for fear of putting her in danger. Such inexperienced or immature superpowered male television characters parallel the mutant superheroes discussed by Bukatman. As Bukatman explains, the mutant superhero functions as an adolescent, lacking social standing and social confidence, with uncontrollable powers that stand in contrast to "Golden Age" superheroes, like Superman, whose "armored bodies" signify "ultimate triumph" (103, 116–17). Similarly, mature superpowered men on television, *i.e.*, those who have mastered their powers, demonstrate their abilities freely, with the self-assurance that such powers will be accepted. For example, *Smallville*'s post-gilded-age series' finale features an adult Clark Kent embracing his superpowered alter ego and heading to the altar with his true love, Lois Lane; while Clark publicly demonstrates his abilities as Superman and not Clark, he has found a way to preserve his own and Lois's safety (or at least mitigate any danger they might be in) without sacrificing his personal life ("Finale"). The concealment of — or rather the fear of revealing — superpowers, then, seems to be a feminine, or at least a feminizing, characteristic. For that reason, the *girl* power exemplified by superpowered women on television from 1996 to 2006 is just that — a depiction of arrested development — as such characters, like the mutant superhero Bukatman describes as a decidedly "feminized figure" (120), must always fear the repercussions resulting from the free and full utilization of their powers.

Despite this fear of exposure, some superpowered women purposely reveal the truth about their powers when they believe doing so is the right thing to do, as on *Bewitched* when Samantha confesses her magical identity to Darrin before consummating their marriage. A gilded-age example of this self-divulgence can be found on *Dark Angel* when Max decides to confide in her friend Original Cindy that she — Max — is a "transgenic," a genetically altered being with exceptional speed and strength. After operatives from Manticore (the secret organization that created Max) kidnap and almost kill Original Cindy in an attempt to flush out Max, Max decides to tell her friend the truth. When Max's boyfriend, Logan, questions whether this decision is "wise," Max replies, "Maybe not. But, after today, I think she's earned it" ("Rising"). Likewise, on *Charmed*, Piper uses her powers in front of a criminal, as noted previously, even though she earlier had chastised Paige for doing the same in front of Glen — a seeming hypocrisy:

> PAIGE: So it's okay to show our powers to a murderer but not to Glen.
> PIPER: Saving an innocent's life is worth the risk. Entertaining friends is not ["Trial by Magic"].

As these examples indicate, a superpowered woman's decision to reveal her powers is often dictated by either conscience or sense of duty.

Regardless of whether superpowered women reveal their powers accidentally or purposely, when they do so they simultaneously reveal that they have been passing as "normal"; such revelations single out these extraordinary women as freaks. As Thomson explains regarding the "grammar" of freaks and beauties, "Both on stage and in reproductions, [...] freaks appea[r] in the singular, whereas beauties appear in the plural"; in other words, the beauty can be mass produced, while the freak is "anomalously unique" ("The Beauty" 468). While the superpowered woman conceals her powers, then, she is just another beautiful woman, but, once she exposes those powers, she is *a* freak — or even *the* freak — and susceptible to the potential rebuke, harassment, and isolation that term conveys. For example, Melinda, the protagonist of *Ghost Whisperer*, faces harassment after her best friend in college, Lexi, tells everyone about her ability; Melinda becomes a laughingstock and leaves school

("On the Wings of a Dove"). *Dark Angel*'s Max fears a similar reaction from Original Cindy when she finally reveals her transgenic identity:

> When you and me hooked up ... it was like, all of a sudden, there was this part of my life where I didn't have to be hiding or fighting or anything else except trying to make a living and kicking it with my homegirl. I never had that before — a friend. I was scared that if I told you what was up it would all change. And that you would look at me like you are right now — like I was some kind of freak you didn't even recognize ["Rising"].

Just as Max postpones telling Original Cindy about her — Max's — true self for fear of being perceived differently by someone with whom she is close, so, too, does Buffy postpone telling her mother, Joyce, that she — Buffy — is the Slayer. When a vampire attacks Joyce, Buffy feels she must tell her mother the truth. Thus informed, Joyce does her best to accept that her daughter is not normal, at times, overcompensating for the anxiety this causes her:

> JOYCE: I just wish you didn't have to be so secretive about things. I mean, it's not your fault you have a special circumstance. They [the high school administration] should make allowances for you.
> BUFFY: Mom, I'm a Slayer. It's not like I need to ride a little bus to school ["Dead Man's Party"].

In the face of such potential rejection, prejudice, or misguided sympathy (as superpowers are even equated with disability), passing then becomes a strategy by which superpowered women attempt to avoid — or at least minimize — these repercussions of being branded freaks. Castelnuovo and Guthrie, building on the work of Erving Goffman, describe the motivation and rationale for this type of passing strategy for individuals who do not meet societal norms: "Persons carrying the signs of abnormality [...] are treated differently from others and often shunned. [...] Moreover, some individuals try to manage stigma by 'passing,' that is, by controlling information about themselves and cultivating facades" (117–18). When the superpowered woman can no longer control this information about herself, as with Prue, Isabel, and Melinda, or when she feels she no longer should control this information, as with Piper (and perhaps Paige), Max, and Buffy, she not only risks censure from others, but she may have to acknowledge that she has censured herself.

Superpowered women, then, in anticipation of the reactions of others, may attempt to identify primarily with the facades they have cultivated. *Birds of Prey*'s Helena serves as an example; as noted in the introduction to this chapter, she often considers herself more human than metahuman, despite her dual heritage. When Barbara, who is fully human, asks Helena to visit a meta-only bar to seek out information about a villain they are tracking, Helena is reluctant, or, as Barbara later notes, Helena "want[ed] to be like other girls" ("Prey for the Hunter"). Likewise, *Roswell*'s Isabel so carefully has constructed her facade of a normal teen that, even when her true identity is revealed, she cannot bear to call herself an "alien" in front of Jesse:

> JESSE: I believed you completely. I mean, strange things would happen, and I never doubted that I knew you — that I knew who my wife really was. I mean, I married Isabel Evans, and there is no Isabel Evans. Isabel is this person you hide behind. I just....
>
> ISABEL: You're right. You're right about everything. And even though I'm a ... a really good liar, I want you to know that I'm telling the truth when I say I love you and I love being your wife ["Chant Down Babylon"].

For these superpowered women, then, embracing a lie, or at least a half-truth, is easier than facing the consequences of being a freak.

Conversely, other superpowered women may readily identify themselves as freaks, but this self-identification, too, may be in anticipation of the reactions of others. For example, Gwen responds to Angel's "What are you?" with a definitive "I'm a freak" ("Ground State"). On the surface, this statement could be viewed as an example of what Foucault, in the first volume of his *History of Sexuality*, terms "'reverse' discourse," or the solicitation of "legitimacy" by some marginalized group by using "the same vocabulary, using the same categories by which [they were ...] disqualified" (101).[1] However, Gwen's proclamation is more a defensive strategy than an empowering one. Gwen self-deprecatingly identifies herself as a freak before others have the chance to do so; this self-branding, though, isolates her to such a degree that she uses

Isabel and Jesse's marriage on *Roswell* begins happily; however, when he learns of her alien origins, his faith in his wife and their relationship is shaken (UPN/Photofest).

her powers not to fight crime, but to commit it: "I'm a freak. Being a thief makes me a part of something ... and not a part ... at the same time" ("Players"). Gwen so craves being a part of something that she even risks her life to steal the prototype for a device that neutralizes electricity so that she will be able to experience human touch for the first time: "The thing [the device] might let me be ... well, not normal, but hold hands maybe. So, yeah. I guess I was willing to die [to obtain it]" ("Players"). Although psychic teen Raven from *That's So Raven* does not go to the extremes that Gwen does to feel connected to others, when Raven meets a group of fellow psychic teens (both female and male), she begins to doubt her long-term friendship with "normie" (the term the psychics call those without powers) pals Chelsea and Eddie. When Raven's telepathic and telekinetic friend Carly tells her that it is "for the best" if they "stick together," since they "know what it's like when [their] friends think [they're] a freak," Raven thinks Carly must be right, as she earlier had lamented that Chelsea and Eddie had "been on [her] case lately" about her abilities. While this episode concludes with a lesson in tolerance for psychics and normies alike, with Raven giving an only-on-Disney "We're all just people" speech ("Saving Psychic Raven"), Raven's insecurities about her abilities that lead her to identify with other freaks indicates her fear of never being considered normal. Therefore, even those superpowered women who self-identify as freaks are doing so preemptively—because they know they will never be accepted fully within mainstream culture. Thus, instead of providing narratives of female characters reclaiming previously pejorative terminology, as the girl-power movement attempted with "girl," television series during this era featuring superpowered women illustrated to viewers that women rarely possess the cultural influence or authority necessary for such a rhetorical reclamation.

Who Versus What Are You?

As the previous discussion indicates, when a male character unexpectedly witnesses a woman's display of superhuman/supernatural powers, he often asks the woman who demonstrates those powers *what* versus *who* she is (in those words or otherwise, as with Darrin's "You're a what?" to Samantha on *Bewitched* ["I Darrin, Take This Witch, Samantha"]). By doing so, he discloses the superpowered woman's alleged transgression, the fact that her power violates traditional gender boundaries. With this question, the male character assumes an authoritative role; he establishes the very boundaries that the superpowered woman allegedly violates. In regard to this idea of who is allowed to establish such boundaries, Robert Bogdan writes, in "The Social

Construction of Freaks," "Whenever we study deviance we have to look at those in charge — whether self-appointed or officially — of telling us who deviants are and what they are like. Their versions of reality are presentations, people filtered through stories and world views" (35). In other words, within television series featuring superpowered women, from the male character's perspective, within his version of reality, he becomes the norm — or at least the embodiment of the beliefs of a male-dominated society — from which the superpowered woman deviates. He is normal; therefore, she is freak, reminiscent of de Beauvoir's "He is the Subject [...] she is the Other" (33). In the examples noted earlier in this chapter, this assumed position of normalcy on the part of the male characters is especially ironic, as Reese is the son of a murderer, Riley is a member of an elite, military special-operations corps, Angel is a 200-plus-year-old vampire with a soul, and Wike and Gallo are murderers. These fictional men who fall outside of societal norms, however, still claim the authority to position extraordinary women as Other.

In contrast, when a female character witnesses an unforeseen display of male power, she, too, may ask "What are you?," but her query may not carry the same significance that a male's would. For example, on *Angel*, the title character, who, like superpowered women, can pass as a normal human, must reveal his vamp face in an attempt to rescue Kate, a homicide detective he has befriended, from another vampire. At the sight of Angel in his demon guise, Kate fearfully asks, "What are you?" Angel arrogantly replies, "You already know the answer, Kate" and begins to berate her, telling her "there are some things in this world," like the existence of demons, that she's "just not ready to face" ("Somnambulist"). During this exchange, Kate does not take the authoritative position that Angel did with Gwen. Instead, Angel is the authority who assumes not only what Kate already knows, but also what she is or is not ready to learn. Similarly, on *Jake 2.0*, when former CIA agent-turned spy Angela Hamilton asks Jake, "What the hell are you?" after he survives exposure to a lethal gas, Jake responds, "I told you. I'm an agent with the NSA" ("The Spy Who Really Liked Me"). When Angela follows up with, "I didn't ask who, I asked what," Jake proceeds to change the subject by attempting to persuade Angela to turn herself in to his superiors. Angela does not ask again. Therefore, if a female character does ask a male character *what* he is, she does not assume the same "illusory position of authoritative normativity," to use Thomson's term ("The Beauty" 461), that the male character does — thus the male character is not deemed a freak (at least not overtly).

Furthermore, for male characters, there exists a separation of *who* versus *what* they are that is not distinguishable for superpowered women. This separation for male characters is demonstrated by Jake's reliance on his professional status to be a sufficient expression of identity, as noted previously, and

2. Misreading the Superpowerful Female Body

by the dual personae of Clark Kent and Superman in pre–gilded-age series *The Adventures of Superman* and *Lois & Clark: The New Adventures of Superman* and, as mentioned earlier, in post–gilded-age episodes of *Smallville*. Fingeroth, drawing from Superman's comic book origins, explains that: "One thing we can say that separates Superman's dual identity from most others is this: Superman is the 'real' person. Clark Kent is the fake," while for other heroes it is the "civilian" persona that is the real (56–57). Such separation, and a potential privileging of the civilian side, is evident in Riley and Buffy's exchange. Even though Riley asks Buffy "What are you?," she counters with "Who are you?" After Riley answers, "You know who I am," he indicates that what he does is another matter ("Doomed"). By invoking this separation, Riley suggests that Buffy should accept him for who

When *Angel*'s title character reveals his vampire identity to homicide detective Kate, he maintains a position of authority by refusing to directly answer her question of "What are you?" Instead, he assumes that Kate will be unable to handle the truth that demons — and other forms of supernatural evil — exist (WB Television/Photofest).

he is — the man she has grown to know — regardless of what he does — which he is not at liberty to tell her (although she has already figured out that he is "part of some military monster squad"). In contrast, Riley is only focused on *what* Buffy is; he is interested in how she has super strength and speed and can take a punch without any visible injury ("Doomed"). Riley's reaction is something of a déjà vu for Buffy, as she once had a date with a boy named Owen that was interrupted by her Slayer duties — duties that resulted in Owen almost losing his life. Owen, however, instead of fearing contact with Buffy after this near-disastrous date, tells Buffy that her contact with danger is the reason he wants to keep seeing her ("I never thought that nearly getting killed would make me feel ... so alive!" ["Never Kill a Boy on the First Date"]). Like Riley, Owen fixates on Buffy's what to the exclusion of her who. For Buffy, the inability to separate her personality from her powers is something she has come to accept — as Kendra, a fellow Slayer, once pointed out to Buffy: "You talk about slaying like it's a job. It's not. It's who you are" ("What's My Line? Part 2"). According to the narratives of television series that feature superpowered women, a superpowered woman's powers transcend all other aspects of her personality and character; her who is conflated with her what — and what she *is* is her powers and not her passion, artistic ability, or inquisitiveness (qualities Buffy also possesses and that she attempts to point out to Riley while he is preoccupied with her "amazing" speed and strength ["Doomed"]).

The viewing of superpowered women primarily in terms of their powers stems from their so-called gender transgression; as their powers prevent them from being defined as "women," the only option left (according to the binary nature of U.S. discourse) is to define them by what prevents them from being "women." Thus, their powers are seen as unnatural and a source of anxiety that male characters have difficulty accepting. For example, Greven contends that *Witchblade*'s Sara is a "strong, tough woman within a homosocial setting" where her "very femininity makes her alien and troublesome" (136). Off-screen women with remarkable abilities may be seen as alien and troublesome, too, as, for example, professional female athletes who participate in historically male-dominated sports may threaten the masculinity of the men who observe their performances.

Although the abilities of professional female athletes may be anxiety-provoking, they may still be perceived as gifts. In contrast, for superpowered women, their extraordinary abilities may be perceived as liabilities — a hard truth that Prue learns on *Charmed*. When Prue casts a twenty-four-hour truth spell to determine whether her boyfriend, Andy, would continue their relationship if he knew she was a witch, she shares the following exchange with him after demonstrating her telekinesis and revealing her magical origins:

ANDY: So, when you have kids [they will have powers, too]...
PRUE: If they're girls, yes.
ANDY: Wow. That's quite a secret you've been hiding.
PRUE: Tell me about it.
ANDY: Can you change? I mean, is it something you can get rid of?
PRUE: No, Andy, I can't change who I am. And that's something I've recently come to accept. The question is, can you?
ANDY: To tell you the truth ... I don't know, Prue. I honestly don't know ["The Truth is Out There ... and It Hurts"].

For Andy, Prue's powers are a defect, something she might be better off without — if not for her sake, then for her future children's sakes. *Ghost Whisperer*'s Melinda, too, fears that her "gift" will be passed on to her children,[2] a fear she expresses to her husband, Jim: "Look at what it [her ability] did to the relationship between me and my mother. I mean, she could hardly speak to me, sometimes barely even look at me. What if I'm like that with our kids?" ("Demon Child"). On *Birds of Prey*, Dinah, a teenage metahuman who lives with Helena and Barbara, explains that her former foster parents had a reaction similar to Melinda's mother; they taught her to be ashamed of her powers, to conceal them: "And when I couldn't hide it anymore, they were going to take me somewhere, somewhere to make my powers stop" ("Slick"). Even on the Disney-fied *That's So Raven*, Raven's psychic abilities often are considered a detriment by her and her friends; when Raven shares one of her visions with Eddie in an attempt to help him, he, armed with such foreknowledge, acts out of character and humiliates himself. Eddie then angrily sputters at Raven: "Your visions are whack. Why can't you just be more..."; Raven dejectedly fills in the blank with "normal?" ("To See or Not to See"). Superpowers, for women, may be viewed by others (and themselves) as more liability than welcomed ability.

In contrast, the powers of superpowered men, while perhaps startling at first, come to be valued and accepted. During the early seasons of *Smallville*, Clark Kent, who, as noted above, has not yet assumed the guise of Superman,[3] reveals to his best friend, Pete, that he — Clark — is from another planet. Pete, naturally, is at first stunned by this revelation ("So you're some sort of... what? You're not a human?") and hurt that Clark took so long to confide in him ("I don't care if you're from the moon. You never trusted me. What kind of friendship is that?"). However, he eventually comes to terms with Clark's powers, telling Clark "That's my boy" when he learns Clark once used his X-ray vision to peer into the girls' locker room and "This is gonna be fun" when Clark uses his powers to jump over Pete to dunk a basketball ("Duplicity"). Clark's powers, likewise, are accepted by his friend Chloe, when Clark, under the influence of red kryptonite (which removes his inhibitions), recklessly demonstrates his powers for her. Chloe, who, like Clark, is being influenced by an alien substance (in her case, a parasite) that renders her uninhibited, is curious, but not afraid. She does ask, "What are you?," but she follows this question with "Oh, my God. This is so cool.... Can you fly?" Chloe then tests Clark's powers by diving out of a loft so he will catch her; when he does, she remarks, "My own personal superhero. I always knew there was something special about you, Clark Kent" ("Rush"). As these examples from the gilded era demonstrate, female powers were depicted as transgression, as something to get rid of or stop, while male powers, as exaggerated masculinity, were depicted as special.

The Freak Tradition, Revisited

Superpowered women on television from 1996 to 2006, as innately powered beings, challenged, by their very presence, hegemonic power structures that traditionally subjugate women's roles to men's. These characters are the heroes of their shows, often saving male characters and rarely needing to be saved themselves. Their innate powers make them physically superior to, *i.e.*, stronger than, most other characters, and they often demonstrate qualities of leadership, resilience, and initiative — they are not just brawn, but brains as well. In addition, some superpowered women embrace their powers as part of their identity, *e.g.*, Helena tells Barbara that she "got over" wanting to be "like other girls"; Dinah tells Helena, "I spent the last fifteen years hating myself because I was different. I'm done with that. I am what I am. I'm never going to be ashamed of it again" ("Prey for the Hunter"); Max proclaims, "Today I'm proud to be a freak" ("Freak Nation"); Viv, Raven's psychic grandmother, tells Raven "It's [the ability to have visions is] what makes us special" ("To See or Not To See"); and Melinda states, "Everybody has a talent; this [communicating with the dead] is mine" ("Undead Comic"). However, despite these empowering attributes of gilded-age superpowered women, these characters also reinforced the same hegemonic power structures that they challenged.

When a superpowered woman unexpectedly demonstrates her powers, she is often met with a "What are you?" from a male character. Thus exposed as "abnormal," the superpowered woman is demoted from subject to object — she resembles the living exhibits of turn-of-the-century freak shows. Her powers are feared or considered a physical defect, and she must conceal them or face the consequences, whether those consequences result in harm to herself or her loved ones, isolation, or self-doubt about her own true identity. For example, when Paige says to Piper, "Okay. So you're saying I have to choose between having any friends and being a witch," Piper's reply is, "Yes. I have" ("Trial by Magic"). Likewise, Greven notes of *Witchblade* that "[u]ltimately, her [Sara's] tough womanliness ensures her isolation, her remove from social ties of any kind" (147). Superpowered women, then, pay a price for their transgression.

As these characters were portrayed by, according to Hollywood standards, extremely beautiful women with perfect, thin bodies, the fact that their powers are not accepted as readily as those of a male character underscored how high this price may be. Any woman who has a body that "stray[s] from what is typical or predictable" (Thomson, *Freakery* 1), even one who would be considered conventionally desirable, is a freak. For example, although Buffy is considered pretty and captures the attention of the aforementioned Owen and another high-school student named Scott, these relationships are short-lived because of Buffy's "special circumstance," to use her mother's term ("Dead Man's Party"); Owen wants the adrenaline rush Buffy can provide, not Buffy's company, and Scott breaks up with Buffy because she "seem[s] distracted all the time" ("Homecoming"). Her only long-term romantic relationships occur with men whose own special circumstances render them disenfranchised to some degree: Riley is the subject of military experiments that attempt to make him a super soldier; Angel, as previously mentioned, is a vampire with a soul; and Spike is a vampire who later acquires a soul (although Buffy never truly loves Spike, she often turns to him for solace). In other words, Buffy as a freak must stick with those closer to her own kind; she cannot escape the designation once it is out there. This "enfreakment" (Thomson, *Freakery* 10) of women with bodies that stray was not confined to the realm of scripted television from 1996 to 2006, either. The enfreakment of superpowered women on television had — and continues to have — many realistic parallels, as "[f]eminist discourses on television tend to correspond to aspects of feminism explored by U.S. culture" (Lotz 107). These aspects of feminism include bodily challenges to traditional gender roles.

Female athletes, in their quest to strengthen and master control over their bodies, most closely parallel superpowered women on television. While women have continued to gain acceptance and garner respect for their athletic abilities in recent years, their participation in certain sports, especially in contact or historically male-dominated sports, may still be viewed as abnormal. As Castelnuovo and Guthrie explain:

> Rarely does one stop to consider the fact that most sports, particularly the heavily commercialized variety — the ones deemed "major" in American society — are structured to highlight the extreme advantages of the male body. As a result, the presence of women in these sports is often viewed as bizarre, certainly less so today than in previous decades and centuries, but still anomalous [93].

For athletes, like superpowered women on television, their very presence challenges traditional roles for women — and causes anxiety from onlookers, as "anomalous," while synonymous with "exceptional," also can mean "deviant."

In some cases, such male anxiety — or cultural anxiety in general about exceptional women — may be lessened by focusing on the femininity versus the physical abilities of the athletes in question. While in these cases, female athletes may not be enfreaked, per se, the focus remains on their "what"s versus their "who"s, except now, *what* they *are* are attractive women more so than athletic powerhouses. For example, tennis phenoms Serena and Venus Williams have received media attention as much for their off-court pursuits as their on-court skills, as evidenced by the 2005 headline "From Racket-

Wielding Warrior Princesses [a reference to Xena] to Designing Women." The subsequent article included a reference to the Williams sisters' interests in interior design, fashion, and acting — more traditionally acceptable pursuits for women — alongside an accounting of their tennis careers. For less-successful, or perhaps less-gifted, female athletes, especially those with less physically imposing bodies (*i.e.*, smaller and toned versus broad-shouldered and obviously muscular), their athletic abilities may be disregarded entirely. Tennis star Anna Kournikova has garnered more fame as a pin-up than as a professional athlete. Her *what* is more often her "sex appeal, attitude and antics" ("Anna Kournikova") and not her backhand. The editors of Ask Men.com, which reaches 19 million readers monthly ("About AskMen"), noted that "we'll give her some credit as a tennis player," but that they are "just fine watching her strut her stuff in magazines and bra ads," referring to Kournikova's high-profile publicity shots and endorsements ("Anna Kournivoka"). For women who possess great athletic ability, such ability and the anxiety it evokes may be downplayed or overlooked in an attempt to present those women in a more stereotypically feminine manner.

In contrast to these more glamorous female athletes who rival the beauty aspect of television's superpowered women, other female athletes rival their fictional television counterparts since their sex and strength are read as oxymoronic. For example, as Fen Coles relates in "Feminine Charms and Outrageous Arms," spectators at female bodybuilding competitions "cannot resolve what she [the female bodybuilder] 'ought' to be — a woman — and what she appears to be: the impossible juxtaposition of feminine/masculine, female/male, femme/butch, female impersonator/male impersonator" (452). Likewise, in "Iron Jane: Chopping Down the Muscle Myth," Dorothea Helms describes how female bodybuilders, in the face of such irresolution, must justify both their gender and professional identities: "Imagine my shock when these two gorgeous women [professional bodybuilders Lenda Murray and Diana Dennis] were called 'freaks' and had to spend the entire hour [of a television program] fighting to defend their femininity and their right to carry the sport to professional levels." As with female bodybuilders, teen golf sensation Michelle Wie was perceived (during the first few years of her career) as a juxtaposition or anomaly, since she was (and still is) a young woman in a sport more known for high-profile male athletes (namely, during the gilded era, Tiger Woods). In a 2004 "Rome is Burning" column on ESPN.com, Jim Rome wrote that "Wie is a 14 year old girl. [...] She hits it like a dude, has a great make up and probably could play the tour one day. She's a freak" (1 Dec. 2004).[4] In the same manner that superpowered women on television are considered freakish for possession of power that is more commonly associated with the masculine domain, so, too, are female athletes considered freaks for being able to be competitive (being able to "hit it like a dude") in historically masculine (or originally male-only) sports.

As with superpowered women on television, this process of real-life enfreakment serves to limit women's empowerment. Although most of the superpowered women described throughout this chapter are considered heroes (or, in Raven's case, at least a good friend) in their fictional worlds — a positive designation — they still often wish to be accepted as normal girls instead of being disenfranchised as freaks, no matter how heroic — or powerful — they may be. Grosz characterizes this limiting effect for those who are enfreaked: "All [those termed freaks] suffer a certain social marginalization" (56). The marginalization of superpowered women communicates to female viewers that they should continue on traditional paths; narratives of enfreakment then become policing or, perhaps, self-policing mechanisms for encouraging women not to stray. Such narratives could be found elsewhere on television from 1996 to 2006 as well (and continue to be found post–2006). In "Fearing the Freak: How Talk TV Articulates Women and Class," Elizabeth Birmingham describes how television talk shows, many of which, she notes, "are simply about women's issues, relationships, and medical issues that become carnivalesque," are one such method of policing: "Talk shows have become the new sideshows, and we watch them to validate our values and beliefs; if not for those values and beliefs, we would be like 'them.' The 'them' that talk shows present are so horrible, and the punishment for their transgressions is so severe, that we are asked to accept the status quo and remain 'us.'" Talk shows, like series featuring superpowered women, serve as regulatory texts for women.

This regulatory effect could also — and can currently — be found in television series and movies aimed at teenagers. As Rachel Moseley explains in "Glamorous Witchcraft: Gender and Magic in Teen Film and Television," "Recent [late 1990s and early 2000s] teen films and television shows have been profoundly engaged in the policing of difference and the construction and validation of hegemonic femininities, in the correcting of 'aberrant' femininity." Moseley, as evidence of this assertion, cites the "'glamour' [sic] makeover and the space of the high school prom" that occurs in many of these texts (405). This policing of aberrant femininity during the gilded age also occurred with adult women, as evidenced by such television fare as *Extreme Makeover* (ABC, 2002–07), which also featured makeovers of men, and *The Swan* (FOX, 2004) — both of these series featured participants seeking cosmetic surgery to correct their so-called bodily anomalies. Regulatory texts, such as the examples above, not only police women's bodies, but their actions and beliefs as well.

While body and appearance are visible indications of a woman's gender transgression, methods of enfreakment are not confined to these outward signifiers. Bogdan explains that the term freak may be applied even to those who would not have been considered a human curiosity in Barnum's day. Since the term freak is "a social construction" and not a description of a physical condition, it "is a way of thinking about and presenting people — a frame of mind and a set of practices" (23–24). A woman's behavior and ideology, therefore, can also earn her freak status. Those who identify themselves as feminists most notably and frequently may receive this moniker. Maria Mitchell writes in "Ambitious Women and Strange Monsters: Simone de Beauvoir and Germaine Greer" that these two feminist icons (de Beauvoir, as referenced previously, is the author of *The Second Sex*, and Greer is the author of *The Whole Woman* et al.) "both inhabit the freak category"; furthermore, descriptions of the two indicate "that some key assumptions about women, behaviour [sic] and appearance still remain firmly entrenched" (98). Similarly, Whelehan addresses this linking of feminists to the abnormal by noting that critics of feminism manipulate the "average observer's belief that to be a feminist one has to be slightly unhinged" to their — the critics' — advantage (78). Espoused ideologies, like powerful bodies and unconventional appearances, can lead to marginalization.

Therefore, all powerful women, whether they are powerful in mind, body, and/or spirit, have the potential to be freaks. As Mitchell opens her article:

> Most female heroines are oddities: adventuresses and originals notable less for the importance of their acts than for the singularity of their fates.... The great man springs from the masses and he is propelled onward by circumstances; the masses of women are on the margin of history, and circumstances are an obstacle for each individual, not a springboard. In order to change the face of the world, it is first necessary to be firmly anchored in it; but the women who are firmly rooted in society are those who are in subjection to it; unless designated for action by divine authority — and then they have shown themselves to be as capable as men — the ambitious woman and the heroine are strange monsters [98].

Hence, women who demonstrate heroism are considered strange monsters, even when such women, to paraphrase Mitchell, have been designated by divine authority and shown to be as or more capable than men, as is the case with many superpowered women on television from 1996 to 2006. If extraordinary women such as Buffy, Gwen, Helena, Piper, and Sara (as well as Isabel, Max, Paige, Prue, Dinah, Raven, and Melinda) cannot avoid such marginalization, then what hope do their ambitious, athletic, and/or feminist real-life counterparts have in the face of similar — albeit sometimes more subtle/less extreme — cultural constrictions? Gilded-age television narratives that depicted women's marginalization as the result of overt (super)power, therefore, both paralleled the experiences of actual women and reinforced — through their questioning of *what* a superpowerful woman is rather than *who* she is— the hegemonic power structures that limited the empowerment of those women in the first place. Clearly, *what* these superpowered women are is misread; *who* they are — and, perhaps more importantly, who they could be — had yet to be fully explored even in the fictional and fantastic realms of mid–1990s to mid–2000s television.

CHAPTER 3

Masquerade of Selflessness

PHOEBE [to Piper]: You are the most sweetest, most caring person I've ever met. [...] You're always there to help anybody, even strangers. You've been doing it your whole life. So there's no way you've been given this ... this gift if it wasn't to do good things with it.—*Charmed*, "I've Got You Under My Skin"

MAX: All I wanted was a normal night out, but I guess for a girl like me normal is too much to ask.—*Dark Angel*, "Boo"

DAVIS: You're saving lives. It's a gift.
TRU: No, candles are gifts. Boots. Bath salts, maybe. But this is ... I don't know what this is. Do you?—*Tru Calling*, "Star Crossed"

"Would an afternoon off cause any harm?"

In "It Came From Next Door," the first segment of the premiere of the animated *My Life as a Teenage Robot*, the back story of the title character, a pubescent automaton named XJ9 who calls herself Jenny, is revealed by her creator, Mrs. Wakeman: "You were built for one purpose: to protect the planet Earth. Unless you're out saving the world, you should stay in your room." Jenny, although physiologically atypical, as she is equipped with ray guns, rocket power, super shields, and numerous other extraordinary gadgets, reacts to this voice of authority (she calls Mrs. Wakeman "Mom") as a stereotypical teen, equipped with sarcasm and high drama: "What's the crisis, anyway? So I left my room for five seconds. Do you hear any alarms going off? [...] You never let me do anything but save the Earth. Would an afternoon off cause any harm?" While Mrs. Wakeman avoids Jenny's question regarding harm and dismisses her tantrum as adolescent angst ("Your powers are still developing, and it's bound to be a confusing time. When you get a little older, you'll see things my way"), by the episode's end both Jenny and the viewer learn the answer to her question: "Would an afternoon off cause any harm?" Almost.

Jenny, it seems, longs to "have friends and hang out like normal teenagers" and, in a moment of teenage rebelliousness, does indeed decide to take the afternoon off to spend time with Brad and Tuck, the two boys who live next door, thereby ignoring her mother's orders to "be a good robot" and destroy a meteor that is headed toward Earth. While, as Jenny points out to her mother, these meteors generally disintegrate before they reach Earth, this meteor proves an exception — due to one of Jenny's leisure-time activities. Jenny's afternoon with her new friends includes a game of hacky sack; Jenny's superpowerful kick launches the miniature beanbag into the solar system, where it collides with the meteor, causing the meteor to gain instead of lose mass. Due to Jenny's remote alarm system (*i.e.*, one of her pigtails), she learns of the meteor's trajectory toward Earth and is able to save the day just in time, although Tuck, the younger of the two neighbor boys, is almost destroyed in the process — his shirt gets caught on Jenny's rocket booster, and she unwittingly takes him along on the mission. The segment, therefore, concludes happily — for the most part. Brad and Tuck (who recovers quickly from his harrowing space flight) think Jenny is a hero, and Mrs. Wakeman acknowledges that, since Jenny "saved the world," "[a]n afternoon off can't cause much harm." However, following Mrs. Wakeman's pronouncement of the minimal risk in Jenny privileging her social life over her purpose, the segment's final shot of unfriendly spacecraft with their ray guns pointed at planet Earth belies the validity of this assessment ("It Came from Next Door").

Jenny's plight — an attempt to momentarily evade her purpose to pursue her own (read "selfish") aspirations, which results in (near-) disaster — resembles that of many other superpowered women on television during the gilded age. Similar themes and storylines to "It Came from Next Door" aired on *Tru Calling*, *Dark Angel*, *Charmed*, and *Birds of Prey*, among others. Although the superpowered women within these live-action series were not built — in the literal sense as Jenny was — to protect the Earth, their powers demand that they shoulder the responsibility of safeguarding the world — or at least some corner of it. Despite these characters' performances of superheroic feats, they do so without the traditional masks and costumes of superheroes; instead, they are masked by their assumed mantle of responsibility. Selflessness is their masquerade.

The absence of literal masking heightens the performance of femininity by superpowered women; these characters enact a masquerade of selflessness to such a degree that, like Jenny, they face repercussions from themselves or others for even temporarily privileging their own interests. Furthermore, the inability (*i.e.*, extreme difficulty) of these characters to take off their heroic personae is underscored by the use of storylines in which physical masking and/or costuming results in danger to themselves or others. Superpowered women's masquerade of femininity, their guise of selflessness, then, results in a circumscribed use of their abilities. Such selflessness is presented as the only — and, therefore, right — course of action for television's superpowered women to take, indicating to viewers that self-sacrifice — never self-indulgence — leads to cultural acceptance for women.

Femininity as Masquerade

In 1929, *The International Journal of Psychoanalysis* published "Womanliness as a Masquerade," an article by Joan Riviere, Freud's first translator and an analyst in her own right (Heath 139–141). Within this article, Riviere examines the psychological motivations for and ramifications of "a particular type of intellectual woman['s]" use of a "mask of womanliness" (Riviere 130). According to Riviere, this particular type of woman excels in the professional world and, therefore, exhibits masculine behaviors; thus, such a woman employs a masquerade of femininity to avoid the potential repercussions that such displays of masculinity might elicit from men — or in the vernacular of Riviere's article, the "father-figures"— these women encounter or seek (130–33).

Although, as Riviere notes, prior to her writing of this article, such intellectual, *i.e.*, "masculine," women would have been perceived as just that— overtly masculine — many professional women could now — in the late 1920s— be recognized as feminine as well. In fact, Riviere notes that women in a variety of vocations "seem to fulfil [sic] every criterion of complete feminine development," criteria that Riviere enumerates as being superior wives, mothers, and housewives; maintaining an active social life; contributing to culture; exhibiting concern about personal appearance; and acting as devoted "mother-substitutes" to copious friends and family members. Working women, therefore, according to Riviere, could execute the above criteria while professionally performing "at least as well as the average man"— a seeming paradox that Riviere found psychologically puzzling (131).

Apparently, for Riviere, the apparatus for addressing such a paradox was the concept of the "masquerade": "[t]he conception of womanliness as a mask, behind which man suspects some hidden danger, throws a little light on this enigma" (138). Such feminine development is a mask, because, as Riviere explains, the fulfillment of these exhausting qualifications of femininity cannot be engaged in authentically. According to Riviere, no distinction may be made between "genuine womanliness" and the masquerade: "they are the same thing" (133). In this regard, motivation for seeking and/or carrying out the necessary elements of feminine development is of no consequence, as the results do not differ. Women who aspire to professional achievement or those who choose more traditionally feminine pursuits may be equally womanly, as both assume the mask.

The masquerade, therefore, can be used by all women to avoid rejection or rebuke from men, whether a woman fears that her professional superiority will not be accepted due to her gender, or, as in one of the cases Riviere notes, a housewife does not want to appear too knowledgeable when a "builder or upholsterer is called in" (134). Since such scenarios of potential rebuff or social exclusion trigger anxiety in women, as Riviere's casework suggests, women assume the masquerade of womanliness to "restore or make good [for]" what they have allegedly stolen, *i.e.*, power, ability, and or knowledge presumably demarcated for the masculine domain (although Riviere also writes of the need for reconciliation with "mother-figures" as well [134, 138]). Riviere asserts that integral to these women's efforts to make good for their alleged appropriation of that which is not theirs for the taking are expressions of "self-sacrifice, devotion, [and] self-abnegation" (138). Selflessness, then, is a hallmark of the masquerade of womanliness.

Therefore, as indicated by Riviere's work and others, there exists a cultural expectation of selflessness for women that is absent for men. In Julia T. Wood's *Who Cares? Women, Care, and Culture*, she notes that women are socialized to bear what she refers to as "the burden of selflessness" (33), *i.e.*, to be perceptive of the needs of others on an ongoing basis and to accept that such caring responsibilities are expected of them but not of men; according to Wood, if such socialization is successful, "women will internalize the expectation and prompt themselves to care for others and to judge themselves as selfish if they don't give generously of their time and of themselves" (5). Similarly, in *Unbearable Weight: Feminism, Western Culture, and The Body*, Susan Bordo terms this expectation for women an "other-oriented emotional economy" and describes how this economy is established via the social construction of femininity; the rules of femininity, Bordo writes, "require that women learn to feed others, not the self, and to construe any desires for self-nurturance and self-feeding as greedy and excessive."[1] She goes on to note that any hunger felt by women, including the desire for power, independence, or sexual satisfaction, must be controlled (171). Television's superpowered women, as their abilities allow them to fulfill their own needs and wishes easily and excessively, become texts on which this cultural expectation is most legible, especially since their abilities and the circumstances under which they may be used are curtailed to an equally excessive degree.[2] Thus, for gilded-age viewers, television's superpowered women became symbols of selflessness and self-sacrifice more so than power and autonomy — even fantasies of female power, then, came (and continue to come) with built-in limitations.

Heroic Femininity

As with Samantha on *Bewitched*, the protagonists of *My Life as a Teenage Robot* (Jenny), *Tru Calling* (Tru), *Dark Angel* (Max), *Charmed* (the sister witches known as "The Charmed Ones"), and *Birds of Prey* (Helena's team) have innate abilities and/or knowledge that others do not, *i.e.*, they have much in their possession, according to Riviere's framework, for which they must "make good." Even though Max sarcastically proposes that the sentiment "Girls kick ass" must be valid due to its sartorial origins ("It says so on a T-shirt" ["Pilot"]), the bodily powers and heroic behaviors of Jenny, Tru, Max, the Charmed Ones, and Helena's team more often are associated with masculinity, as discussed in the previous chapter. The possession of said powers and behaviors by such women, therefore, requires compensation. The masquerade these characters enact, then, includes the hyperfemininity also discussed in the previous chapter — the wearing of form-fitting clothing and the maintaining of perfect hair and make-up in all scenarios, including combat (even Jenny maintains a stereotypically feminine — although mechanical — appearance, complete with metallic pigtails and miniskirt). Such enactments can be read, on this level, similarly to the way in which Riviere interpreted her case subjects, *i.e.*, as women "wish[ing] for masculinity" who assume traditionally feminine appearances and behaviors to alleviate the anxiety triggered by or the vengeance that may result from their non-traditional actions (Riviere 130); in the case of superpowered women, their break from traditional gender roles occurs, in part, through their service as crime fighters and protectors. However, Riviere's framework refers to the anxiety that women themselves feel, while the previous chapter focuses primarily on the anxiety that superpowered women raise in others (most often in men). The fear of potential repercussions, specifically from men, though, remains consistent from both perspectives; the masquerade is a form of passing, a way for superpowered women to "'hide in plain sight' in the patriarchal order," to borrow a phrase from Kerry Maguire's "The Cloak of Definition: Fantasies of Feminine Identity" (55).

While more contemporary scholars, such as Stephen Heath and Mary Ann Doane, conceive of the masquerade of womanliness as the "donning of hyperfemininity" (Maguire 54), which, as noted previously, can be applied to superpowered women on television, it is Riviere's idea of "self-sacrifice, devotion, [and] self-abnegation" (138) that is most applicable to an analysis of the gilded-age manifestation of this character type. Jenny's, Tru's, Max's, the Charmed Ones', and Helena's bodily inscribed powers combined with their sex, their femaleness, ostensibly predestine their roles as heroes within their respective series, as heroes are, by definition, selfless. Just as women historically have been inscribed as maternal figures due to their biological capacity for childbearing, so, too have these characters been inscribed a type of maternalism, *i.e.*, the prioritizing of others' needs above their own due to the physical embodiment of their powers. For example, in the pilot episode of *Dark Angel*, social crusader Logan (who is not yet Max's boyfriend) solicits Max's help to bring justice to a corrupt dock worker. When Max balks at the idea of getting involved in such an operation, as the dock worker's crimes do not directly affect her, Logan chides her by saying, "By being alive, you're involved" ("Pilot"). While Logan's reproach directly refers to Max's responsibility as a member of the human race, the indirect message is clear: Max's inherent ability, her very existence, requires that she provide her assistance whenever and wherever it is needed, regardless of her personal feelings on the matter. Her powers necessitate her caregiving. Likewise, on *Tru Calling*, Tru has no choice but to answer each call of the dead. Her life automatically rewinds one day so that she can seek to prevent the demise of the person who sought her aid, no matter the consequences to her own personal or professional pursuits. Tru's power, then, like a woman's ability to bear children, is a life-giving one (or at least a life-saving one)—a power that brings with it the obligation to prioritize others' needs above her own. In contrast, Tru's morgue co-worker Jack, who also re-lives days, seeks to end lives not save them, a purpose he zealously pursues without any outward appearance of guilt or crisis of conscience.

Selflessness as a Sign of Maturity

Personal sacrifices, such as the preceding examples, are common for superpowered women. As the majority of these characters, like the feminized mutant superheroes Bukatman describes (100), come into their powers as teenagers or young adults (even if they were born with or destined for their abilities, such abilities often remain latent until puberty), the assumption of this masquerade of selflessness, then, becomes a sign of emotional and intellectual maturity that corresponds with their physical maturity (with an obvious correlation to their capacity for childbearing). This timeframe parallels Riviere's theory, as it describes *womanliness* as a mask; girlhood, presumably, can be navigated genuinely. This equating of selflessness with maturity is underscored by the fact that these characters accept their heroic roles with varying degrees of reluctance. For example, the Charmed Ones (who at the start of the series are comprised of Prue, Piper, and Phoebe) were born with their abilities; however, their grandmother, in an effort to protect them from demon attacks, bound the sisters' powers when they were children. Their powers are restored to them as young adults after Phoebe inadvertently reads a reversal of the binding spell, but the revelation that they are witches is not necessarily a welcome one. Piper so fears her new powers at first that she is scared to enter a church, for fear that such abilities must make her evil. Piper eventually comes to terms with both her abilities and her charge to save innocents (joyfully exclaiming, "I'm good," when she sets foot in a church without any negative consequences ["I've Got You Under My Skin"]); she then devotes herself to this calling to the detriment of her social life. As noted in the previous chapter, Piper chooses being a witch over her friends — a life lesson that as the older, more mature sister, she can then pass on to half-sister Paige; it is a lesson that Paige, like her half-sisters, at first stubbornly refuses to learn. (Paige's powers are activated upon Prue's death so that Paige can complete the triad of the "Charmed Ones.")

As Paige's and other superpowered women's reluctance to accept the sacrifices that accompany their abilities illustrates, such reluctance is depicted within the narratives of these series as a symbol of immaturity that must be overcome for these women to fulfill their heroic destinies. To apply Riviere's term, selflessness marks the completion of their "feminine development" (131), just as, for Riviere's patients, marriage and motherhood (among other things) marked theirs. A scene from *Birds of Prey* between Barbara (who does not have superhuman abilities, but who was once Batgirl and now assists Helena and Dinah in their crime-fighting efforts through her near superhuman knowledge of technology) and Alfred, the trio's butler/father figure, best illustrates this equating of selflessness with womanly maturity:

> BARBARA: [staring at her Batgirl costume] I'm not the hero I once was, Alfred.
> ALFRED: Oh, thank goodness. Batgirl was strong, but impetuous. You've grown into a thoughtful, beautiful woman with the capacity to care more for others than you do for yourself. And, if that's not a hero, then I don't know what is ["Lady Shiva"].

Similarly, on *Dark Angel*, Logan comments on Max's personal growth from selfish to selfless by noting that when he first met her, "She was just looking out for herself. No responsibilities. No entanglements" ("The Berrisford Agenda"); Logan's admiration for the new Max who empathizes with and assists others, even those who have harmed her, is evident. For superpowered women, therefore, an awareness of their extraordinary abilities signals the end of the impetuousness of youth and the need to accept a mature, inordinate capacity to care, just as, for young women off screen, there is often a realization that the bodily changes brought on by puberty carry with them the potential for motherhood and its related caregiving responsibilities.

The Power of Personal Sacrifice

In fact, this capacity to care, this willingness to set aside one's own needs to meet others' needs, aptly describes the powers of *Bewitched*'s Samantha, as she rarely uses her magical abilities in pursuit of her own agenda. The extraordinary ability to be of service to others, though, is demonstrated more markedly by the superpowered women on *Tru Calling, Joan of Arcadia,* and *Wonderfalls*. The protagonists of these three series—Tru, Joan, and Jaye— have no special abilities that enable them to assist others. Instead, they serve as instruments or vessels of some greater good. As referenced previously, Tru hears the call of the dead (who usually say "Help me" or sometimes "Save me"), and her day rewinds so that she can try to prevent the death of the person who solicited her aid (or someone that person failed to help before she/he died). However, Tru has no extraordinary ability or insider knowledge that allows her to help or save the individual in question. Unlike Gary, the male protagonist of CBS' *Early Edition* (1996–2000), who receives tomorrow's newspaper today and thus has black-and-white information from which to begin his quest to prevent the reported deaths and disasters,[3] Tru must rely on her instincts, as her boss, Davis, suggests, as well as her memory of the deceased's personal effects, the time of death, and any other details she was able to observe in the few moments between the body's arrival at the morgue where she works and the body's plea for her aid. On *Joan of Arcadia*, the title character can see and hear God in various human forms; the Almighty may be a fellow high-school student one day and a utilities worker the next. God, in whichever form, persuades Joan to perform an ostensibly random and/or irrational act that ultimately leads to the benefit of another. Then Joan, armed only with typical teenage awkwardness, does her bumbling best to answer each cryptic charge, leaving her parents, brothers, and friends questioning her seemingly erratic behavior. Likewise, in the short-lived *Wonderfalls*, the Brown-educated but apathetic Jaye, who works in a Niagara Falls souvenir shop, contends with talking tchotchke animals, such as a wax lion and a brass monkey, who instruct her, as God does with Joan, in a round-about manner, to help strangers. Jaye reluctantly carries out each good deed, relying solely on her sarcasm and desire to silence the relentless voices of these normally inanimate objects.

The premiere of the similarly premised *Tru Calling, Joan of Arcadia,* and *Wonderfalls* within a single television season (2003–04) could be considered a coincidence rather than a programming trend. However, *The New York Times*'s Alessandra Stanley asserted that these three series "about young girls who hear voices" was the effect of "lockstep network brainstorming." This particular lockstep resulted in three superpowered women who have the power to be selfless, *i.e.*, they possess a willingness — or at least a deference — to be used as a vessel for what they consider to be a greater good. The fact that the three self-sacrificing and cosmically linked protagonists in question are women cannot be overlooked; as Tucker opened his combined review of *Joan of Arcadia* and *Wonderfalls*, "It sounds at first like a sexist trend, or the premise for a very evil FOX reality show: Vulnerable young women receive signs or hear voices that give them orders they feel they must obey" ("Guided by Voices" 55). Selflessness, itself, therefore, can be a power for female television characters and actual women alike, as women who meet this cultural expectation are afforded greater social acceptance.

Selflessness Begins at Home

This power of selflessness must be enacted on a large-scale, as the responsibilities that accompany superpowered women's abilities often include saving the world, as Mrs. Wakeman reminds Jenny or as Buffy's tombstone attests ("She saved the world. A lot" ["The Gift"]). Along with these large-scale responsibilities, though, many superpowered women also fulfill more traditional caregiver roles, à la Samantha, their progenitor from *Bewitched*. Such traditional caregiving roles can be equated with the "mother-substitutes" Riviere describes (131), since superpowered women on television often serve as surrogate parents to siblings and/or others who are struggling to understand their own powers and place in the world. These additional, maternal responsibilities frequently distract superpowered women from their larger-scale responsibilities of protecting innocents and/or preventing the apocalypse. The resulting anxiety experienced by these on-screen characters due to their split focus in purposes and responsibilities echoes that of many off-screen women experiencing anxiety from their own split focus between the personal and the professional.

For example, on *Tru Calling*, Tru uses her "rewind days" not only to save the lives of the dead who seek her aid, but to protect her substance-abusing sister Meredith (*e.g.*, Tru warns Meredith of an upcoming temptation ["Pilot"]) and her reckless, unemployed brother Harrison (*e.g.*, Tru slips him the card he needs for a winning poker hand so that he does not face violent retribution from the criminals to whom he is indebted ["Pilot"]). In fact, Harrison relies on and feels entitled to this sororal duty. When Tru warns Harrison that she will not always be there to save him, he replies, "Of course you will, Tru. You're my sister" ("Murder in the Morgue"). Similarly, on *Buffy the Vampire Slayer*, Buffy becomes her sister's, Dawn's, guardian upon the death of their mother; school lunches and parent-teacher meetings then must be worked in alongside Buffy's efforts to stave off that week's apocalypse. Likewise, on *Birds of Prey*, Barbara and Helena serve as teenage Dinah's foster mother and honorary big sister, respectively, as they simultaneously battle the supervillains of New Gotham. On *Charmed*, first Prue and then Piper fulfill the role of big sister/caregiver for their younger sisters in between and amidst their battles with the dark side; for Piper, such caregiving duties multiply when she later becomes the mother of two sons. Next, on *Dark Angel*, Max first seeks out her X5 "siblings" (the other genetically engineered individuals who escaped from Manitcore with her when they were children) and, later, becomes a maternal figure and leader for the Manticore refugees she releases from captivity when she destroys that institution's compound. Max willingly makes sacrifices for all of her Manticore relations, and, in a scene reminiscent of John Steinbeck's *Of Mice and Men* ("Tell me about the good place" ["Pollo Loco"]), she even tearfully takes the life of her brother Ben, who, injured and mentally unstable, begs her to kill him lest he be taken back to Manticore. Finally, even *My Life as a Teenage Robot*'s Jenny acts as a big sister/ protector for neighbor Tuck on occasion.

In all of these examples, the superpowered women's willing or obligatory performances of caregiving roles for family and friends allow these otherwise nontraditional women the opportunity to fulfill traditional feminine roles. Or, as Joan remarks when God requests that she help out around her family's busy household, "What's with God the sexist? [...] How come the girl in the family always has to do all of the cooking and running around? How old school is that?" ("Requiem for a Third Grade Ashtray"). Such old-school roles offer superpowered women yet another way to make good for their extraordinary powers— powers that generally are associated with men. The ability of superpowered women convincingly to portray mother figures while concurrently being full-time Good Samaritans, preventing crime, and/or battling evil for the betterment of their communities or possibly their worlds underscores the essentialist component of Riviere's concept of the masquerade. As Véronique Machelidon explains in "Masquerade: A Feminine or Feminist Strategy," for Riviere, femininity "may not be completely innate [...], but it is there all along from the beginning as essence, as potential to be activated in every woman through 'normal' development" (105). While superpowered women do not undergo what Riviere — or Machelidon — perhaps would deem normal development, the result is the same: even abnormal development, such as that experienced by superpowered women, leads to an assumption of the culturally acceptable face of femininity— the guise of selflessness. According to psychoanalytic theorists, such as Riviere, then, women are socialized to assume this guise, but the capability to carry it out — the capacity for self-sacrifice — may have biological/ psychological roots. Selflessness for women, therefore, as with other elements of their so-called feminine development, may be predetermined to some degree as based on Riviere's observations. Thus, from this theoretical perspective, the gendered destinies of superpowered and actual women during the gilded age were difficult to escape or even temporarily evade.

No Time Off for Good Behavior

Once the guise of selflessness is assumed by superpowered women, they quickly learn that this mantle cannot be taken off easily or without consequences, as self-interest is not "a mask that fits within the cultural norms" for women, to use Maguire's phrase (55). Therefore, these characters, like Jenny, face chastisement when they decide to take — or even ask for — a day away from their responsibilities. For example, when Logan and Max make plans to go away for a weekend, Max plans on down time; Logan, however, plans to investigate a group of protestors who died ten years before. When Max complains, "This was supposed to be a vacation," Logan asks how he could enjoy himself when the person responsible for the protestors' deaths has not yet come to justice. Max's insistence on "kick[ing] back, [and] mak[ing] S'mores" is met with a passive-aggressive remark ("Have fun. Because that *is* the most important thing") from Logan ("Haven"). Max, though, foregoes her relaxation when she befriends a young boy who witnessed the death of his parents and is now in danger from their killers.

Likewise, when Tru plans a party for her first night off since starting work at the morgue (thirty-eight days previously), Tru's supervisor, Davis, who knows about her supernatural moonlighting, questions the wisdom of such revelry:

DAVIS: So you're absolutely, positively, 100 percent sure about this whole day off thing?
TRU: For the last time, yes.
DAVIS: Okay. But what if a dead body comes in and asks for help ... what do I do? [...]
TRU: Did you hear what I said? I have worked eight days this week. Literally. [...] Davis, I need a break ["Morning After"].

Tru's festivities, however, turn into another occasion for her to save a life when she awakens a few hours after the party with the dead body of her exboyfriend in her bed asking for her help. The selflessness necessitated by superpowered women's abilities is, as Tru notes, an eight-day-a-week responsibility; likewise, the caring responsibilities expected of off-screen women rarely allow for any downtime.

No Powers for Personal Gain

For superpowered women, such responsibility also dictates that they use their abilities solely for their prescribed purposes, as they face negative repercussions for using their abilities for their own benefit. While on *Bewitched*, Samantha's occasional — and initially covert — use of her powers for her own pleasure causes marital discord, as when she and her mother fly to Paris (sans plane) for lunch and run into Darrin's vacationing boss ("Witch or Wife?"); such discord, in sitcom tradition, however, is resolved by episode's end. For more contemporary depictions of superpowered women, though, using their abilities for self-benefit may result in more long-term and/or dangerous repercussions. For this reason, the Charmed Ones' mantra is "no powers for personal gain," as spells cast for their own reward create havoc at the least and near-peril at the worst, such as when Phoebe and Piper cast a spell that makes them irresistible to men — so irresistible that a league of overly ardent admirers almost kills the sisters in pursuit of their affections ("Dream Sorcerer"). As Melissa Levine relates in "Charmed and Dangerous: The So-Called Power of Celluloid Witches," movies and television series, like *Charmed*, that feature supernaturally powered women only allow such women to use their powers in defense of themselves or others (61).

In contrast, on *The Dead Zone*, Johnny, whose six-year, car-accident-induced coma left him with the ability to receive premonitions by touching people and objects, does choose to use his unusual ability to help others, but he also does not hesitate to use his powers for his own purposes, such as selecting the perfect birthday present for his son ("Total Awareness"). Similarly, on *Smallville*, Clark uses his super speed to get to school on time when he misses the bus, and, as noted in the previous chapter, he confides to Pete that he — Clark — once used his X-ray vision to peer into the girls' locker room; Pete's response is encouragement, not chastisement ("Duplicity"). Unlike the Charmed Ones, Johnny and Clark face no repercussions for such personal gain.[4]

Superpowered women may also face consequences — most often censure from others and/or self-imposed guilt — for withholding their powers, as well. When Max, during her "no entanglements" days, refuses to help Logan protect a woman and her child, Logan is shot, and the child is kidnapped. Logan's injury leaves him paralyzed from the waist down, and, even though Max tells an unconscious, hospitalized Logan that she does not feel guilty for his condition ("Pilot"), she later confesses to Original Cindy that Logan "has to spend the rest of his life in a wheelchair because of me," noting "[t]hat's on me 100%" ("Meow"). On *Dead Like Me*, in the aptly titled episode "Reapercussions," grim reaper George's evasion of her current purpose — to assist the

The teenage Clark Kent on *Smallville* receives the admiration of best friend Pete when Clark reveals that his abilities allow him to see into the girls' locker room; Clark, unlike his female counterparts, does not receive admonishment for using his powers for selfish purposes (WB Television/Photofest).

soul of a CEO at the time of his death — while, done out of compassion (she feels preventing his death is "right[ing] a universal wrong"), results in even more deaths. The recently deceased George has trouble accepting her undead role of easing the passing of those who are fated to die; she feels like she is bringing death to her "appointments."[5] Therefore, George concocts a distraction that prevents the CEO from arriving at the allotted time and location for his predestined demise, but also prevents him from issuing a product recall; thus, dozens of the product's users die before their fated times. When George's superior, Rube (the reaper who assigns the appointments), finds her guilt-stricken and sobbing in a public restroom, he admonishes not only George's error in judgment but also her lack of maturity by telling her to "Grow the fuck up" and "You pulled the wrong piece out of the Jenga tower, little girl." Once again, self-interest for these characters (even when combined with good intentions) is not allowed, in part because it signals immaturity, but more so because it signals egocentrism for women. Thus, superpowered women on television from the gilded era serve as recurrent examples of Bordo's concept of other-oriented emotional economy (171), as they are not allowed to pursue their own desires. Selflessness for women was (and continues to be) a cultural expectation on screen as well as off.

Trying on Another Guise

The removal (or attempted removal) of the masquerade of selflessness, then, becomes a type of protest by superpowered women. In *Femme Fatales: Feminism, Film, Psychoanalysis*, Doane describes this oppositional function of the masquerade of femininity (once again, Doane defines the masquerade as the assumption of hyperfemininity) as "resistance to patriarchal positioning"; however, she makes no distinction between the taking off or the putting on of the masquerade in regard to its fulfillment of this function. As Doane explains, a woman's ability to wear or to remove the masquerade of femininity disallows the genuineness—and, in contrast to Riviere's position, any essential nature—of femininity. Since femininity is a mask, women may use it to distance themselves from their culturally imposed images and behaviors and, therefore, gain both perspective and autonomy (25–26).[6]

For superpowered women, a removal of the masquerade indicates an attempt to oppose their heroic destinies and indeed may allow for increased autonomy, but, such autonomy, like a day off for these characters, is short-lived. For example, after Buffy must kill former boyfriend Angel to save the world from demonic rule, she attempts to quit being the Slayer and runs away; in a new town, Buffy now calls herself "Anne" and works as a waitress who longs, Eliza-Doolittle style, "to be alone and quiet in a room with a chair and a fireplace and a tea cozy" ("Anne"). While such a life is far from enviable, for Buffy, focusing on basic needs and living day to day without the burden of her prophesied responsibilities is a welcome change. However, after a homeless girl recognizes Buffy as the Slayer and solicits Buffy's aid to locate a missing boy, Buffy reluctantly, although dutifully, resumes her role as Slayer and its accompanying responsibilities to save the day (again). She then returns to Sunnydale and all of the burdens of Slayerhood, illustrating the cultural inducement for women to enact femininity in the form of selflessness.

One of the more egregious forms of removing the masquerade of selflessness for superpowered women is the putting on of physical masks and costumes. As Bukatman explains in his discussion of mutant superheroes, costumes and logos represent a public marking of the body (101); however, for superpowered women, their bodies—their biologically female bodies—are already publicly marked by their sex. Within the psychoanalytic—which coincides with a patriarchal—framework, the binary of male/female privileges male over female; hence, "[h]e is the norm and therefore unremarkable" and "as the Other, it is she whom he marks" (Phelan 5), an accounting of the sexes that resembles de Beauvoir's, as discussed in the previous chapter. According to Peggy Phelan in *Unmarked: The Politics of Performance*, as marked Others, women remain invisible; to bring attention to themselves, to become visible, invites surveillance, voyeurism, and fetishism (6).[7] The visibility of physical masking for superpowered women, *i.e.*, when they attempt to replace their selflessness with some other guise, no matter how seemingly beneficial, does indeed expose them to danger, as such costuming distracts them from the execution of their responsibilities. In one episode of *Charmed*, for example, the Charmed Ones are transformed into comic-book superheroes, complete with mask-and-cape costumes— they literally become the embodiment of a teenage boy's fantasies when a supernaturally inclined adolescent makes his drawings of the sisters as superheroes become reality. While the costumes provide the sisters with additional powers to employ in saving innocents, the guises also have a side effect. As Phoebe explains, "It's like the masks are clouding our judgment, making us feel like we're invincible"; this feeling of invincibility leads to carelessness, and a slumlord that Phoebe forced into improving his tenants' living conditions catches the Charmed Ones and their "cute little outfits" on tape ("Witches in Tights"). Similarly, on *Birds of Prey*, Barbara's temporary resumption of her Batgirl role — including putting back on that persona's cape and cowl — results in disaster, endangering both Barbara and Dinah. In this regard, then, Barbara's retired Batgirl costume and the Charmed Ones' comic-book–inspired garb become symbols of girlish immaturity that must be overcome by donning a womanly masquerade of selflessness— one that is not only culturally acceptable for women but culturally required. Power suits for women — whether worn by superheroes or female executives— are not acceptable if such attire distracts these women from fulfilling their expected cultural roles.

In less extreme cases of superpowered women donning physical costumes, the characters are merely seeking normalcy, or a method of passing, as discussed in the previous chapter. Since Jenny longs to be accepted, she dons an exoskeleton that transforms her appearance into that of a "normal girl," which, she at first thinks is "bliss"; however, when her stereotypically girlish exoskeleton begins to take over her actions as well as her appearance (an eerie, animated representation of Naomi Wolf's "beauty myth"), this costume puts her friends in danger when a group of space bikers attack the local malt shop. Since normal girls do not fight, Jenny must short-circuit the exoskeleton and return to her usual appearance before she can defeat the bikers ("The Return of the Raggedy Android"). Like Jenny, Buffy and Dinah lament the lack of normalcy in their lives. For this reason, on Halloween, Buffy decides to wear an eighteenth-century noblewoman's costume, because, as she explains, Halloween is "come as you aren't night." When Buffy is magically turned into her costume, her resulting performance as a fainting female leads to the endangerment of the entire town; after the spell is broken, she explains that her choice of costume stemmed from her desire "to be a real girl for once"

Jenny (left), the title character of *My Life as a Teenage Robot*, often must forego the typical teenage experience to fulfill the purpose for which she was created: to save the earth. However, she longs to be "normal" like friends Brad (center) and Tuck (Nickelodeon/Photofest).

("Halloween"). Dinah, too, assumes a costume in a quest for normalcy, although hers is more subtle; after reading the mind of a boy she has a crush on, she dresses in the type of sexy clothing that she learns he likes, with the hope that he will ask her to the school dance — a dance she earlier pointed out to Barbara was "for normal girls" ("Lady Shiva"). Dinah soon, though, feels sufficiently guilty for both using her powers on a civilian and for trying to be someone she is not: "Reading a guy's mind to get him to like you is like the lowest form of metahuman existence" ("Lady Shiva"). Ironically, then, when superpowered women seek to replace their guise of selflessness, they may turn to yet another masquerade of femininity — that of a "normal girl" who "worr[ies] about outfits and make-up tips," as Dinah explains ("Lady Shiva"), and not "ambush tactics [and] beheading," as Buffy notes ("Halloween"). This superficial hyperfemininity, which relates to Riviere's criterion of interest in personal appearance, offers these characters a much less burdensome — and more pleasurable — masquerade than the one of selflessness that their powers have destined them to assume.[8]

(Alternate) Reality Break

Despite superpowered women's intense yearning for normalcy, their indoctrination to the self-sacrifice that accompanies their powers ultimately overrides their desire to drop the mantle of selflessness. While breaking from a destiny that requires constant self-abnegation would be the ultimate protest against the masquerade, when superpowered women face an opportunity to make such a break, they question their sanity. *Charmed*, *Buffy the Vampire Slayer*, and *Joan of Arcadia* all featured episodes in which primary characters experience some type of emotional breakdown when faced with the possibility that an alternate reality exists—a reality in which they do not have to protect innocents, save the world, or follow obscure orders from a higher power.

On *Charmed*, in the episode "Brain Drain," Piper proposes to her sisters that they call a truce with the Source, the ultimate evil within the Charmed Ones' universe, so that they can "get out of the demon fighting business once and for all." When Leo, Piper's husband and Whitelighter (a guardian angel for witches), asks if this means that she is willing to give up her destiny, Piper notes that the countless innocents they have saved may have already fulfilled that destiny. The Source then recognizes Piper's desire for the mundane as the chink in her superpowered armor and exploits it in an attempt to rid the sisters of their extraordinary abilities. After an attack by the Source (who has altered Piper's perceptions), she awakens in the family manor, which is now a mental hospital. Piper learns from Leo, who is now her doctor, that she has episodes in which she believes that she and her roommates—Phoebe and Paige—are witches who save innocents. Furthermore, in this reality, Piper's sister Prue is still alive; she has apparently been cured of her own magical delusions and released from the hospital. While Piper fights valiantly against accepting this alternate world as reality, the Source's mind games eventually weaken her resistance, and, at his urging, she begins to recite the spell that will relinquish the Charmed Ones' powers; however, before she can complete the recitation, Phoebe, Paige, and Leo enter her mind and convince her that the hospital is the false reality.

In the similarly premised episode "Normal Again" on *Buffy the Vampire Slayer*, Buffy experiences hallucinations after being wounded in a fight with a demon. Buffy alternates between her world (the one in which she is the Slayer) and what the viewer is led to believe, at least initially, is a delusional world (one in which Buffy, like Piper, is a patient in a mental institution, and a deceased relative, in this case her mother, is still alive). Within the hospital world, Buffy is told that she does not have special abilities, that her memories of slaying vampires and preventing apocalypse are schizophrenic hallucinations, or, as a doctor explains to Buffy's parents: "She believes she's some type of hero. [...] She's also created an intricate latticework to support her primary delusion. In her mind, she's the central figure in a fantastic world beyond imagination." Within the hospital world, Buffy fights to maintain her grasp on the reality she knows, but, like Piper, the mental and emotional anguish becomes too much to bear, and she gives in to the delusion. Then, following her doctor's orders to rid herself of all ties to her fantastic world, Buffy binds her sister and friends Xander and Willow and locks them in the basement with the demon that wounded her. (Buffy's friend Willow was using the demon's blood to create an antidote for Buffy.) Before the demon can kill the helpless Dawn, Xander, and Willow, another friend, Tara, arrives and unbinds them so they can defend themselves; as Slayer Buffy watches her loved ones battle the demon, hospital Buffy is urged by her mother to believe in herself.

Hospital Buffy then tearfully says goodbye to her parents, and Slayer Buffy joins the fight, kills the demon, apologizes, and asks Willow for the antidote. Unlike "Brain Drain" on *Charmed*, though, "Normal Again" questions but does not confirm its protagonist's reality; the episode's final scene reveals hospital Buffy catatonic in a corner of her room while her doctor tells her distressed parents, "I'm afraid we lost her."

Finally in "Silence," the season-one finale of *Joan of Arcadia*, Joan, after a year of believing she was interacting with the Almighty, learns that she has a severe case of Lyme disease, which brings with it hallucinations. When Joan's parents explain that her sickness may have caused her to imagine some things and they fail to acknowledge the individuals Joan knows as God leaving her hospital room, Joan tearfully asks, "It was never real? I've

Joan of Arcadia's title character feels burdened by her "gift"— the ability to talk to God — but when faced with the possibility that such a gift is actually a hallucination, she grieves the loss of her purpose, her direction in life (CBS/Photofest).

always been sick?" Later Joan confesses to her boyfriend, Adam, that she has been talking to God, thinking that if someone else believes her then maybe she is not sick or crazy after all: "I've been talking to ... to God. [...] It's scary and ... annoying. But the thing is, when I obey ... things turns out okay. [...] You have to believe me. If you believe me, then ... I know it's not crazy, but if you don't...." When the only reassurance Adam can provide is that he believes Joan believes, Joan is despondent; the episode and the first season end with Joan and her parents asleep in her hospital room with God — in the first guise revealed to Joan, that of a cute, high-school boy — standing by Joan's bedside.

For Piper, Buffy, and Joan, their abilities (or in Joan's case, her connection with the supernatural) define them, since it is their abilities that prevent them from being normal, as discussed in the previous chapter; thus, when faced with the opportunity to forego such abilities, whether the opportunity is real or imagined (as the *Charmed* episode is the only one of the three described above that definitively validates one reality over another), these superpowered women experience a crisis of identity and emotional breakdown. Such a breakdown can be equated with hysteria, as it historically has been ascribed to women. While Freud's definition of hysteria as physical symptoms resulting from repressed sexual trauma is not applicable to an analysis of the aforementioned characters, feminist psychoanalytic theorists Hélène Cixous and Catherine Clément's description, in *The Newly Born Woman*, of Dora, Freud's hysterical patient, as "the one who resists the system, the one who cannot stand that the family and society are founded on the body of women" does apply (154), as does Heath's explanation of hysteria as "*[f]ailed* masquerade" (145). Piper, Buffy, and Joan each struggle with the self-sacrifice required by their abilities; each longs for a life free of the system that has designated them full-time protectors, caregivers, and/or Good Samaritans. However, as the need for and the alleged nobility (a type of martyrdom) inherent in these selfless roles are constantly reinforced by those who sanction their powers and/or their loved ones, superpowered women such as Piper, Buffy, and Joan cannot imagine a world where their calling does not exist; faced with the possibility of such a world, they experience emotional and mental collapse. Who are they if not those who help others? While, in each of the narratives described above, this collapse comes from an outside influence — whether demonic or bacterial in nature — the subconscious wrestling with their destinies indicates a degree of protest — a resistance to and not a blind acceptance of — their culturally expected roles. The short-lived nature of their hallucinatory breaks from their burdensome real lives, though, indicates the strength of the pull exerted by such forces, or, more specifically the gendered expectations therein. As Cixous and Clément explain regarding hysteria, while the hysteric temporarily can disrupt patriarchy (or, in their terms, the patriarchal family), the hysterical state ultimately binds her more closely to patriarchal forces: "The hysteric, dolefully reclining, tended and surrounded by doctors and worried family, is a prisoner inside the family" (8). Consequently, it is Piper's family and Buffy's sister and friends who reintegrate them into their roles as a witch and a Slayer, respectively, and Joan's family and friends who gather in the hospital as a show of support. So, for superpowered women, a permanent removal of the masquerade of selflessness — a severance from the abilities that require the sacrifice of a normal life — can only be experienced through delusion, and even that temporary respite ultimately underscores their inability to escape their destinies. The hysteria of superpowered women on television parallels the anxiety and depression faced by many real-life women who likewise struggle with potentially competing emotional forces — their own desires and the expectations of family members, friends, colleagues, and the culture at large.

Gift Versus Obligation

While all heroism requires selflessness, as noted previously, the degree of selflessness required of superpowered women exceeds that of superpowered men. Superpowered women on television are often chosen or predestined for their powers and accompanying savior roles, while superpowered men often exhibit a higher degree of autonomy in terms of when and how to use their extraordinary abilities. For example, superpowered female characters such as Jenny, Tru, and the Charmed Ones are fated (or built, in Jenny's case) to serve others, while male superpowered characters such as Clark Kent of *Smallville* and Jake of *Jake 2.0* choose to use their remarkable abilities to help others even though such assistance has not been cosmically predetermined. Thus, Davis tells Tru, "You were chosen for a reason. [...] Curse or calling, love it or hate it, you are the right person for the job. No doubt in my mind" ("Valentine"), while Jonathan, Clark's father, tells the teenage Clark, "[Y]ou choose your own destiny. Nobody can decide that for you, son" ("Exodus"). In fact, on *Smallville*, when Jor-El, Clark's Kryptonian (*i.e.*, biological) father, attempts to control Clark and his abilities so that the superpowered teenager will "accept [his] destiny," Clark resists both the otherworldly parental control and said destiny ("Exodus"); for Clark, the imposition of such a destiny is considered a malevolent force, rather than the fulfillment of a divine prophecy.

Furthermore, superpowered women may be coerced into using their abilities for the betterment of others by being told it is the right thing to do, while superpowered men may be encouraged to do the same but also are told what is in it for them. In the debut episode of *Missing*, Jess, who gains psychic abilities after she is struck by lightning, is held in custody by the FBI after she calls in the locations of three missing persons; to be released from custody, Jess must agree to serve as a special consultant to the Bureau:

> MALE AGENT: We believe you have a special gift, but with a gift comes responsibility.[9] Now if you can help people — really help people — wouldn't you want to?
> JESS: Yes. Obviously ["Pilot"].

For Jess, her abilities require the fulfillment of the cultural expectation of selflessness.

In contrast, when a male character unexpectedly gains extraordinary abilities, the use of these abilities for the greater good is presented as an opportunity for advancement. When, as noted previously, a laboratory accident transforms NSA computer technician Jake Foley into "a universal remote" with enhanced physical abilities, he, like Jess, becomes the object of recruitment efforts by a federal agency; however, Jake's NSA recruiters use different tactics than Jess's FBI handlers. NSA officials, after learning of Jake's new skills, do, initially, hold Jake against his will, but, ultimately offer him an upgrade in his security clearance — a privilege for which he twice before applied and had been denied:

> DEPUTY DIRECTOR: I have just been authorized to create a special ops team — with you at its core.
> JAKE: Whoa. Hold on. Hold on. I didn't ask for any of this, okay?
> DEPUTY DIRECTOR: Yes, you did. Twice.
> SPECIAL AGENT: This is your big chance. Don't waste it.
> JAKE: [smiles] ["The Tech"].

For women with supernatural or superhuman abilities, then, such gifts are synonymous with obligation, while, for men, such powers may result in opportunity with the choice of added responsibility.

The autonomy of superpowered men during the gilded age is also greater than that of their female counterparts because they rarely answer to sanctioning organizations. While the Charmed Ones must answer to their Whitelighter, the Elders (guardians of good), and the Tribunal (guardians of both white and dark magic), Buffy to her Watcher (appointed mentor) and the Watchers' Council (at least for her first five seasons), George to Rube, and Joan to the Almighty Himself (or Herself depending on the incarnation), *Smallville*'s Clark and *The Dead Zone*'s Johnny face no such institutional accountability or chain of command. While these male characters may feel a personal obligation to help others, no formal structure is in place to demand or ensure such a philanthropic use of their powers. For this reason, superpowered men are often reminded that they do not have to do it all. Therefore, Johnny's friend Rebecca (who later becomes his girlfriend) urges him to reconsider his self-imposed mission to save the world, especially since the continued use of his powers is taking a physical toll: "[T]he truth is, despite your abilities, you're just one man. Maybe it's not your visions causing these symptoms; maybe it's this burden you carry around with you. This enormous responsibility you've taken on. You can't save everyone, Johnny" ("Collision"), while, in contrast, the Charmed Ones are reminded constantly by the authorities in their lives that they have been granted their abilities to save any and all innocents they encounter. Superpowered men, therefore, do not face the cultural expectation of selflessness that superpowered women do; male self-sacrifice is admirable, but optional.

Because constant selflessness is not demanded from or expected of superpowered men, they are forgiven more readily for selfish acts, even when such acts cause harm to others. On *Smallville*, when Clark attempts to break from Jor-El's influence by destroying the spaceship that brought him — Clark — to earth, the resulting explosion causes Martha, his adoptive mother, to miscarry. Clark, unable to face the repercussions of his actions, runs away to Metropolis and begins using his abilities for criminal purposes. Jonathan, determined to bring Clark home, seeks Jor-El's assistance. Although this assistance temporarily empowers Jonathan to return Clark to Smallville, the loan of such heightened physical abilities causes Jonathan to collapse. Later, as the Kents gather at Jonathan's bedside, Martha tells Clark that they "never blamed [him]" and Jonathan tells Clark that "[t]he important thing is that [he] is back home" ("Phoenix"). Unfortunately, Buffy faces no such homecoming when she returns from her sabbatical as Anne; her friends, Watcher, and mother all express more hurt and resentment than forgiveness and a welcoming of the prodigal. When Buffy inquires whether Giles is "mad at [her]," Xander sarcastically replies: "Mad? Just because you ran away and abandoned your post and your friends and your mom and made him [Giles] lay awake every night worrying about you?"; Buffy even overhears her mother telling a friend that, as difficult as it was when Buffy was away, "having Buffy home [...] in some ways, it's almost worse" ("Dead Man's Party"). The laying aside of a heroic, selfless persona is forgiven more readily for superpowered men than for their female counterparts. Such allowances for selfish behavior are more often granted for men than women off-screen, as well, since, for example, there is no culturally acceptable female equivalent to "boys will be boys."

Finally, in contrast to superpowered women, superpowered men more often are able to lead separate lives — to have both heroic and everyday personae, or as described in the previous chapter, to separate their "what"s from their "who"s. As Fingeroth notes, "Only the superhero disguises his identity for a noble purpose and is able to maintain his integrity while so doing" (53). For this reason, Clark Kent and Superman easily can be distinguished on the pre–gilded-age *Lois & Clark: The New Adventures of Superman*; Clark is the mild-mannered newspaper reporter, while Superman is the costumed superhero. (Buffy uses this well-known fact as a bargaining chip when she tries to convince Giles to give her the night off: "Clark Kent has a job. I just want to go on a date" ["Never Kill a Boy on the First Date"].) Traditionally, for superpowered men, such costumes have not been seen as the signs of immaturity that they are for superpowered women; instead, for men, such costumes are a sign of physical maturity. Therefore, on *Smallville*, the teenage Clark Kent's lack of costume and accompanying Superman persona are reflective of his developing powers.[10] This use of costuming for superpowered men reflects Heath's contention that masculinity, like femininity, is a masquerade, although masculinity is a "charade of power" (150). Such a charade, apparently, cannot be successfully executed by women, as Helena attempts to separate her personal life from her heroism through her use of the name Huntress while crime fighting. When Reese almost discovers that Helena and Huntress are one and the same, Helena complains to Dinah and Barbara:

> HELENA: My life was this close to becoming a French farce.
> DINAH: Hey, Molière. I think you're making way too much of this secret identity thing.
> HELENA: Really? You try keeping a secret with my schedule.
> DINAH: What secret? You have no secret identity. You don't wear a mask.
> BARBARA: She's kind of got a point. [...]
> HELENA: Can't I have two lives without looking like an overgrown trick-or-treater? ["Reunion"].

The answer to Helena's question is, of course, "No," as superpowered women do not have the luxury of taking off the masquerade of selflessness in the same manner that superpowered men do, just as actual women face a cultural expectation of selflessness that men do not.

The Cultural Expectation of Selflessness

Superpowered women on television, then, must enact a masquerade of selflessness to "restore or make good," to use Riviere's phrasing (138), for their remarkable abilities—abilities that traditionally have been associated with the masculine domain. Just as women's physical ability to bear children

3. Masquerade of Selflessness 91

brings with it the cultural expectation of the possession of maternal instincts (the strongest of which is a mother's willingness to sacrifice herself for her child),[11] so, too, do superpowered women's innate powers bring with them the cultural expectation of selflessness. The fulfillment of this expectation becomes a sign of maturity for superpowered women; these women, therefore, must privilege their selfless roles, which often include domestic caregiving in addition to saving the world (literally or symbolically). Attempts to lay aside such fated responsibilities are chastised or punished; superpowered women, then, must use their powers only as directed. Any autonomy they may gain from pursuing their own agendas is short-lived, as they seemingly cannot escape or change their destinies. While superpowered men demonstrate agency vis-à-vis their powers and may reap benefits from such powers, for superpowered women, such abilities are indicative of obligation and responsibility, not agency. Theirs is a gift that only can be given to others.

The prevalence of such scenarios in series that feature superpowered women from 1996 to 2006 suggested the rightness of women following such culturally prescribed paths and taking on such culturally expected responsibilities, perhaps then communicating to those series' predominantly female viewers that they, too, should "obviously" want to "really help people" with their own abilities (as Jess is told ["Pilot"]) since doing so will make "things turn out okay" (as Joan explains ["Silence"]). For this reason, it is not surprising that the "superheroine," which was designated by *TV Guide* as the "decade's latest pop-culture obsession" in 2002 ("Best of" 72), an obsession that produced the superpowered women noted above, gave way to the "next big television thing," as forecasted by Stanley in 2004: scripted and reality series that feature housewives and mothers (specifically, *Desperate Housewives* [ABC, 2004–2012], *Trading Spouses* [FOX, 2004–07], and *Wife Swap* [ABC, 2004–]). The legacy of the gilded-age superwoman was, apparently, at least in the short term, the soccer mom, a legacy further reinforced by the 2003 Dodge Caravan ad with the tagline "Some superheroes use a phone booth. Moms have this [the Caravan]" referenced in the Introduction. Whether armed with remote alarm systems in their pigtails or in their minivans, both superpowered women and soccer moms enact the masquerade of selflessness.

The narratives of selflessness contained within television series featuring superpowered women — or swapped spouses, for that matter — reinforce the expectation of selflessness imposed upon women through other cultural trends and texts. Mothers are often the target of such trends and texts, since, as Karlyn notes, American culture has a "tradition of mother-blaming"; working mothers are targeted even more frequently in advertisements and other texts, perhaps because they possess more economic power than stay-at-home moms or perhaps because they pursue what are considered non-traditional roles for women. Despite the financial need for two-income families during the gilded age, working mothers still faced (and continue to face) censure for their alleged privileging of their careers over their families. Researchers even linked "absent mothers with teen crime"; the National Bureau of Economic Research in Cambridge, Massachusetts, published a 1999 study that found "the long-run effect of a one percentage point rise in the female labour [sic] force participation rate increases the crime rate by just over five percent" (qtd. in McLean).

Such data, then, perhaps justified the increase in options during this time period that offered working mothers help in enacting their caring responsibilities. Business casual apparel can be interpreted as one such option, as it allows working mothers to wear more comfortable, easier-to-launder clothing, saving on transition time between home and office. However, some sources indicate that "women may be negatively affected by casual dress codes" (Chaney and Lyden), as women who dress casually may not be viewed as professionally as those dressed in more formal clothing. In addition, telecommuting, which was once "heralded as the liberation of working mothers" (Star 571), blurs the boundaries between familial and professional environments to the detriment of women. While in-home work hours are supposed to allow working mothers flexible schedules so that they can devote more time to their families with less guilt, telecommuting women "miss promotion and social aspects of the job, and often are expected to do finicky tasks such as data entry along with full-time child care" (571). Such options seem to encourage working mothers to maintain their mask of nurturing — of selflessness — at all times and in all situations.

The cultural pressure to maintain such a masquerade took its toll on the health of some working women during the gilded age. A late–1990s survey of female employees of a British University indicated that there is a link between women's caring responsibilities (whether for children, spouses, aging parents or some other loved one) and the level of pressure they experience: "pressures increase as caring responsibilities increase" (Field and Bramwell 166, 168). Some working women, therefore, may feel burdened by the negotiation of their dual — and seemingly opposing — masquerades of "carer" and "worker" (to use the terms of the aforementioned survey). This feeling of burden may be a factor contributing to the mental disorders experienced by many women. As Brant Wenegrat explains in "Illness and Power: Women's Mental Disorders as Illness Roles," the number of women who suffer from mental disorders may be higher than the number of men who suffer the same "because women in fact have lacked needed social power." Both women's greater propensity toward mental illness and their lack of social power have been capitalized upon by pharmaceutical companies.

Along with women's higher risk in suffering mental illness comes a greater likelihood for women to be featured in advertisements for anti-anxiety or anti-depressant medications.[12] While these linked phenomena, in part, can be attributed to the overall cultural trend of medicalizing women's bodies, the taglines and images of women used in these advertisements often specifically address women's caring responsibilities and the increased difficulty of fulfilling these responsibilities due to illness. For example, the Web site for Sarafem, a pink-coated, repackaged version of Prozac used for treating premenstrual dysphoric disorder, asks women if "juggling work, family and personal commitments leave[s] [them] feeling frazzled and stressed out?" (qtd. in Koerner). In addition, an advertisement for the anti-depressant/anti-anxiety medication Paxil not only references a woman's caring responsibilities, but the text and images suggest that the woman's illness has caused her to fail at these responsibilities: the tagline "What's standing between you and your life?" appears above the image of a woman with cast-down head physically separated from her visibly sad and concerned husband and son by words such as "Depressed Mood," "Agitation," and "Restlessness." An image of the same woman smiling while cuddling with her son appears next to the product description and the message, "Feeling balanced, more like 'yourself,' is within reach" (Paxil CR). Such advertisements indicate that illness is not a culturally acceptable mask for women, as illness focuses on the self and not others. Therefore, depression for women can be read as allowing them to remove their own masquerade — making depression akin to Heath's explanation of hysteria as failed masquerade by a woman who "will not play the game" (145).

The cultural expectation of selflessness for women, then, is perpetuated by both formal institutions, such as the media and the medical community, and informal ones, which include women themselves. Women who will not play the game of meeting this expectation, either by choice or by some force beyond their control, such as illness, are met with reproach, whether in the form of criticism (*e.g.*, working women cause increased crime) or assistance (*e.g.*, the opportunity to telecommute). During the gilded age, then, selflessness was, indeed, the ultimate sign of feminine development; as communicated by cultural trends and texts, it was clearly the right thing for women to do. Karlyn even notes that for contemporary young women, in reflection of third-wave ideology, "family life (or their fantasies about motherhood and domesticity)" is (are) looked to as "an option or 'luxury' that may appear frustratingly out of reach." Such ideology, therefore, idealizes rather than contests the cultural expectation of selflessness. Or, as Whelehan explains, "women are being emotionally blackmailed by the new/old patriarchs and the backlashers to return to their role as moral guardians of society and the family to the point of utter self-effacement" (174). Moreover, feminism, itself, is not even exempt from the association of such guardianship, as Gloria Steinem relates that "it will take a while before feminists succeed enough so that feminism is not perceived as a gigantic mother who is held responsible for almost everything, while the patriarchy receives terminal gratitude for the small favors it bestows" (xix).

Narratives of superpowered women struggling against their own (physical or moral) roles as guardians of society — or as extraordinarily abled mothers — from 1996 to 2006 reinforced the cultural expectation of selflessness. This expectation was further underscored by the fact that these characters predominantly exist in the fantasy genre — a genre that, by definition, should be escapist. However, for women on screen and off, there was no apparent escape from this cultural expectation of selflessness, from the assumption of this particular masquerade of femininity. After all, how can a woman take the afternoon off when unfriendly spacecraft have their ray guns pointed at the Earth?

CHAPTER 4

Surveillance of Female Superpower

WARREN: We got nine high-resolution surveillance cameras hooked in, super-wide angle, infrared, auto-iris, plus six types of audio matrix monitoring ... that's filtered through a dual quad DVS system, and a...
JONATHAN: [...] Are you sure with all of this stuff that we'll be able to watch Buffy without her noticing us?
WARREN: Absolutely.—*Buffy the Vampire Slayer*, "Life Serial"

MAX: [pointing to a classified advertisement] Those numbers are me.
LOGAN: This is your bar code?
MAX: Black and white for the whole world to see. It's like opening the paper and finding my panties.
LOGAN: Who else knows this number?
MAX: Only someone from Manticore.—*Dark Angel*, "411 on the DL"

IRONS: What is your recommendation?
IAN: To watch her [Sara] closely. [...]
IRONS: You are a good and faithful servant, Ian.—*Witchblade*, "Periculum"

Can't Afford to Be Photographed

Max, the genetically engineered protagonist of *Dark Angel*, lives in a futuristic Seattle; the year is 2019, and, as Max explains, a terrorist-triggered electromagnetic pulse ten years earlier turned the United States into "just another broke ex-superpower looking for a handout and wondering why" ("Pilot"). Within this post-apocalyptic America, Max "liv[es] on the run always looking over [her] shoulder" ("Pilot") for fear that Manticore—the secret military operation that created her and from which she escaped as a child—will locate her. For Max, the pulse can be counted as both blessing and curse. The shockwave obliterated existing computer data, making it all the harder for Manticore to discover her whereabouts; however, the resulting conditions also transformed the city into a police state. Seattle citizens must now have passes to be cleared through sector checkpoints, and flying-saucer-like "hoverdrones" patrol the city with electronic eyes (and, in one episode, are programmed to execute people ["I and I Am a Camera"]). Since Max's escape from Manticore, she has strived to be "just another one of the huddled masses yearning to go by unnoticed" ("Flushed"). And while Max is an expert at bypassing checkpoints and dodging hoverdrones, she learns in the series' third episode, titled "Flushed," that she should have been looking over her shoulder for more than just Manticore.

Although Manticore's engineering of Max's DNA made her a "revved up female," it also left behind a "design flaw" ("Flushed"). Max occasionally has seizures due to lack of serotonin; to combat the seizures, Max takes tryptophan, a food supplement. When Max experiences a particularly "bad patch" ("Flushed") of seizures, her roommate Kendra and Original Cindy observe her atypical behavior and conclude that Max must be taking drugs; after searching Max's possessions, Kendra and Original Cindy find the tryptophan and flush it down the toilet, telling Max they did so because they "love [her] very much" ("Flushed"). As Max's condition worsens, she attempts to steal tryptophan from a medical clinic and, in her weakened state, fails to evade the clinic's security guards; she is then arrested and placed in an overcrowded prison.

Logan, now Max's love interest, who anonymously broadcasts "streaming freedom video bulletins" as "Eyes Only," eventually locates Max and devises a plan to rescue her — with some help from the now-contrite Original Cindy, who has learned from Logan that Max was taking the tryptophan due to a life-threatening neurological condition. Logan uses his considerable technical skills to hack into the prison's security system to locate Max, noting when he sees her mug shot that "she's one girl that can't afford to be photographed" ("Flushed"). As the undercover Original Cindy attempts to help the now feverish and hallucinating Max break out of prison, Lydecker, a Manticore operative, learns of Max's location. Before Lydecker can capture Max, though, she and Original Cindy are able to escape — on their way out, they even save a young girl named Maria who was being abused by the warden. Thus the episode concludes happily — or as happily as Max's escapades can conclude; Max's health is restored for the time being (thanks to the tryptophan Original Cindy gave her before the escape), Original Cindy and Kendra apologize for their actions, Logan praises Max for her good deed in protecting Maria, and Maria is placed with adoptive parents. This narrow escape, however, only can be cause for relief and not celebration, as the episode illustrates that the spying eyes of well-intentioned loved ones imperil the superpowered Max as readily as those of her enemies — since both have the capacity to flush her into the visible and into danger.

Max is not the only superpowered woman on television who must protect herself from spying eyes; the surveillance of superpowered women is a common element within the narratives of gilded-age series, including *Witchblade*, *Buffy the Vampire Slayer*, *Sabrina, the Teenage Witch*, and *Roswell*. On *Witchblade*, millionaire Kenneth Irons, who is obsessed with the titular magical gauntlet's power, surveys Sara personally, psychically, and by proxy; on *Buffy the Vampire Slayer*, Buffy's Watchers Giles and Wesley and the Watchers' Council, the institution to which they report, scrutinize the Slayer's performance; on *Sabrina, the Teenage Witch*, Sabrina's aunts and the Council of Witches survey her actions; and on *Roswell*, alien Isabel's parents and husband closely monitor — and, in the case of her mother, even secretly videotape — her behavior. Regardless of the formality or familiarity of this surveillance, whether it is conducted by a bureaucratic and perhaps impersonal institution such as the Watchers' Council or a less official and more personal one such as the family unit, this relentless observation of superpowered women renders their extraordinary abilities a cause for inconvenience, paranoia, danger, and a mechanism by which they can be controlled.

Ultimately, superpowered women internalize the omnipresent gaze of those who, whether well-intentioned or not, seek to influence or dominate their behavior. Thus, even if such surveillance is not present, it is still felt. Whether actual or anticipated, surveillance indoctrinates superpowered women into policing themselves; superpowered women, therefore, censor their own actions, or, more specifically, hide or curtail their abilities for fear of exposure. Surveillance narratives within series featuring superpowered women from 1996 to 2006 then conveyed to female viewers — who themselves may have suffered the effects of the gaze of medical professionals, supervisors, and even the general public — that the politics of visibility operate to the detriment of women.

The Panopticon

Feminist theoretical accounts of surveillance primarily stem from Foucault's writing on "Panopticism" in his *Discipline and Punish*. The Panopticon, as proposed by philosopher Jeremy Bentham in the eighteenth century, is a circular prison with an observation tower at its center, thus providing guards with simultaneous visible access to all prisoners (Germov and Williams 126). Foucault describes the Panopticon as allowing for ceaseless inspection, as a structure in which "[t]he gaze is alert everywhere" (*Discipline* 195). Therefore, prisoners entering the Panopticon become objects only; they, in effect, leave their subjectivity outside its walls. Within the Panopticon, they exist to be seen, not to see; for these prisoners, visibility means vulnerability (200). In contrast, for the Panopticon guards, visibility is their means of power. This power, as Foucault relates, must not only be "visible" but "unverifiable": visible because the observation tower remains the only fixture in the prisoners' landscape, a constant reminder that there is no escaping the gaze; and unverifiable because the prisoners can never confirm the precise moment at which they are under observation — they must assume such observation is occurring at every moment. Thus, the guards may discontinue their gaze without the prisoners' knowledge or without any effect; whether an assumed or actual gaze, the power relations between guards and prisoners remain the same (201–02).

These power relations within the Panopticon are established and maintained via surveillance. Such surveillance is not an end unto itself, though; rather, it is a means to an end. Surveillance ultimately serves a corrective purpose, as, according to Foucault, surveillance allows for punishment (*Discipline* 184–85), or, in the case of the Panopticon, altered behavior (203). The corrective practices imposed via the Panopticon relate to Foucault's concept of "normalizing judgments," as he notes that surveillance and normalization are both "great instruments of power" (184). The power of normalizing judgments, such as disciplinary practices within schools, is the power to impose conformity (182). Such judgments therefore establish both the norm and any deviations from it (183) — deviations that then must be erased to reassert the norm. As Foucault explains, "The 'shameful' class exist[s] only to disappear" (182). Within the Panopticon, the shameful class disappears under the guards' normalizing judgment; prisoners under the panoptic gaze must conform to the institution's regulations and, therefore, one another. Foucault describes this resulting uniformity as the "homogeneous effects of power" (202).

To achieve such homogenizing effects, the panoptic gaze does not require active oversight; once the power structure is in place, it is self-perpetuating. In Foucault's words, "[T]his architectural apparatus [the Panopticon] should be a machine for creating and sustaining a power relation independent of the person who exercises it" (*Discipline* 201). Thus, inmates, or any individuals subject to a panoptic gaze, become self-policing — modifying their own behavior unprompted. As Christian Parenti explains in *The Soft Cage: Surveillance in America from Slavery to the War on Terror*, "[S]urveillance instills discipline by forcing self-regulation. Constant surveillance brings forth loyal citizens, trained soldiers, obedient patients, productive workers, and docile, useful bodies" (9). Surveillance, then, or even the perception of surveillance, serves as a "'generative' force," to borrow a phrase from Parenti (9); in other words, surveillance is a power that influences, evokes, and creates.

Therefore, just as Foucault describes power, in general, as producing reality for those subjected to it (*Discipline* 194), so, too, can surveillance as a power produce reality for those who fall under its gaze. It is at this point where feminist scholarship on surveillance diverges from Foucault's, as feminist scholars recognize that a power such as surveillance produces a different reality for women than it does for men. For example, Bartky argues in "Foucault, Femininity, and the Modernization of Patriarchal Power" that, especially in regard to bodily disciplinary practices, women's experiences are distinct from men's. Bartky even notes that, while Foucault's "critique of power" contains a "liberatory note," his overall analysis "reproduces that sexism which is endemic throughout Western political theory" (131–32). Other feminist scholarship that draws from Foucault's writing on the Panopticon offers a less-critical assessment of his work but nevertheless indicates the differences between men's and women's subjection to the gaze. In John Germov and Lauren Williams's "Dieting Women: Self-Surveillance and the Body Panopticon," they assert that in cases where women are pressured to conform to ideal body types, it is unlikely that resistance will emerge, despite Foucault's contention that where there is power there is also resistance (126). Feminist scholarship on surveillance, therefore, seeks to recognize and deconstruct the ways in which the power of the gaze can be more pervasive and intrusive for women—and thus a greater factor in the production of their reality—than it is for men.

Women's reality, then, includes subjection to a panoptic gaze, although the origins of this gaze are more difficult to locate and name than the guards in Bentham's observation tower. As Bartky notes, "Woman lives her body as seen by another, by an anonymous patriarchal Other" (140). Consequently, there is a cultural association between women and visibility—the state of being seen (or the potential thereof)—and, conversely, another between men and vision—the power to see. Television's superpowered women from 1996 to 2006 exemplified the persistence of such associations, as even those characters with extraordinary abilities, many of whom possess enhanced or alternate forms of vision, are spied upon surreptitiously and/or openly. The message to viewers is clear: the greater a woman's power, the more eyes there are upon her. Power for women does not automatically gain them the privileged position of seeing—their perspective cannot be considered universal or representative, as it remains at/from the periphery.

Institutionally Bound Surveillance

Dark Angel, Witchblade, Buffy the Vampire Slayer, Sabrina, the Teenage Witch, and *Roswell* all include narratives in which an extraordinary female

Dark Angel's Max faces institutional surveillance from Manticore, the secret government agency that created her; at times, her attempts to elude Manticore require the hacking assistance of love interest, Logan, whose upper-class background affords him the privilege of such cyber-voyeurism (FOX/Photofest).

protagonist is subject to surveillance, a disciplinary method that can reinforce the cultural expectation of selflessness. The surveillance of these characters, following a pattern established by *Bewitched*, may be conducted by institutions, individuals, or both. Such fictional surveillance illustrates two organizational structures for disciplinary practices that Bartky names "institutionally bound" and "institutionally *unbound*" (143). Institutionally bound surveillance within these characters' universes generally originates with the organizations that sanction superpowered women's abilities. For *Bewitched*'s Samantha, this organization is the Witches Council, an unseen group (whose presence often is indicated by thunder and lightning) that disapproves of and, therefore, monitors Samantha's chosen life in suburbia with a mortal husband. Similarly, *Dark Angel*'s Max and *Buffy the Vampire Slayer*'s title character also are scrutinized under an institutionally bound gaze. In Max's case, this institutional surveillance is enacted first by Manticore and, then, upon her dismantling of that organization, by a breeding cult known as the Familiars; while in Buffy's case, such surveillance comes from her Watchers and the Watchers' Council.

4. Surveillance of Female Superpower

For Max, since Manticore is a black-ops division of the Department of Defense, that institution has access to all available surveillance technology and endless personnel to operate it. Manticore, then, is as all-seeing and ever-present as the guards in the Panopticon tower; it serves as an example of what Foucault refers to as an "automatize[d] and "disindividualize[d]" exertion of power — by "see[ing] everything without ever being seen" (*Discipline* 202). While Max has managed to elude Manticore agents in the ten years since her escape, her life is fraught with near misses whenever she falls under their gaze, *e.g.*, when she breaks from prison only minutes before Lydecker can locate the room in which she is being held ("Flushed"), as described earlier in this chapter, or when Lydecker and his men track Max and her X5 brother Ben, as discussed in the previous chapter ("Pollo Loco").

Buffy, too, suffers the effects of a persistent institutional gaze. The gaze of the Watchers' Council is established in the premiere of *Buffy the Vampire Slayer*. In this episode, Buffy, on her first day at Sunnydale High, meets Watcher Giles, who, after taking one look at Buffy, identifies her as the Slayer and urges her to embrace that role. Buffy, who is hoping for a fresh start sans vampires in her new town and school, angrily urges Giles to fulfill that role himself; Giles, taken aback, stammers, "I-I'm a Watcher, I haven't the skill." Recovering slightly, Giles tries a different tack, beginning with "A Slayer slays, a Watcher...," but before he can finish that thought, Buffy interrupts with "watches" ("Welcome to the Hellmouth"). Although Giles then argues that Watchers fulfill a more active role than just watching, as they also train and prepare the Slayer, it is clear that watching is the central component of these other functions as well. The watching done by the Watchers, and, on occasion, the Watchers' Council to which they report, takes the form of examination, as they evaluate the Slayer's development of her skills and the execution of her responsibilities. Examination that accompanies surveillance, as Foucault describes it in *Discipline and Punish*, is "a mechanism of objectification" that allows those in power to maintain control over their subjects (187). Buffy's experiences with the Watchers' Council, then, serve as an illustration of Foucault's correlation between examination and objectification, as the examinations Buffy faces are used to maintain the dynamic of watcher/watched between Watchers and Slayer. More specifically, one of the Council's primary mechanisms for objectifying the Slayer is a formal assessment of the Slayer's abilities on her eighteenth birthday. When Buffy is forced to undergo this examination, both she and her mother are endangered — a circumstance that Council representatives do nothing to prevent, as "[a] Watcher watches" ("Checkpoint").[1] Thus, within series featuring superpowered women, examination serves as periodic or constant reminder of the pervasiveness and influence of the institutional gaze — a gaze that is not merely a passive form of looking but has the potential for (perhaps violent) intervention in its subjects' lives. Off-screen women, too, may face examination with possibly dangerous repercussions, as public scrutiny can quickly turn to public harassment.

Along with examination, a system of registration is central to the success of institutional surveillance — registration that allows for both the marking and tracking of the objects of the organized gaze. *Dark Angel*'s Max is the best example of this type of registration, as Manticore brands its human experiments with bar codes on their necks. To Manticore, therefore, Max is known as "452," the last three digits in her bar code (Max is the name by which she was known to her X5 siblings). When Logan suggests that Max remove this bar code so that it will be more difficult for Manticore to locate her, Max explains that such a removal is not possible. Max's bar code exemplifies Foucault's contention that surveillance is based on a system of *permanent* registration (*Discipline*, 196). As Max explains to Logan:

> MAX: I tried once [to remove the bar code]. It feels like someone's pouring acid on your skin after it's been sandblasted. Came back in a couple weeks. It's etched into our genetic code.
> LOGAN: The mark of Cain ["411 on the DL"].

The permanence of Manticore's registration serves as a constant reminder to Max that, as a superpowered woman (or, in Max's words, a "revved-up female" ["Flushed"]), there is no escaping surveillance; even after Manticore is destroyed, a breeding cult known as the Familiars pick up the search for 452 where Max's creators left off, as viewers learn Max is exceptional even among her X5 siblings. (Her DNA contains no unassigned chromosomal pairings.) Max and other superpowered women, then, may be marked further by institutional surveillance, since, as noted in the previous chapter, women already are publicly marked by their sex. For real-life women, physical marking likewise may occur as the result of institutional surveillance, *e.g.*, when women subject themselves to the medicalized gaze of plastic surgeons — a gaze that remains permanently imprinted on their bodies.

Registration, though, does not necessarily leave a visible imprint. In the fictional worlds of superpowered women, the effects of registration may not be as obvious as Max's bar code; however, such seemingly invisible registration may be no less permanent. For example, as the Slayer, Buffy's powers, themselves, serve as a type of bar code. Once a Slayer's powers are activated upon the death of her predecessor, she remains the Slayer until her own demise; there is no removal or transferal of power (although, as discussed in the following chapter, a sharing of this power is possible). The Watchers' Council is able to track the Slayer and prospective Slayers via these powers (or, in the case of the prospective Slayers, the potential for such abilities). Although it is never made clear in the series how the Council recognizes these powers, it is clear that their system of surveillance and registration is longstanding, highly organized, and magical in nature. (Giles refers to the Council's records as containing "[t]he mystic secrets of the Watchers" ["Bring on the Night"].) All Slayers, both potentials and actives, therefore, can be tracked without physical branding; their powers serve as supernatural serial numbers.

More conventional forms of registration exist in other series featuring superpowered women. On *Sabrina, the Teenage Witch*, for example, the title character must, on her seventeenth birthday, take an examination for her witch's license. When Sabrina fails her first attempt at this examination, she is sent to a weekend boot camp for witches (where she is addressed as S-2103411819-577K) and learns that if she fails the exam a second time she will spend a year at the camp. At her aunts' urging, Sabrina seeks to avoid this unpleasant fate by giving up many of her favorite activities, including editing the school newspaper and spending time with her boyfriend, Harvey, so that she has more time to study for the exam. Such sacrifices pay off when she passes the exam on her second try and receives a learner's permit — although not the license she is expecting. Apparently the Council of Witches functions similarly to the Department of Motor Vehicles, as Sabrina learns from her Aunt Zelda that she will be tested "on and off for the next year" before she can get her actual witch's license when she turns eighteen "and can pay for insurance" ("Sabrina Gets Her License, Parts 1 and 2"). Along with this disappointing news, Sabrina discovers that if she fails to obtain this license by age eighteen, she will become completely mortal (Sabrina is half-human/half-witch). Sabrina's understandable response is, "Great. If I study I may lose Harvey, and if I don't study I'll lose my powers. This is gonna leave no time for TV" ("Sabrina Gets Her License, Part 2"). As indicated by *Dark Angel, Buffy the Vampire Slayer,* and *Sabrina, the Teenage Witch*, institutionally bound surveillance, including its accompanying examinations and registration, positions superpowered women as objects of a persistent gaze that may endanger them, mark them physically or supernaturally, and/or remind them that their powers may be lost.

The Institutionally Unbound Gaze

Not all superpowered women are surveyed by formal or institutional means; other superpowered women are under the gaze of individuals. This convention has its roots in *Bewitched*, as Samantha's neighbor Gladys Kravitz maintains a vigilant watch over the Stephens's household, always attempting to convince her husband, Abner, that all is not normal in Samantha and Darrin's home (see, *e.g.*, "Mother Meet What's His Name"). Although less-structured in nature, the gaze of spying individuals is no less pervasive, as exemplified by Gladys, and may be obsessive, wary, or well-intentioned. As an example from a more contemporary series, *Witchblade*'s Sara is perhaps the most frequent object of an individual's gaze, as the mysterious Kenneth Irons has made it his life's mission to follow the witchblade and, therefore, all of its wielders. Irons, who once attempted to wear the powerful gauntlet only to learn that it will only adorn a woman's arm, now has a supernatural connection to the weapon. As he explains, his brief exposure to the witchblade allows him to "see some of what it sees, but not all" (*Witchblade*). For this reason, Irons, at times, is able to experience what Sara is not only seeing but feeling; for example, when the power of the witchblade tests Sara's worthiness to wield it, Irons vicariously experiences this magical rite of passage ("Periculum").[2] In addition to his psychic surveillance, Irons employs more traditional methods to keep Sara under his gaze. In some instances, Irons observes Sara in person, inviting her to his home under the pretense of assisting her with a police investigation or providing her with additional information about the witchblade. More often, though, Irons watches Sara via his proxy, Ian Nottingham. Ian, a mysterious warrior with a connection to Irons, follows Sara almost constantly; his reports allow Irons to follow Sara's progress as she learns to develop and control her new abilities. Both Irons's obsession with the witchblade and its power and Ian's obsession with Sara herself serve as examples of scopophilia, or pleasure derived from the act of looking. In Laura Mulvey's landmark *Screen* article "Visual Pleasure and Narrative Cinema," first published in 1975, she addresses scopophilia by explaining that female film characters "connote *to-be-looked-at-ness*," *i.e.*, they serve as erotic objects upon which the male gaze can project its fantasy both intra- and extratextually (24, 27). The male gaze, as defined by Zeisler, is "the idea that when we look at images in art or on screen, we're seeing them as a man might — even if we are women — because those images are constructed to be seen by men" (7). In *Witchblade*, intratextual scopophilia occurs, as Sara, through the powers bestowed upon her by the witchblade, unwittingly invites the gaze of Irons and Ian, serving, for Irons, as a fantasy of power and, for Ian, a fantasy of desire. For viewers of *Witchblade*, whether female or male, the same type of scopophilia may occur extratextually, as Zeisler contends that "[s]eeing the visual cues of the male gaze,[3] in turn, affects how women understand images of other women on the screen" (9). The male gaze that is embedded in televised representations of superpowered women invites all viewers to objectify these characters, with such objectification underscored by narratives that directly address superpowered women as the focus of obsessive surveillance.

On *Witchblade*, Sara (center) falls under the watchful eyes of (from left) henchman Ian Nottingham; her friend Gabriel; slain partner, Danny (who maintains a spectral presence); current partner, Jake; and millionaire Kenneth Irons. However, Irons and his proxy, Ian, maintain surveillance on a regular basis; Sara's powers, which are channeled through the witchblade, even allow Irons to have a psychic connection with her, as he once possessed the magical gauntlet (TNT/Photofest).

In other series, the abilities of superpowered women may not invite surveillance that is as obsessive in nature as that directed at Sara, but the extraordinary powers of other female characters may invite a gaze that is suspicious in nature. As noted in Chapter 2, when the abilities of a superpowered woman are witnessed unexpectedly, the woman is often met first with disbelief and then with intolerance. However, often, such shock and prejudice are fostered by others even *before* they witness a superpowered woman's abilities. In other words, when the family, friends, or neighbors of a superpowered woman sense that there is something atypical about her, they make the superpowered woman the object of their wary gaze; their surveillance then becomes a mechanism by which they confirm their suspicions. This wariness can be found in *Roswell*, as teenage alien Isabel comes under the scrutiny of those she loves best — both her husband, Jesse, and her parents, Diane and Phillip. Before Jesse learns of Isabel's alien origins, he, as noted in Chapter 2, questions whether Isabel is psychic. After Isabel pretends to laugh at the thought of having such extraordinary abilities, Jesse is embarrassed by his misgivings ("I Married an Alien"). Jesse, though, resumes his suspicions a short time later and surveys Isabel as she meets Michael to help rescue Max. It is through this surveillance that Jesse verifies his suspicions about his wife, when he, as noted in Chapter 2, learns that she is an alien after she is shot in the rescue attempt ("Panacea," "Chant Down Babylon"). Jesse's positioning of Isabel as the object of his gaze takes away her privacy. David Lyon, in *The Electronic Eye: The Rise of Surveillance Society*, discusses the connection between gender and privacy, which he defines as "freedom to reveal only what, and to whom, one wishes"; in this discussion, he notes that women "have reason to be less sure" of their privacy than men (184). Isabel serves as one such example — albeit a fictional one — of a woman who has no reason to be sure of her privacy. Although Isabel has long wanted to share with Jesse the truth about her background and abilities, Jesse's furtive sleuthing denies Isabel the agency to select the time, place, and manner in which such information is revealed.

Isabel's adoptive parents encroach upon her privacy, as well, when they become determined to discover the secret they are certain their children are keeping. As loving, but suspicious parents, Diane and Phillip's investigation into their children's private lives is well-meaning in nature, as they are afraid Isabel and Max are in trouble. However, while Diane and Phillip are curious about both Isabel's and Max's behavior, it is Isabel whom Diane chooses to observe surreptitiously (while Phillip trains his gaze on Max in less furtive, and less-intrusive, ways). After inviting Isabel to spend the night when Jesse is out of town, Diane hides a video camera in Isabel's former bedroom; when Isabel later becomes upset after a phone call from Jesse warning her that her parents are "on to [her]," she uses her powers in a fit of anger. Unbeknownst to Isabel, the camera catches this display on tape ("Crash"). Diane and Phillip, shocked at the contents of the videotape, later confront Isabel, asking her to explain what the tape means. Isabel is justifiably angry, although her parents defend their behavior, claiming their actions were out of parental concern:

> ISABEL: I ... oh, God, I can't believe that you spied on me.
> DIANE: I'm sorry, honey, but we didn't know what else to do ["Four Aliens and a Baby"].

Although Isabel eventually forgives her parents' actions and her parents eventually overcome their shock and accept their children's alien origins (Isabel and Max were adopted as young children), Diane's surveillance tape falls into the hands of a secret military organization (coincidentally there seems to be at least one of those in nearly every series featuring a superpowered woman) that poses a threat to Isabel (and, subsequently, Max ["Four Aliens and a Baby"]). While Isabel, in her short life, has grown used to being watched by police officers and government agents trying to uncover her secret, she was unprepared for Jesse's suspicious gaze and her parents' well-meaning one. Isabel's situation can be read as an illustration of Carol Brooks Gardner's assessment, in *Passing By: Gender and Public Harassment*, of the public versus the private scrutiny of women. Since, as Gardner notes, public harassment "is a regular and lifelong occurrence for women" (41), the home, according to what she terms "popular wisdom," should serve as "a bastion" against such public scrutiny (28). For Isabel, and perhaps for many of *Roswell*'s female viewers, this is not the case, as surveillance blurs the boundaries between the public and the private.

Internalizing the Gaze

Whether superpowered women suffer the effects of institutionally bound or unbound surveillance (or both), one of the resulting effects is the internalization of another's gaze. Superpowered women, therefore, can be compared to the inhabitants of Bentham's proposed prison. Just as the inmates of the Panopticon become self-policing under the assumed gaze of the guards in the tower, so, too, do superpowered women preempt their own behavior in anticipation of the spying eyes of others. These characters' self-censorship in anticipation of being surveyed by others parallels the experiences of off-screen women. As Bartky explains, such an internalization of an outside gaze is common for women: "In contemporary patriarchal culture, a panoptical male connoisseur resides within the consciousness of most women" (140). While Bartky is describing women who discipline themselves to appear and act in the traditionally feminine manner expected of them by a patriarchal society (in which the male gaze is omnipresent), superpowered women, likewise, discipline themselves according to the constant surveillance in their own lives. This discipline includes the proscribed or limited use of their powers for fear of the rejection or retribution of others, as discussed in previous chapters. In contrast to Bartky's description of the gaze of an unnamed panoptical male connoisseur, though, for superpowered women, as noted previously, the source of the gaze is far from anonymous—the purveyor of the panoptical gaze trained upon them frequently can be identified. Knowing their voyeurs by name, however, does not preclude the embedding of the panoptical gaze within the consciousness of superpowered women; the lack of anonymity perhaps allows the gaze to be felt even more acutely. With the gaze emanating from within, superpowered women often resign themselves to the inescapability of surveillance and the limitations such surveillance places on their abilities and their personal lives.

This concept of the inescapability of the gaze can be illustrated by *Charmed*, as the Charmed Ones are under constant surveillance by the Elders, the universal guardians of good. The Elders are supernaturally powerful, omnipresent, and, allegedly, benevolent; thus, the sisters have little hope of evading them or protesting their interference. Piper, who falls in love with Whitelighter Leo, suffers the most from the Elders' presence in their lives. According to the Elders, it is against the rules for a Whitelighter and a witch to be involved romantically; therefore, Piper and Leo try to marry secretly — during an eclipse. As Piper's sister Phoebe explains, "If we can't look up, that must mean that they [the Elders] can't look down." Unfortunately, before Piper and Leo can take their vows, the eclipse ends, and the Elders magically remove Leo from the ceremony ("Magic Hour"). When Leo returns, he explains to Piper that they can no longer be together, that the Elders have forbidden their relationship. While the Elders eventually acquiesce and let Piper and Leo resume their relationship on a probationary basis (and eventually allow them to marry because Piper acts in an extraordinarily selfless manner — she is willing to give up Leo if that means more innocents will be saved), Piper is at first too self-conscious to be intimate with Leo. Even though Leo assures Piper that the Elders are not watching, their calls to Leo regarding his duties occur too often at inopportune moments for Piper to believe him:

> PIPER: [as Leo kisses her] Okay, um, how about you tell them to look the other way?
> LEO: They're not looking. How many times do we have to have this conversation? [...] Look, come on, Piper, we need to get past this.
> PIPER: Yeah, and I need to feel like it's just you and me and not the whole universe watching ["Sight Unseen"].

Piper's avoidance of intimate moments with Leo indicates her internalization of the Elders' gaze; even if the Elders are not looking, as Leo asserts (although, ironically, an invisible demon is present in the above scene), Piper feels as if they are, noting she is "so tired of living under this scrutiny," and alters her behavior accordingly. When she finally does get past this problem and she and Leo make love, she is still not convinced that they have done so without an otherworldly audience, as indicated by the post-coital "I hope you enjoyed the show" she addresses skyward ("Sight Unseen"). Even the most private of moments for superpowered women, then, cannot be experienced without the presence — or the expectation of the presence — of the intrusive gaze of others.

While the Elders' gaze is embedded within Piper's consciousness, Manticore's gaze is embedded in more than Max's mind. Manticore's genetic engineering of Max included the incorporation of feline DNA into her chromosomal makeup; as a result, Max goes into heat a few times a year. For Max, this overwhelming biological urge to mate is degrading and humiliating. Despite Max's efforts to fight the urge, she has sex with a stranger on the night she and Logan are supposed to celebrate the anniversary of the day they met. She later confesses this indiscretion to Logan and explains that she feels helpless against Manticore and its influence: "It's just something Manticore tricked up inside of me that I can't control. Makes me feel like no matter what I do or how far I run I can never get away from them. Never" ("Meow"). In this regard, Manticore's gaze and its accompanying methods of discipline and punishment are physically embodied in Max; she is genetically programmed to behave in the manner that they prescribe. Therefore, Manticore's malevolent gaze (which Max describes in another episode as "The darkness. Right on my tail" ["I and I Am a Camera"]) is literally inescapable; even after the institution is destroyed, its physical hold on Max remains. She lives her body as seen by Manticore, to paraphrase Bartky's assessment of how women experience their physicality via an unnamed patriarchal Other (140). For superpowered women, then, the internalization of the gaze, whether consciously or physically, prevents them from living their lives in the manner that they choose. The all-seeing Other, whether benevolent or malevolent, is unavoidable, as it resides within. As Bartky indicates, such an internalization of another's gaze is a status with which off-screen women can readily identify.

In the fictional worlds of superpowered women, if these characters embody the gaze, then, their only recourse to avoid such surveillance is to be disembodied. In other words, if visibility is indeed a trap, as both Phelan (6) and Foucault (*Discipline* 200) assert, then invisibility is the escape hatch. One example of the potential advantage of invisibility for women can be found in *Buffy the Vampire Slayer*. Buffy, in the aptly titled episode "Gone," discovers the freedom of not being seen when her arch nemeses (or "nemesis-es" as they describe themselves), Warren, Jonathan, and Andrew, zap her with an invisibility ray. For most of this episode, Buffy, who ironically had gotten her hair cut minutes before her forced disappearing act, revels in her imperceptibility, enjoying a "giddy-fest," as she later describes it, for the first time since her friends resurrected her. (In the finale of the previous season, Buffy sacrificed herself to close a portal to a demon dimension that could bring hell on earth.) While Buffy's friends and sister frantically search for a way to reverse the Slayer's invisibility, Buffy does not share their urgency — instead, she spends her time playing practical jokes on the Social Services agent who questioned her competency in caring for her sister and rendezvousing with Spike, with whom she is having a physical relationship. It is not until Buffy learns that prolonged invisibility could result in her fading from existence entirely[4] that she gains possession of the ray gun from Warren, Jonathan, and Andrew so that she can reverse her condition. For Buffy, the price for escaping surveillance, then, is too high, as such a cost would entail disappearing permanently. The only option for superpowered women to avoid an external — and resulting internalized — gaze, then, is to erase their bodies completely; for these extraordinary women, like the prisoners in the Panopticon, visibility will always equal vulnerability. Invisibility may hold a similar appeal for real-life women who have internalized the gaze of others, especially in regard to body image, since disciplinary practices such as excessive dieting and exercise literally are designed to decrease women's visibility.

For Male Eyes Only

Although some superpowered women, like Max, are endowed with exceptional sight, the discourse of vision within series featuring these characters often is coded as masculine. As Lyon explains regarding the rhetorical implications of systematic watching, "the language of surveillance all too often classifies, divides, and excludes" (197). In the case of *Dark Angel* and *Buffy the Vampire Slayer*, such language classifies, divides, and excludes along gendered — and socioeconomic and ethnic — lines. In *Dark Angel*, Logan, as mentioned previously, is a social crusader who airs cable hacks under his alter ego "Eyes Only"; each broadcast's audio begins with "Do not attempt to adjust your set. This is a streaming freedom video bulletin. The cable hack will last exactly 60 seconds. It cannot be traced, it cannot be stopped, and it is the only free voice left in the city" ("Pilot") and, as his screen name indicates, visually features only Logan's eyes. The implication is that Eyes Only sees all and reports all — that vision is necessary to discern truth. As the one who watches, Eyes Only is righteous; hence, those who Eyes Only watches, in contrast, must be suspect at best and guilty at worst. While Logan, as the man behind Eyes Only, is depicted as sincere in his quest to expose corruption and rectify social injustice, his identity as a white, educated, upper-class, heterosexual male cannot be ignored, especially since those who fall under his cybergaze often have what would be considered less-than-desirable upbringings. Therefore, Logan's vision and judgment — his eyes — are the only ones that matter in *Dark Angel*'s social hierarchy. The fact that Logan often uses both his Eyes

Only connections and technology to assist Max when she lands in dangerous situations, such as when he helps her escape from prison, does not undermine this privileged viewing position. It is the white Logan, who lives in a penthouse (where the view is, of course, extraordinary), who watches, and the Latina Max, who lives in a condemned building, who is watched.[5]

Likewise, on *Buffy the Vampire Slayer*, as noted earlier in this chapter, it is the Watchers' Council that watches, and it is the Slayer who is watched. While the Watchers' Council is made up of a number of individuals and therefore cannot be classified as easily as Logan in terms of socioeconomic identity, Buffy's two Watchers, Giles and Wesley, are upper-class Brits who are classically educated; Quentin Travers, the head of the Watchers' Council, presumably has a similar background. The only female Watcher featured prominently in the series (for one episode) is fellow Slayer Faith's Watcher Gwendolyn Post, who was expelled from the Council for practicing dark magic; Faith's Watcher before Gwendolyn, who was also a woman, was killed by a demon before Faith's arrival in Sunnydale. The predominantly upper-class masculine force of the Watchers' Council stands in stark contrast to the Slayers, who must be female, as Giles indicates in his "Into each generation a Slayer is born, one girl in all the world, a Chosen One" expository speech in the series' first episode ("Welcome to the Hellmouth"),[6] and of various ethnic, socioeconomic, and educational backgrounds (although Buffy, who perhaps is considered the chosen even among the chosen, is, as discussed in the Introduction, white and middle-class). Perhaps illogically, then, the Watchers—who, like Logan, have a privileged position from which to view others—are empowered more fully than the Slayers they watch—who, like Max, have exceptional abilities. This disparity in empowerment between those who watch and those who are watched is addressed by Donna Haraway in "The Persistence of Vision." Haraway notes that the gaze that marks bodies as Other "signifies the unmarked positions of Man and White" (283). As examples of the unmarked, the Watchers Council and Eyes Only, therefore, reinforce gender- and ethnicity-based power structures; the power to see is only afforded the privileged.[7] On screen and off, the rhetoric of vision remains rooted in patriarchy, positioning men's vision as universal and women's as peripheral.

Vision by Any Other Name

Since the power to see is often denied superpowered women, series featuring these characters often depict repercussions equated with women's vision—or the act of their seeing. For example, on an episode of *Tru Calling*, an elderly woman accuses Tru of stalking her, since Tru has been watching the woman in an attempt to prevent her death ("Murder in the Morgue"). Bartky argues that the criticism women receive for attempting to claim the power of sight — which, in contrast to the above example, she describes as "male scrutiny" — trains women to adopt an "expression of deference"; in other words, she notes, "the female gaze is trained to abandon its claim to the sovereign status of seer" (135). Thus, in the pre–gilded-age television universes inhabited by the superpowered, it is *The Six Million Dollar Man*'s Steve Austin who is equipped with a bionic eye and *The Bionic Woman*'s Jaime Sommers who is equipped with a bionic ear.[8] When superpowered women do attempt to claim or reclaim their status as seers (via their version of the bionic eye or human sight), they often face extreme repercussions. Consequently such narratives reinforce the idea that such a status should not be occupied by women.

One such narrative may be found in "End of Days," one of the final episodes of *Buffy the Vampire Slayer*, in which Buffy learns from an old woman that an all-female group known as Guardians has existed alongside the Watchers; this unnamed woman explains that she is the last of the Guardians and describes the dynamic between Guardians and Watchers: "[T]he Watchers watched the Slayers. But we were watching them." Before Buffy can process the information that the Watchers have been under watch all these years, Caleb, an agent of the First, the ultimate evil Buffy is fighting, snaps the old woman's neck. Hence, moments after the old woman explains to Buffy that the matriarchal Guardians kept the patriarchal Watchers under their gaze, the old woman's life ends. Apparently, women who not only return the gaze but initiate it do so at their own risk. Tru, too, illustrates the risks of active looking. When Tru was a child, she witnessed her mother's murder; understandably, Tru never fully recovers from this event. Consequently, when she begins reliving days, each life she saves is a reminder of the one that she could not — the one that she merely stood and watched slip away. Furthermore, the man who killed her mother later tries to kill Tru, as he knows that she witnessed his previous crime ("Daddy's Girl"). The cost of seeing for superpowered women, like the cost of avoiding being seen, may be the ultimate one. While real-life women may not suffer such extreme repercussions for active looking, their gaze may be met with cultural disapproval, since deference, as Bartky notes, rather than eye contact, is expected of women.

As traditional sight — the power of seeing rather than the state of being seen — is not available to superpowered women or comes with too great a cost, many of these extraordinary women, therefore, possess alternative methods of seeing. According to Beeler, women throughout myth and history have been associated with alternate forms of sight (what Beeler terms "intuition") more so than men, "perhaps because of their [women's] more limited roles in the physical world of male activity" (6). Although many of television's superpowered women with alternate sight fulfill more than limited roles in the physical world, these characters continue in the tradition of the Cassandra and Joan of Arc prototypes about which Beeler writes (3). Consequently, Sara can see and communicate with her deceased partner, Danny, and has flashes of memories that belong to former wielders of the witchblade; Isabel can see into others' dreams; and *Charmed*'s Phoebe, *Missing*'s Jess, and *That's So Raven*'s title character all have the power of premonition. The powers of these women allow them to, as Irons explains regarding the abilities Sara gains from the witchblade, "see in an entirely new way" (*Witchblade*). These alternative forms of sight possessed by superpowered women parallel a feminist perspective on vision, as described by Haraway. Since, as Haraway notes, "Vision is *always* a question of the power to see" (287–88) and that power has long been afforded men via their privileged positions as the disembodied and unmarked, feminism, in contrast, must entail a "view from a body" and embrace a multiple subject with "(at least) double vision" (283, 291). As examples of women who possess at least double vision, superpowered women's flashes and premonitions emanate from their bodies, as their powers are innate, and compound their perspective. Such perspective, unlike traditional vision and its "conquering gaze from nowhere," as Haraway describes it (283), arms these characters with insight and intuition not available through their "Eyes Only." Unfortunately, such double vision, since it often lacks control, precision, and/or predictability, is not accepted as readily within society as traditional vision or power;[9] in other words, these characters "with the gift of special sight still share some limitations of their mythic or historical prototypes [...] they may be viewed as mad or their legitimacy as women who have access to the supernatural may be questioned" (Beeler 3). Hence, Sara is considered eccentric, Isabel is sometimes feared, and Phoebe, Jess, and Raven are viewed as crazy or anomalous. Women's vision, on screen and off, is coded as outside of the mainstream.

Superpowered men, too, may be enabled with alternate forms of vision. However, for these men, such sight may be considered more asset than eccentricity. For example, on *That's So Raven*, Raven's friend Eddie temporarily has visions after an astronomical occurrence. Eddie, unlike Raven, who only shares her visions with Eddie and Chelsea, flaunts his new ability freely, enjoying the attention and admiration the premonitions bring him ("He's Got the Power"). Although Eddie eventually sees the downside to having visions when his foresight begins to fade and he faces the anger of an older teen who lost a bet based on one of Eddie's predictions, his initial impulse to display his abilities openly and the acceptance by which such abilities are met stand in direct contrast to Raven's own experiences. As Eddie remarks to Raven, "What is the big deal? I mean, they [his fellow students] have questions, and I have answers" ("He's Got the Power"). Furthermore, Eddie can summon his visions by making a certain facial expression; Raven's visions, although accompanied by a similar expression, come unbidden. As with Eddie's premonitions, *Smallville*'s Clark's X-ray vision, which Clark can use at will, is met with approval from his peers, or at least his best friend, Pete, as referenced in Chapter 3. While Clark's ability to see through buildings and other structures can be considered an alternative form of vision, it can also be considered an enhanced form of traditional vision — his gaze merely extends further and penetrates more deeply. Regardless, Clark's superpowered sight, like Eddie's clairvoyance, is considered a benefit and not a compensation.

Furthermore, superpowered men who possess alternative forms of vision, such as the power of premonition (on a more regular basis than Eddie) or intermittent visions, are afforded more agency than superpowered women with similar abilities. For example, on *The Dead Zone*, the local authorities solicit Johnny's help on their cases; so, even though Johnny possesses a stereotypically feminine power, his privileged position to see is reestablished via this connection with the legal system.[10] Likewise, on *Roswell*, Isabel's brother, Max, gets flashes of his past life on their home planet. As with Raven's premonitions, Max cannot fully control these flashes; however, Max's visions occur when he kisses his girlfriend, Liz, thereby reconfirming his masculinity despite the association of an unpredictable power with the feminine. Therefore, based on these examples, superpowered men can use such passive powers to their advantage in ways that their female counterparts cannot. Beeler, however, offers a counterargument, maintaining that contemporary television and film representations of visionary women employ their alternate sight in an active manner, despite the perception of such sight as a passive ability (3), since such women often are depicted as "savior figures and mediators who initiate change in the lives of others" (9) or even their own (10). More often than not, though, during the gilded age, television's superpowered women utilized their supernatural vision only in the service of others, keeping in line with the cultural expectation of selflessness addressed in the previous chapter.

Adversarial Versus Objectifying Gazes

As with superpowered women, superpowered men often find themselves under surveillance, whether via an institutionally bound or unbound gaze. The experiences of these male characters versus the aforementioned female characters in regard to this surveillance, though, differ greatly. As Bartky notes regarding gender and surveillance, women are conscious of the fact that they are under surveillance in ways that men are not (149). Therefore, where women are "object and prey," to use Bartky's phrase (140), men are worthy opponents. In the fictional televised worlds inhabited by the superpowered, extraordinary female characters are subject to an objectifying gaze while extraordinary male characters invite an adversarial one. The title character of *Angel*, who originated on *Buffy the Vampire Slayer*, best exemplifies this oppositional gaze; Angel, who was first introduced as a shadowy figure watching Buffy, finds himself, upon his relocation to Los Angeles, watched by the institutionally bound gaze of Wolfram and Hart, a law firm with supernatural connections that represents the most notorious of clients. When Angel encounters one of Wolfram and Hart's vampire clients, an encounter that ends with said client's rapid descent — and immolation — from the firm's high-rise offices, the attorneys realize that there is "a new player in town" ("City of...") — one they plan to watch closely. Later, when the senior partners learn via a prophecy that Angel will be a key figure in the apocalypse, the firm's members strengthen their resolve to track Angel's whereabouts and actions, albeit as a fellow player in town. Despite the vast resources at the firm's disposal, the at-first solo Angel clearly establishes himself as Wolfram and Hart's opponent and not their object — the attorneys, therefore, consider Angel's steely eyed return of their gaze a power with which to be reckoned. For the Wolfram and Hart attorneys, Angel's role as adversary is so ingrained within their consciousness that when one of Angel's team follows Angel's instructions to kill Lindsey, a former member of the firm, Lindsey's dying words are, "Angel ... kills me. You don't ... Angel..." ("Not Fade Away").

Likewise, *Jake 2.0*'s NSA agent Jake is respected as a worthy opponent by his superiors when a board of inquiry convenes to question his team's actions on a recent mission. After the board members announce that Jake's team will be put on desk duty until the board's decision has

Jake 2.0 follows the adventures of Jake Foley, an NSA computer technician who becomes superpowered as the result of a laboratory accident; although such abilities draw the careful attention of his superiors, he refuses to give in to their scrutiny, even resorting to blackmail to swing the balance of power (UPN/Photofest).

been made, Jake, refusing to acknowledge the board's authority, uses his abilities to blackmail the board members into backing down.[11,12] While the board members are, of course, indignant and vow to keep Jake under surveillance, they respect him as an adversary; one board member even remarks, "Did you see the way he stood up to us? As a soldier" ("The Spy Who Really Liked Me"). Superpowered men, by returning the gaze, are acknowledged as worthy opponents and good soldiers, unlike superpowered women, who, by attempting to evade the gaze, are positioned as objects and, as metaphors for Bartky's description of real-life women's positioning under surveillance, sometimes as prey.

Furthermore, while superpowered men potentially may suffer the effects of surveillance, the fear of inviting the gaze — by engaging in what culturally would be considered normal pursuits— is not as great as it is for superpowered women. Once again, visibility — although in this case an intentional and not an inadvertent drawing of the gaze — proves problematic for women in different ways than men. As Russo notes of women's visibility, "Making a spectacle out of oneself seem[s] a specifically feminine danger" (318). As a fictional example, Clark's father will not give him permission to play football at Smallville High since he is afraid that Clark accidentally will expose his powers or hurt one of the other players, but Clark defies his father and joins the team. As Clark explains to his father, he believes he deserves some normal high-school memories; his father, although still worried, supports Clark's decision and even teaches him to play ("Façade"). Buffy, in contrast, does not receive the same support from Giles, the father figure in her life, when she attempts to create her own high-school memories by trying out for cheerleading in one episode and running for homecoming queen in another — both of which nearly result in the Slayer's demise. Giles's response to Buffy's cheerleading interest is, "You have a sacred birthright, Buffy. You were chosen to destroy vampires, not to ... wave pompoms at people" ("Witch"), while his response to her royal aspiration is, "Seems like a lot of fuss for one little title"— although Giles does attend the dance to console Buffy when she loses the aforementioned little title ("Homecoming"). In this regard, superpowered men may receive an admiring gaze in their quest for normalcy, while superpowered women remain under an admonishing one. The same dynamic vis-à-vis men and women and the inviting of a public gaze may be present off screen as well, since men who actively seek public recognition are accepted more readily than women who do the same.

The Politics of Visibility

Superpowered women on television frequently are subject to a panoptic gaze, whether from a formal institution, such as the government, or a more personal one, such as the family unit. When this surveillance is institutionally bound, it may include examinations that maintain the dynamic between the perpetrator of the gaze and superpowered women as objects of that gaze; in addition, it may include a system of permanent registration that further marks the superpowered women's already-marked female bodies. With institutionally unbound surveillance, individuals may fix superpowered women as the objects of their erotic gaze, eliminate the superpowered women's privacy, or confirm their suspicions about the superpowered women's alleged abnormality. Due to the nearly omnipresent surveillance in the lives of superpowered women, they internalize the gaze of others consciously or bodily; thus, even when such surveillance is not physically present, it is duly felt. Superpowered women, therefore, resign themselves to the inescapability of the gaze and its accompanying limitations on their abilities; invisibility — or ceasing to exist — is their only recourse. According to the narratives of superpowered women on television, vision primarily belongs to the masculine domain — it is a privilege rarely afforded women. Because of this masculine connotation of vision, superpowered women may experience repercussions for active looking or be compensated for lack of vision with alternative, more passive, methods of seeing. Finally, while superpowered women's male counterparts also may find themselves subject to surveillance, they do not suffer the same effects as superpowered women. Superpowered men often are able to return the gaze, thereby establishing themselves as adversaries to versus objects of those who attempt to survey them.

The gilded-age storylines of superpowered women who are subject to near-constant surveillance parallels the lived reality of many women; such representations for female viewers of these series then serve as a type of surveillance and discipline in their own right. As Robyn Wiegman explains in *American Anatomies: Theorizing Race and Gender*, the "disciplinarity so deeply woven in systems of representation" can be found when

> one turns to cinema, television, and video where the circulation of representational images partake in a panoptic terrain by serving up bodies as narrative commodities, detached from the old economy of corporeal enslavement and situated instead in the panoply of signs, texts, and images through which the discourse of race functions now to affirm the referential illusion of an organic real [41].

Although Wiegman is specifically referring to race, as indicated by the above quotation, the same can be said of gender, as televised representations of women with extraordinary abilities who cannot escape the gaze of others contribute to a discourse that both reflects and influences cultural perceptions and expectations of gender. The "panoply of signs, texts, and images through which" this particular discourse of gender — a discourse of surveillance — functions includes the medical procedures that women elect or require, the spaces in which they work, their relationships with their bodies, and the public places they frequent. Such discourse of surveillance prescribes for women an accompanying discipline of self-control.

Pregnant women perhaps best exemplify the effects of such discourse on real-life women, as these women are expected to enact a high degree of self-discipline. As Bordo explains, women's bodies have increasingly been seen as gestational vessels, and this "ideology of woman-as-fetal-incubator" leads to increased scrutiny of pregnant women's lifestyles (81). Since pregnant women potentially, then, are subject to surveillance from anyone they come in contact with—friends, family members, coworkers, medical professionals, and even strangers—their behavior must be above reproach. Since their bodies are marked by their reproductive abilities (superpowers in their own right), they cannot escape the allegedly well-meaning, but often accusatory or judgmental, gaze of others; therefore, their every choice must be in the best interest of their unborn child. For this reason, Bordo notes that pregnant women take "extraordinary levels of vigilance [...] upon themselves" (83). In other words, pregnant women police their own actions in anticipation of the disapproving gaze of others.

The anticipation of the disapproval of others also motivates—or coerces—women to seek cosmetic surgery. Due to the elective nature of these procedures, they are often promoted as empowering for women; women who are unsatisfied with their appearances literally have the power to transform how others view them. As Kathy Davis explains in "'My Body Is My Art': Cosmetic Surgery as Feminist Utopia," women who have undergone cosmetic surgery did so because others would then be able to "see them as they saw themselves" (460). The others women (at least heterosexual women) are most concerned with, of course, are men; for this reason, women who elect cosmetic surgery underscore Bartky's argument, as stated previously, that women live under the panoptical gaze of a male connoisseur (140). In contrast to Bartky, though, for women who cosmetically modify their bodies, this male connoisseur does not just reside in their consciousness. Instead this expert exists, in the flesh, so to speak, in the person of their surgeon. In *Technologies of the Gendered Body: Reading Cyborg Women*, Anne Balsamo describes this relationship between patient and cosmetic surgeon as being based on a normative gaze (160): "In its encounters with the cosmetic surgeon and the discourse of cosmetic surgery, the female body becomes an object of heightened personal surveillance; this scrutiny results in an internalized image of a fractured, fragmented body" (78). The internalized gaze of the surgeon, who is often male, alters these women's perceptions of themselves; following their surgery, these women literally embody this gaze, as their new faces and/or bodies bear its imprint. Consequently, women who elect cosmetic surgery illustrate the

4. Surveillance of Female Superpower 119

inescapability of surveillance, of the panoptic gaze trained upon women, as an all-seeing Other has physically marked their bodies.

Women's workspaces may also allow for constant exposure to surveillance. While women who work have greater cultural power, at least economically, than women who do not, women are more likely to hold administrative positions than men; therefore, women are more likely to work in open-floor (versus closed-door) spaces. Such open-floor workspaces eliminate women's privacy and invite surveillance (Spain 443–44), reinforcing the idea that the rhetoric of vision positions women as the ones who are watched and men, who are more often in supervisory positions, as the ones who watch. In the workplace, as in other cultural spaces, vision and the privacy that accompanies the act of looking belongs to the privileged domain of the masculine.

The surveillance women are subject to in the workplace extends beyond the observation of their professional performance; their bodies are under scrutiny as well. Women that reach executive positions and, therefore, cannot be observed as readily in their workspaces as women who are in administrative positions still are unable to escape the gaze. These women are, instead, judged by their physical bodies in ways that their male counterparts are not. As Germov and Williams note, "'success' for a woman is still measured by her appearance, where economic success needs to be matched with 'body success'" (120). Women executives, then, are not exempt from internalizing the "thin ideal," to use Germov and Williams's term (118).

Although the thin ideal originates in patriarchal institutions and thus stems from the critical gaze of others, women, themselves, play a role in propagating this unrealistic body standard through self-surveillance and self-regulation (124–25). This form of body policing (125) may take the form of disciplinary practices such as dieting and exercise (Bartky 133, Bordo 171). While many women are aware of the discourse and social structures that position them as "objects to be improved upon for the male other, rather than to view themselves as subjects of their own femaleness" (Shields 106), this awareness does not translate into the resistance necessary to rewrite this discourse or dismantle these social structures. Despite the power women might exercise in other avenues of their life, their internalization of the thin ideal causes them to alter their behavior and/or curtail their actions. In extreme cases, such as with women who have eating disorders, altered behaviors due to this internalization may lead to women's attempted erasure of their bodies altogether.

Finally, any public space may serve as a forum for the surveillance of women. In this regard, women must always be on alert for the gaze of others, most often male others, as women are expected to abide by a certain code of behavior whenever they are in public. This code may require, for example, that women never smoke in public, never venture out unaccompanied, never wear clothing meant to attract attention, and never raise their voices (Gardner 17). This code, although inflexible, is not static; the code varies according to the preferences of whomever is in the privileged patriarchal position of watching women.[13] Compliance with this code is mandatory; failure to comply results in social exclusion — women may cease to be considered "women." As Gardner explains,

> Women can come to understand tacitly or explicitly that their claims as members of the category "women" are something that they need to work constantly at achieving, with the hope that this achievement will prove satisfactory to their current audience — and that audience in the public realm may rapidly shift and thus change its standards, making it hard to know how to please reliably [10].

While there are no formal sanctions in place for women who fail to achieve satisfactorily, to employ Gardner's vernacular, there are repercussions. As Bartky notes in regard to women who do not "submit [themselves] to the appropriate body discipline," such women may face the "refusal of male patronage," which, in a patriarchal society, may result in personal and/or professional losses (144). The social power of women thereby is limited via the omnipresent gaze of a presumably male Other.

All women, then, like *Dark Angel*'s Max, cannot afford to be photographed, as such representations contribute to a discourse of surveillance that perpetuates the hegemonic structures that objectify women in the first place. Ironically, women also cannot afford *not* to be photographed, as women's societal contributions have traditionally been invisible. As Alison Adam, drawing from the work of Sandra Harding, explains in *Artificial Knowing: Gender and the Thinking Machine*, "the better women are at it [taking care of others in both the personal and professional spheres], the more invisible it becomes" (134). Thus a paradox emerges: how do women expose their cultural contributions, whether as caregivers or as executives, without objectifying themselves in the process? As *Charmed*'s Prue sarcastically remarks to Phoebe upon seeing that sister's Elvira Halloween costume, which Phoebe claims she has donned in opposition to popular culture's representations of witches: "I am so impressed that you can make a protest statement and show cleavage all at the same time" ("All Halliwell's Eve"). Prue's sarcasm and Phoebe's cleavage aside, even real-life women's efforts to resolve this paradox through legitimate activism, as "voice and the visibilisation [*sic*] of women's experiences are foundation stones of the Women's Movement" (McFadden 49), have not been exempt from the panoptic gaze. According to Patricia McFadden in "Why Women's Spaces Are Critical to Feminist Autonomy," "Surveillance of women's political consciousness is a key objective of the patriarchal backlash" (49). Thus, despite Haraway's urging for women to reclaim vision (283), the act of seeing — of engaging in surveillance — remains in the masculine domain. During the gilded age, television narratives of superpowered women facing the dangers and degradation of being the objects of such surveillance, of being perpetually photographed, contributed to a larger cultural discourse of surveillance that operated (and continues to operate) to the disadvantage of women, fictional or otherwise.

CHAPTER 5

Female Empowerment on Trial[1]

> GIDEON: [an Elder, to the Charmed Ones] Listen to me. You have to stop this. Do you understand? They [the Tribunal members] haven't taken away your powers yet, but they still can.—*Charmed*, "Crimes and Witch Demeanors"
>
> SABRINA: [to her friend Jenny on a field trip to historic Salem] They think you're a witch.
> JENNY: Really? Cool.
> SABRINA: Maybe in some circumstances, but not right now. [...]
> JENNY: Why are you getting so worked up?
> SABRINA: Because they're persecuting you, and, if they can do this to you, they could do it to anyone.—*Sabrina, the Teenage Witch*, "The Crucible"
>
> BUFFY: In every generation, one Slayer is born ... because a bunch of men who died thousands of years ago made up that rule. [...] So I say we change the rule.—*Buffy the Vampire Slayer*, "Chosen"

"You can keep our stupid powers"

On *Charmed*, the magical destiny of sister witches Piper, Phoebe, and Paige brings with it a mission of ministration and an edict of imperceptibility. Their mission as the Charmed Ones to protect innocents must be fulfilled with minimal magical evidence, in accordance with a law agreed upon by the Elders and demon leaders. In compliance with this law, and in keeping with the tradition of the invisibility of women's work, the sisters have a long history of "clean[ing] up" their own "magical messes" when exposure occurs ("Crimes and Witch-Demeanors"), and it does occur, frequently, since the Charmed Ones are subject to near-constant surveillance, as discussed previously. However, in a sixth-season episode titled "Crimes and Witch-Demeanors" that the WB promoted as "Charmed on Trial," the Charmed Ones learn that their preternatural housekeeping is unsatisfactory to the magical powers that be when "The Cleaners" intervene after the sisters' vanquishing of a demon is caught on tape by a police officer.

5. Female Empowerment on Trial 123

The Cleaners are two white-suited gentlemen who were created by and operate under the auspices of the Tribunal, a council composed of two Elders and two demons whose mandate is to ensure magic's secrecy "at whatever cost" ("Crimes and Witch-Demeanors"). The potential cost in this case is Darryl Morris, the sisters' police-inspector friend and confidant who assisted them in the vanquishing; to conceal the Charmed Ones' capture of the demon (a phantasm), the Cleaners have changed past events to make it appear that Darryl shot a helpless victim instead of the possessed and not-so-innocent man he was forced to shoot in self-defense. (According to Phoebe, "the phantasm only possesses bad guys" ["Crimes and Witch-Demeanors"].) To save Darryl from execution for this alleged crime, Piper, Phoebe, and Paige must convince the Tribunal to reverse the Cleaners' actions.

When the sisters' trial before the Tribunal begins, they learn that the opposing counsel is Barbas, the Demon of Fear, whom they previously defeated and sent to a hell dimension. Barbas has made a deal with the Tribunal; if the Charmed Ones are found guilty, he will be reprieved. Although the Charmed Ones protest Barbas's presence, since he previously made multiple attempts on their lives, he counters that his past is not in question. Instead, he explains, "What is in question here is these three witches' so-called right to be continually cleaning up after their own magical asses" ("Crimes and Witch-Demeanors"). Through the course of the trial, Barbas replays the sisters' magical mistakes via holographic images and convinces the all-male members of the Tribunal that, in addition to considering a reversal of the Cleaners' actions, they should decide the "fate of the Charmed Ones and if they should be allowed to practice magic again" ("Crimes and Witch-Demeanors").

Although the sisters believe that Barbas orchestrated the magical exposure in question, they are not able to prove it before the Tribunal passes judgment. The Tribunal declares that the Charmed Ones may continue to practice magic but Darryl must die, as "the trail of exposure must end with him." Paige responds in outrage: "If this is the thanks that we get for all of our good work ... if this is the way the system works, then you can keep our stupid powers" ("Crimes and Witch-Demeanors"). Before the Tribunal can respond to Paige's words or Piper's announcement that they "quit," Leo, who is now an Elder, and Chris, the sisters' current Whitelighter, arrive with evidence of Barbas's treachery. The Tribunal then reverses the actions of the Cleaners— Darryl is saved—but the Tribunal has further words for the Charmed Ones. Since Barbas had demonstrated that Phoebe had been using her powers for personal gain, specifically employing her power of premonition to determine if she has a future with potential romantic partners,[2] the Tribunal strips Phoebe of her active powers, noting that she can "earn them back" if she— and her sisters—are more careful with their abilities. While Paige and Piper protest this pronouncement, Phoebe acquiesces, telling her sisters: "It's okay. I mean, it might be kind of refreshing to not rely on my powers so much anymore, you know? Besides, they're not the only ones who think I have been misusing them" ("Crimes and Witch-Demeanors").

Phoebe's repentant attitude toward the Tribunal's final judgment contrasts with the anger she expressed during the proceedings, as she had noted, "If all the good we've done in the last six years isn't good enough, then nothing is" ("Crimes and Witch-Demeanors"). Apparently, for the Charmed Ones, their multiple years of philanthropy are not good enough to allow them to make their own rules regarding when it is appropriate to use their powers or which actions are appropriate when such powers are observed by others. Thus, the supernatural legal system that governs the sisters' universe does not work in their favor; as women, even superpowered women, they stand little chance of fair adjudication from an apparently male-administered (by the four Tribunal members) and male-manipulated (by Barbas) institution. Their representation is even questionable, as their — male — counsel is Gideon, an Elder who, unbeknownst to the Charmed Ones at this point, is plotting to kill Leo and Piper's son.

Charmed's Paige (left) and Phoebe (along with sister Piper) have to defend their magical actions before the Tribunal, a supernatural judicial system composed of representatives of both good and evil that are charged with preserving magic's secrecy (WB Television/Photofest).

Piper, Phoebe, and Paige's trouble with the legal systems and authorities in their universe parallels that of many other superpowered women on television during the gilded age, including Buffy, Sara, Wonder Woman, and Sabrina. On *Buffy the Vampire Slayer*, Buffy's role as Slayer falls under the sanction of the Watchers' Council, the stipulations of which jeopardize or hamper her on more than one occasion; on *Witchblade*, Sara's power gained through that magical gauntlet acts as a system of justice in and of itself — one that often conflicts with the official system she serves as a homicide detective; on *Justice League Unlimited*, Wonder Woman's status as a hero and favor with her mother the Queen is subject to Amazonian law, which, ironically, Wonder Woman must break to protect the Amazons; and on *Sabrina, the Teenage Witch*, Sabrina's rights as a magical being are regulated by the Witches Council, with such regulations rarely working to her benefit. In addition to these judicial institutions, superpowered women also may face family members, peers, and/or strangers who stand as these characters' judges, juries, and would-be executioners. Superpowered women's relationship with the law — however legal and judicial authority may be defined within these characters' universes — is problematic, as sanctions by such authorities endanger superpowered women's lives, restrict or strip their abilities, require them to justify possession of their conferred powers, and/or position them as public examples of the dangers for women who have too much power. Gilded-age series featuring superpowered women, who, despite their extraordinary abilities, often face, if not impotence, than subordination under the law, indicate to viewers that women in general, regardless of their abilities, face difficulty in having such abilities recognized culturally. In other words, power for women does not equal empowerment.

Feminist Legal Theory

Feminist legal theory stems from a body of literature known as critical legal studies. Critical legal scholars focus on the politics of law and the way that law recreates social power structures, *i.e.*, the "ways law legitimates, maintains, and serves the distribution and retention of power in society" (Wishik 22). Law, therefore, serves what Janet Rifkin, in "Toward a Theory of Law and Patriarchy," terms "hegemonic ideology." As Rifkin explains, one purpose of ideology is to prevent change in society (412) or, in other words, to "rationalize the status quo" (Rothenberg 322). Central to the work of critical legal scholars, then, is the deconstruction of law as ideology in an effort to destabilize the law's political and philosophical influence on this rationalization (Hutchinson 3). Hence, based on critical legal studies, the law acts as an agent or system that sustains disparity — underscoring the differences between dominant and subordinate groups — rather than one that promotes egalitarianism — ensuring equal opportunity.

The law's distinction between dominant and subordinate groups demonstrates that institution's power to classify, or to establish a norm and its aberrations. In Martha Albertson Fineman's "Feminist Theory in Law: The Difference It Makes," she explains that such classification is inherently limited, since lawmaking operates on "broad generalizations about groups or classes of things and people at the legislative level" (218). For feminist legal scholars, more so than their critical legal scholar colleagues, it is the law's "broad generalizations" about the classification "women" that most concern them. Historically, the law has positioned men as the norm and women as "different," as the aberration, basing this classification on both biological (primarily reproductive) differences and perceived distinctions between the sexes (Maschke vii, Taub and Schneider 9). The law then is a point of disunion between women and men.

According to feminist legal scholars, the law's discriminatory classification of the sexes stems from the law's embodiment of the masculine; they argue that the law personifies male speech, vision, behavior, thought, and knowledge. In terms of speech, Lucinda M. Finley, in "Breaking Women's Silence in Law: The Dilemma of the Gendered Nature of Legal Reasoning," asserts that the language of Anglo-American law is male, since, historically, the law has been defined and interpreted by men (571). Nadine Taub and Elizabeth M. Schneider further this assertion, in "Women's Subordination and the Role of Law," by noting that the language of the law is superficially a "language of equality," but such language, in reality, serves to justify gender discrimination (19). The law's masculine voice is accompanied by masculine sight and behavior, as Catharine MacKinnon, in "Feminism, Marxism, Method, and the State: Toward Feminist Jurisprudence," writes that "[t]he law sees and treats women the way men see and treat women" (61). Furthermore, feminist legal scholars who subscribe to difference feminism, which stems, in part, from the work of Carol Gilligan, contend that the law is also structured on male systems of thought and knowledge (Baer 162). The overall embodiment of the law as male, then, aligns the political nature of the law most closely with the political interests of men; the law, therefore, represents a masculine perspective.

For feminist legal scholars, it is not the gendered nature of this perspective that is most troubling, as scholars such as Fineman argue that feminist legal theory cannot and should not be gender-neutral (227), rather it is the presentation of this male perspective as objective that most concerns them. The male perspective represented by law becomes "the standard for point-of-viewlessness" (MacKinnon, "Feminism" 57). Although neutrality is impossible to achieve, the law continues to be presented and to present itself as possessing this elusive quality — to the detriment of women. Feminist legal scholars' method, then, includes making visible those regulations and practices under the law that are, on the surface, neutral, but, in reality, are biased in favor of men. In "Feminist Legal Methods," Katharine T. Bartlett describes this approach as asking "the woman question" or "examining how the law fails to take into account the experiences and values that seem more typical of women than of men" (551). Based on the work of feminist legal scholars, the underlying answer to this query, regardless of which aspect of law it is applied to, is that law is a patriarchal system. Therefore, "feminist jurisprudential inquiry" investigates the "harms" generated by such a patriarchy (Wishik 23), specifically how this power system results in the discrimination and oppression of women (Maschke xi). Hence, feminist legal scholars do not only consider the theoretical effects of the law on women; instead, they base such theory on the actual effects that the law has on women's lives.

Feminist legal theory, in its consideration of how the law affects women, exposes the gender inequities inherent in that institution, with the intent that such exposure will lead to women's increased consciousness about the law's hegemonic ideology, as Rifkin terms it (412). By applying the method of feminist legal theorists to the gilded-age televised representations of superpowered women, by asking Bartlett's "woman question" (551) of these narratives, the same exposure occurs via these televised cultural texts that include multiple and complex systems of "the law." Even in these fictional and often fantastic series, the law serves as a roadblock to women's empowerment. Although created primarily for entertainment and not necessarily as reflections of reality, these series featuring superpowered women, as noted throughout this study, do include many scenarios that parallel the experiences of their female audience members. Thus, episodes of these series that depict superpowered women struggling to find legitimacy under the law or that propose seemingly feminist but un-empowering systems of justice can affect viewers', specifically female viewers', perceptions of the law and women's relationship to/within it by exposing the hegemonic nature of the law and/or by reinforcing its ideology of subordination vis-à-vis women.

Traditional Law and Order

Despite their extraordinary abilities, superpowered women are still subject to such mundane judicial authorities as school officials, police officers, and parents, however antagonistic or misguided such authorities may be. For

Bewitched's Samantha, this type of authority is represented by her mother, Endora (although Endora could never be considered mundane in appearance or ability). While Samantha is an adult when the series begins, Endora is not willing to relinquish her parental influence over Samantha; after Samantha defies Endora by marrying the mortal Darrin, Endora continues to interfere in Samantha's life, often using her magical abilities on the less-powerful Samantha to ensure her daughter's compliance or at least to prevent additional defiance. In contrast to *Bewitched*, but in accordance with feminist legal theory's assertion that the law is a patriarchal institution, the authority figures encountered by superpowered women from 1996 to 2006 are almost always male (although Wonder Woman, as will be discussed later, proves an exception).

Consequently, Sabrina and Buffy have run-ins with their vice-principal and principal, respectively, and must follow the rules of these men who clearly hold personal grudges against them. For example, when Sabrina writes an editorial for the school paper that criticizes the school's emphasis on athletics over academics, Vice-Principal Kraft demands that she write a retraction, since the school's largest endowments come from sports donations. When Sabrina refuses, since she logically argues that you "can't retract an opinion" and doing so would compromise her journalistic integrity, Kraft's response is, "Look, I am in charge here, and in order to maintain a free press you will write whatever I tell you to" ("Dummy for Love"). For Sabrina, the letter of the law, academically speaking, is spelled out by this not-quite-ethical authority figure. Similarly, for Buffy, Principal Snyder dictates her status—or non-status—as a Sunnydale High student. Principal Snyder expels Buffy after she is wrongfully accused of causing the death of fellow Slayer Kendra (who is killed by a vampire); even after the charges are dropped, Snyder refuses to allow Buffy to re-enroll, taking pleasure in this unfair imposition of his authority. When Joyce argues that he does not have the right to refuse her daughter's re-admittance, he retorts, "I have not only the right, but also a nearly physical sensation of pleasure at the thought of keeping her out of school" ("Dead Man's Party"). While Buffy is eventually reinstated at Sunnydale High, Principal Snyder continues to make life difficult for her. Vice-Principal Kraft and Principal Snyder both command the language of the law in their respective academic settings. These male authority figures' appropriation of the law, as they can speak for it within their respective institutions, illustrates Finley's argument that the language of law is so powerful that it will only hear those who speak it in kind (578). Since the law speaks with a masculine voice, as attested by feminist legal scholars, Buffy and Sabrina remain voiceless against their academic adjudicators. Therefore, regardless of Sabrina's ability to point her finger to change her appearance, summon objects, and zap herself from place to place (or Vice-Principal Kraft to another galaxy) or Buffy's aptitude for staking vampires (which could be applied to pummeling principals), these superpowered women are subject to the less-powerful but more-empowered authorities who write and rewrite the rules to serve their own purposes. Superpowered women, as with actual women in regard to the law, do not have the cultural power to manipulate the law in the manner that men do; historically, the language of the law and its related cultural power have been — and continue to be — associated with men (Finley 571) on screen and off. Therefore, real-life women who seek to use the law to protect their own rights or interests may be maligned publicly for such attempts.

In regard to superpowered women, when these characters do attempt to subvert the patriarchal legal system — when they try to claim the language of the law — such attempts are presented as dangerous not only to the superpowered women in question but to society as a whole. Such an attempt occurs on *Buffy the Vampire Slayer* when Buffy's fellow Slayer Faith accidentally kills a man when she mistakes him for a vampire. When Faith refuses to confess to or repent for her misguided action, Buffy asks Faith how she can live with herself; Faith's reply is that all the good she and Buffy have done as Slayers clearly puts them "in the plus column." When Buffy counters that their call to help people does not allow them to do whatever they want, Faith asks, "Why not?" ("Consequences"). As Faith continues to evade the formal structures that try to judge and punish her for her actions — the Watchers' Council and the police — she tries to convert Buffy to her way of thinking, telling her, "You know in your gut that I'm right. We don't need the law. We *are* the law" ("Consequences"). Soon after, Faith joins forces with Sunnydale's evil mayor; an evil Slayer apparently cannot be, though, and when Faith poisons Angel, Buffy stabs Faith in an attempt to put an end to Faith's evildoing and save Angel's life. (Angel needs a Slayer's blood to recover — as a last resort, Buffy provides her own ["Graduation Day, Part 1"].) Although Faith lives, she is in a coma for eight months; when Faith regains consciousness, she resumes her nefarious lifestyle — for a short time. After traveling to Los Angeles and failing to kill Angel (again), Faith eventually solicits that vampire's help in her quest for redemption — a quest that ends when Faith surrenders to the police (*Angel*, "Sanctuary"). Faith's effort to take the law into her own hands fails miserably, as such a system is not designed to represent women's interests as well as men's nor, apparently, to be manipulated by women for their own purposes. Faith's attitude toward the law exemplifies a strategy available to women vis-à-vis the law. As MacKinnon explains in "Difference and Domination: On Sex Discrimination," when women are faced with their "different" status under the law, one option available to them is to "be the same as men" (276);

however, since gender-neutral experiences are not possible (MacKinnon, "Feminism" 56–57), especially within the patriarchal legal system, this option is not a viable one. Despite her bravado to the contrary, then, Faith cannot *be* the law. Likewise, actual women who attempt to act in a stereotypically masculine manner in regard to the law, *e.g.*, skirting ethics and the rules when making business decisions, face punishment for their attempted assumption of this masculine power.

In the fictional worlds of superpowered women, even matriarchal legal systems do not afford these characters a greater degree of agency. Therefore, Wonder Woman, like Faith, cannot circumvent or assume the voice of the law when she breaks Amazonian statutes. In the two-part *Justice League Unlimited* episode titled "Paradise Lost," Wonder Woman returns to her island home feeling guilty that she last left without her mother's approval. Upon her arrival, she finds that her mother, Queen Hippolyta, and her Amazon sisters have been turned to stone by the evil Faust, a henchman of Hades. To save her mother's and sisters' lives, Wonder Woman must, of course, strike a Faustian bargain; if she recovers the artifacts that serve as the key to the underworld, her loved ones will survive, but the gates of hell will be opened. As she cannot battle Hades alone, Wonder Woman accepts the help of fellow Justice League members Superman, the Flash, and the Martian Manhunter. The superhero quartet indeed saves the day, both defeating Hades and saving the Amazons, and Queen Hippolyta is appropriately grateful — to the male members of the League, noting that they "are all truly heroes" ("Paradise Lost, Part 2"). For Wonder Woman, however, Hippolyta has these words: "As your mother, I am overjoyed that you have finally returned to us. But as your Queen, I am obliged to uphold the laws ... and, in bringing these outsiders to our island, you have broken our most sacred law [that men shall never set foot on the island]. It is with a heavy heart that I must exile you" ("Paradise Lost, Part 2"). Despite the protests of Superman and the Flash, Wonder Woman dutifully accepts her mother's judgment — she is exiled from the very civilization that she fought to protect. As with Sabrina, Buffy, and Faith, Wonder Woman's extraordinary abilities do not translate into agency under the law; she remains subject to the actions— or potentially the whims— of those who establish, interpret, and administer the law. Thus, even a matriarchal legal system that represents itself as a universal objective, as "the standard for point-of-viewlessness" that MacKinnon accuses the patriarchal legal system of assuming ("Feminism" 57), cannot accurately represent women's perspectives. The law within the universes of superpowered women and, as a parallel, the law within actual women's lives, reflects a masculine standpoint.

Supernatural Jurisprudence

In addition to the more traditional judicial systems that television's superpowered women are subject to, they also must face more otherworldly jurisprudence. For superpowered women, their extraordinary abilities—their gifts—are often sanctioned by an institution; therefore, to maintain their powers and/or supernatural status, superpowered women are obligated to follow the rules and regulations of the sanctioning institution. While these institutions do not represent themselves as the law per se, they do function as such, since they meet Fineman's definition of "the law" as a system of rules, *i.e.*, legal processes that produce and employ "coercive rules" (217). On *Bewitched*, Samantha must contend with the rules and rulings of the Witches Council, including their decree that she send her daughter, Tabitha, to witches' school, despite Samantha and Darrin's opinions on that matter ("Witches and Warlocks Are My Favorite Things"), and their order for her to end her marriage to Darrin ("Samantha's Power Failure"). While Samantha eventually discovers ways to disobey such pronouncements, her disobedience comes with a price, since, in the first example, her mother and aunts (who are serving as representatives of the Witches Council) attempt to kidnap Tabitha and, in the second, Samantha temporarily loses her powers.

Gilded-age superpowered women face similar experiences when challenging the supernatural authorities that establish the rules within their universes. For the Charmed Ones, the rules are delineated by the Elders and, further up the hierarchy, as described earlier, by the Tribunal. Piper and Leo's relationship, as discussed previously, breaks one such rule, as the Elders have forbidden witch/Whitelighter romances. When Piper and Leo first attempt to marry without the Elders' consent, Piper's sisters differ in their reactions to this infraction; Prue contends that rules are made to be broken, while Phoebe counters that "these are the rules that we live by now. I'm just not so sure that we should be helping Piper break them" ("Magic Hour"). The sisters, however, all later agree that the rules necessarily do not serve them when they are fighting evil. While the Charmed Ones are temporarily under the guidance of a by-the-book Whitelighter named Natalie, said Whitelighter is killed by a Darklighter (a Whitelighter's evil counterpart) even though the sisters follow Natalie's instructions to the letter. The sisters then agree that following the Elders' ordinances should not supersede their intuition, voicing protests about the supernatural statutes in their lives:

> PIPER: We followed the stupid rules and look what happened.
> PHOEBE: I hate rules.
> PRUE: I knew something was wrong. Why didn't I trust my instincts?
> ["Blinded by the Whitelighter"].

For the Charmed Ones, the "stupid rules" of the supernatural authorities that govern them represent a catch-22, as their compliance with these rules proves costly — Natalie's life is lost — as does their defiance of such authorities— their trial before the Tribunal strips Phoebe of her powers and nearly ends Darryl's life.[3] Hence, the sisters' experiences with the Elders exemplify Fineman's argument that most rules of law are designed to be universally rather than circumstantially applied (218); as feminist legal scholars and the Charmed Ones' (mis)adventures attest, such rules, therefore, rarely reflect women's lived — or scripted — experiences.

On the scripted *Buffy the Vampire Slayer*, Giles, one of the supernatural authorities to which Buffy must answer, does recognize that the Watchers' Council's regulations do not reflect the experiences of — and therefore cannot be followed verbatim by — the Slayer with whom he has been charged. Giles's first impressions of Buffy allow him to ascertain that the Council's rules do not complement Buffy's attitude or improvisational methods; as Giles explains to his charge, "After meeting you, Buffy, I realized that, uh, the [Slayer] Handbook would be of no use in your case" ("What's My Line, Part 2"). Despite the flexibility Giles demonstrates in regard to the Slayer Handbook, he is not so dismissive, initially at least, of the Council's other dictates, one of which is a test that Slayers must undergo on their eighteenth birthday, as referenced in the previous chapter.

This test, called the "Tento de Cruciamentum" (Latin for "test of torture"), pits Buffy against "a psychotic vampire [named Zachary Kralik] with mother issues" (Golden, Bissette, and Sniegoski 134). While, under normal circumstances, facing a vampire — even one this monstrous— would be only minimally challenging for Buffy, the Cruciamentum requires that she face this creature without her Slayer skills; the Council has ordered Giles to inject her — without her knowledge — with an organic compound that renders her normal, *i.e.*, not superpowered. When Giles has doubts about the test — and his role in it — he shares the following exchange with Quentin, the head of the Watchers' Council:

> GILES: It's an archaic exercise in cruelty. To lock her in this ... tomb ... weakened, defenseless. And to unleash "that" [Kralik] on her. [...]
> QUENTIN: A Slayer is not just physical prowess. She must have cunning, imagination, a confidence derived from self-reliance. And believe me, once this is all over, your Buffy will be stronger for it.
> GILES: Or she'll be dead for it ["Helpless"].

When Buffy begs Giles to help her discover why she has lost her Slayer skills, noting that she "can't be helpless like that," Giles decides to defy the Council's orders and tell Buffy about the Cruciamentum, an act for which he is fired

5. Female Empowerment on Trial

("Helpless"). However, after Kralik kidnaps Buffy's mother, the Slayer has no choice but to go through with the test. She succeeds in rescuing her mother and killing Kralik, much to the Council's satisfaction. Despite Quentin's earlier prediction to Giles, Buffy survives the Cruciamentum shaken, not stronger. The Cruciamentum, then, serves as a physical trial that positions Buffy as the subordinate in the power dynamic between supernatural law and superpowered agent of that law (although Buffy eventually reverses this dynamic). In Buffy's helpless days preceding the Cruciamentum, she is even depicted in a red-hooded cloak, à la Little Red Riding Hood — an incongruous image for a Slayer who already has staved off more than one apocalyptic wolf and even death. As Buffy's, along with Piper, Phoebe, and Paige's, experiences with the law indicates, the institutions that sanction these characters' abilities use trials — whether assessments of innocence or tests of mettle — to maintain their influence, thereby serving as illustrations of critical legal theorists' assertion that the law reinforces the societal status quo vis-à-vis power (Wishik 22). Within these characters' fictional universes, supernatural authorities justify the need for such trials by enforcing the regulations and requirements they have established as law — regulations and requirements that reproduce the authority of these authorities; similarly, within actual women's realities, the law underscores existing power structures by advantaging those who already have cultural power.

On *Witchblade*, the existing power structures include one that emanates from the witchblade itself. Although Sara's superhuman abilities are not sanctioned by a formal institution like the Watchers' Council, her powers themselves exert authority over her. The witchblade, it seems, selected Sara to be its wielder, just as it selected its previous wielders, and has an agenda of its own. When Sara and her partner, Danny, follow Gallo, who is under suspicion for the murder of Sara's friend Maria, into a deserted theater, Gallo's men capture and kill Danny. In the ensuing shootout, the witchblade both protects Sara and kills three of Gallo's men (the gauntlet serves as protective armor and sword during battle). When Sara's superior questions her about these deaths, she cannot provide a sufficient account of how they occurred; Sara cannot remember or explain how the men died from sword wounds (*Witchblade*). The magical bracelet that is the source of Sara's power presumably operates according to its own system of justice — one that conflicts with the traditional system of justice that, as a homicide detective, she is sworn to uphold; hence, her sketchy report of the events at the theater almost cost Sara her badge (*Witchblade*). Consequently, the witchblade's supernatural authority is exerted similarly to that of the Watchers' Council, by subjecting its agent to a test of worthiness.

Although the test of the witchblade occurs via no human or even demonic hand, Sara, like Buffy, has no choice but to undergo it. This test, known as the "Periculum" (Latin for "peril" or "trial"— apparently women's superpowers should include a working knowledge of Latin), begins while Sara sleeps; as she slumbers, root-like tentacles bind Sara to her bed — it is revealed later that the witchblade is "a branch ripped from the tree of the knowledge of good and evil" ("Periculum"). When Sara awakens to find that she is bound, she struggles against her constraints; Irons, through his psychic connection to the witchblade, mimics Sara's movements. As Sara drifts in and out of consciousness, she encounters past wielders of the blade (although in the *Witchblade* mythology, time is not linear)— who are all identical to Sara in appearance. The first, Joan of Arc, explains to Sara that she is undergoing a "test of [her] worthiness to wear ... the witchblade. A trial by fire — life or death" ("Periculum"). This trial by fire requires Sara to define her battlefield (the insanity of the human race) and the sacrifice she would make willingly to achieve victory on that front (giving her life); Sara, although uncertain that her responses have been sufficient, learns from Elizabeth Bronte, a World War II spy who was the last woman to wear the bracelet before Sara, that she has passed the test and is worthy to wear the witchblade: "Today, Sara Pezzini, you have become a true warrior" ("Periculum"). When Sara wakes from her dream state, she finds the witchblade has embedded itself in her arm; Sara literally has become the witchblade's "long arm"— of its particular brand — "of the law." Even though Sara emerges from the Periculum with a renewed sense of purpose in her life, this purpose seems to define her as an agent of the supernatural authority that sanctions her powers. The witchblade essentially subordinates Sara to its cause by subjecting her to this test of worthiness. Sara, therefore, can enforce traditional law and order in her role as a homicide detective and can enact the witchblade's supernatural form of justice as its human agent, but she cannot claim agency — the empowerment to establish her own rules— under either system of authority.

Public Sentencing

In addition to the trials imposed by the authorities that sanction superpowered women's abilities, these extraordinary characters may also be tried in or by the public. Public sentencing, like a test of worthiness, often subordinates superpowered women to a more socially acceptable or long-standing authority; such authorities may allow public trials to proceed so that superpowered women may learn some type of lesson. Furthermore, in addition to reaffirming societal power structures, public trials may also position superpowered women as cautionary examples of what happens to those who fall

5. Female Empowerment on Trial

outside of the law's classification of the norm or who attempt to challenge the law's authority—or whose very existence automatically serves as that challenge. Such trials, then, serve as an example of Foucault's concept of "normalizing judgment" (*Discipline* 184), as discussed in the previous chapter, since, through these trials, the public attempts or witnesses the attempt to impose conformity upon superpowered women.

On *Sabrina, the Teenage Witch*, the title character undergoes this type of public trial, although it is a simulated one. When Sabrina goes on a field trip to historic Salem (a location that *Bewitched*'s Samantha also frequents in several episodes), she and her classmates are encouraged to take their Puritanical playacting seriously to "make history come alive"; according to Mrs. Hecht, one of the teachers chaperoning the field trip, most students have been assigned the role of "townsperson," while one or more students have been designated "witch" ("The Crucible"). With this seed of suspicion planted, it does not take one student long to cry witch. Libby, Sabrina's nemesis, accuses Sabrina's friend Jenny of being a witch after Libby witnesses Jenny talking privately with Adam, the boy Libby likes; the other students, tired of doing such period chores as butter churning and candle dipping, are quick to join Libby's cause. Although Jenny casually refutes such accusations, Sabrina, who,

On ***Sabrina, the Teenage Witch***, Sabrina's field trip to Salem includes a mock witch trial that hits too close to home for the teen, who wonders if her classmates would accept her if they knew of her magical heritage (WB Television/Photofest).

of course, has reason to take such accusations to heart, is outraged for her friend. Sabrina's subsequent defense of her friend at Jenny's mock trial turns her classmates' suspicion on her; at the prospect of facing her own trial, Sabrina calls her aunts to take her home. When her aunts, who serve as Sabrina's guardians, insist that she stay, noting that "[t]here's a lesson to be learned" about accepting who she is, Sabrina has no choice but to be put on trial ("The Crucible"). At her trial, Sabrina pleads guilty to the charges and offers her classmates an impassioned plea for tolerance: "I mean maybe there are witches among us right now, but we're so close minded, they can't tell us who they are ... and we're the ones missing out, because if we just accepted witches maybe there'd be a big pizza party right now. So I ask you, can we accept witches?" ("The Crucible"). When Sabrina's query is met with a resounding "No" from the courtroom's occupants, Sabrina has indeed learned a lesson; although she may accept herself as a witch, society will not. She does not meet society's—the law's—classification of normal. Even though Mrs. Hecht explains to the students that no one actually had a witch card, telling them, "I didn't create the witches; you did" ("The Crucible"), Sabrina's mock trial provides a fictional — although perhaps accurate accounting — of how the law provided a justification and a forum for the persecution of women that occurred in the seventeenth century. In contemporary U.S. society, the law is perhaps no longer used to persecute women publicly and violently; however, as noted by feminist legal scholars, it continues to provide a justification for the naming and policing of women's so-called difference.

On *Charmed*, Phoebe stands trial for her difference — her witchcraft — when she faces judgment for a crime she has committed, or at least a crime her future self has committed. When Phoebe receives a premonition of her future self being burned alive, she, Piper, and Prue travel ten years forward in time to prevent this execution. By inhabiting the bodies and lives of their future selves, the sisters learn that Phoebe used her magic to kill a professional athlete who, through a technicality, eluded conviction for the brutal assault of one of Phoebe's friends. Thus exposed as a witch, and a murderous one at that, Phoebe's subsequent death sentence becomes the cornerstone of the platform for an ambitious— and McCarthy-esque — district attorney named Nathaniel Pratt. Due to Pratt's prosecutorial zeal, Phoebe's crime and impending capital punishment comprise the lead story on television newscasts, with Pratt never failing to find the spotlight: "Now, some people say this is a victory for me. But I say, here's a victory for us all. For today the blight on everything that is good in our world will be extinguished. Tonight, the witch will burn" ("Morality Bites"). While Pratt makes a public example of Phoebe and the illegal use of her power, Prue and Piper enlist the aid of the future Leo to prevent Phoebe's death. Leo, however, believes Phoebe should die for her crime, as she "crossed the line from protecting the innocent to punishing the guilty" ("Morality Bites"). Phoebe agrees with Leo, and, seconds before she is burned at the stake, she tearfully tells her sisters that she must die, because "wrong things done for the right reason" are still wrong ("Morality Bites"); as the flames begin to engulf Phoebe, the sisters (including Phoebe) find themselves back in their home in the present. Apparently, the sisters have learned the "valuable lesson" that the Elders had planned for them; as Leo explains, the Elders would not have returned them to their time if they had not ("Morality Bites"). Phoebe's trial — or, more specifically, its results, as the sisters arrive in the future after sentencing has occurred — then serves a double purpose: Pratt, a representative of traditional law and order, makes a public example of Phoebe as a woman who attempted to take the law into her own hands and thus must pay the price, while the Elders, as supernatural authorities, provide the sisters with a graphic illustration of the consequences that await if they overstep their supernatural mission to protect the innocent.[4] The fact that the system failed to convict the athlete who attacked Phoebe's friend and that Pratt is clearly manipulating the system for his own political gain are referenced in this storyline, but downplayed; it is Phoebe's transgression that is the primary concern of all parties. This focus on Phoebe's wrongdoings typifies the experiences of actual women, as many women who participate in trials, even when they technically occupy the role of the accuser rather than the accused, may be indicted publicly or by the public.

While Sabrina's mock trial and Phoebe's actual one both have the pretense of occurring within the confines of the traditional legal system, other superpowered women face charges and sentencing at the hands of the public. One such sentencing occurs on *Firefly*, a science-fiction/western hybrid that follows the adventures of the ragtag crew of a transport ship, which includes River, a psychic (and perhaps schizophrenic) young woman. During the crew's visit to a remote community, the locals accuse River of witchcraft after she reads the minds of a mute girl and the town leader. A hysterical mob soon ties River to a stake; in an attempt to save River, her brother, Simon, offers to sacrifice himself in her place, but the town leader notes that "[t]here is no other way"— as River is the witch, it is she who must be destroyed. While the backwoods town has no formal court system, its denizens do appeal to a higher power, claiming they are following God's commands to destroy evil ("Safe"). Fortunately, before the fire engulfs River and Simon (who has climbed onto the pyre to die with his sister), they are saved by the rest of their crew. The townspeople show no remorse; they only release River because the crew has greater firepower. Likewise, Buffy and her friend Willow, who practices witchcraft, narrowly escape burning at the stake when their mothers, of all people, attempt to execute them for their alleged connection with the occult.

Although their mothers are under demonic influence and not acting of their own accord, the demon in question specifically is targeting women who have supernatural powers. The demon, who first appears as the ghosts of two children who allegedly were killed in an occult ritual, urges Joyce and Willow's mother, Sheila, to "kill the bad girls"; when Buffy logically points out to her mother that "dead people are talking to you. Do the math!," Joyce's response is, "You toyed with unnatural forces. What kind of mother would I be if I didn't punish you?" ("Gingerbread"). When the demon reveals its true self and the spell over Joyce and Sheila is broken, they, understandably, are horrified by the evil entity that has been controlling them, and Joyce, at least, expresses fear for her daughter's safety. After Buffy defeats the demon and all returns to Sunnydale's version of normal, Willow notes that the only thing her mother claims to remember from the last few days is that Willow is dating a musician ("Gingerbread"). River and Simon's and Buffy and Willow's witch trials, reminiscent of the actual Salem witch trials, allow the community to serve in the role of accuser (Karlsen 78), a role not afforded the superpowered women in question, even though they are innocent of the crimes for which they have been accused. Furthermore, the lesson to be learned is the same for superpowered women and their accusers (as well as for viewers): women who possess such extraordinary abilities are dangerous. Thus, highly public fictional trials and highly publicized actual ones serve the same ends in regard to their female defendants—they temper women's power.

Men with extraordinary abilities may be considered dangerous, too, although when superpowered men are put on trial for their abilities, their accusers learn the lesson instead. On *The Dead Zone*, when Johnny and his friend Bruce are passing through the small Massachusetts town of Hobbs Landing, Johnny, like Phoebe, has a premonition of himself being burned at the stake. Despite his instinct to leave town as quickly as possible, Johnny attempts to use his powers to help the local authorities solve a double murder and locate a missing girl. The local deputy ostensibly welcomes Johnny's assistance, but actually considers him a suspect, since, in her mind, his supernatural abilities must connect him to the pentagram found at the crime scene. Johnny soon finds himself on trial for witchcraft, an archaic crime that is still on the books in Hobbs Landing. While the judge pronounces Johnny innocent of any enforceable crime, since "[h]e does not appear to have used his powers for personal gain or to harm others," the townspeople, convinced that Johnny knows where to find the missing girl, forcibly remove him from the courthouse and take him to the crime scene ("Here There Be Monsters"). When Johnny has additional premonitions that reveal that the missing girl's father knows where his daughter is, the father, who cannot admit that it was his wife who killed their other child and their surviving daughter killed her mother in self-defense, leads the charge to kill Johnny. The sheriff intervenes before Johnny, tied to a stake, can be burned; the sheriff's dismayed response at witnessing the mob's near-execution of an innocent man is, "Holy Judas, mother of God. What have you people done?" ("Here There Be Monsters"). As Johnny, Bruce, and Dana, Johnny's reporter friend who came to assist Johnny with his defense, leave Hobbs Landing, Johnny's attorney, Gabe, a Hobbs Landing native, expresses his regret to Johnny: "I'm sorry doesn't begin to cover it. [...] [T]his town has always been a place of ideals and principles ... I wish I knew when we lost that" ("Here There Be Monsters"). In contrast to narratives featuring superpowered women, when a superpowered man faces public trial for his extraordinary, and perhaps frightening, abilities, the community not only accuses, but also realizes the short-sightedness of such accusations. Once again, the law, as indicated by feminist legal scholars, works to the advantage of men, even allowing them to progress from accuser to accused — in this fictional example and in real life.

Johnny (left), the protagonist of *The Dead Zone*, has the power of premonition; this ability often causes him to be judged unfairly (and dangerously). However, Johnny, with friend Bruce as his staunchest ally, is able to turn the tables on his accusers in ways his female counterparts cannot (USA Network/ Photofest).

Working the System

Johnny's witch trial is not his only experience with the law — whether enforced by authorized representatives or vigilantes — that differs from his female counterparts. Along with other superpowered men on television, Johnny is afforded more status and agency under the law than superpowered women. For example, Johnny often uses his abilities to assist Walt, the town sheriff; this relationship is both reciprocal and publicly recognized. Johnny seeks Walt's aid when he has a premonition of an impending crime, and Walt seeks Johnny's aid when traditional evidence-gathering methods fail. Johnny's affiliation with the sheriff is known and accepted by area citizens; such an open relationship with the local authorities lends credence to Johnny's premonitions. With Walt's official endorsement, Johnny's abilities often garner praise rather than suspicion.

On *Charmed*, the sisters, like Johnny, have a relationship with the local police. The sisters' relationship with Darryl, though, is not a public one. Darryl cannot advertise the use of supernatural assistance to solve his cases, nor can the Charmed Ones risk the exposure. The sisters' off-the-record relationship with this police officer, therefore, does not increase their credibility; instead, their frequent involvement with unsolved cases, since Darryl cannot document that certain crimes have been committed by demons, arouses the suspicions of his colleagues. Therefore, the sisters, themselves, often become suspects. On *Birds of Prey*, Helena and Reese share a similar relationship to the one between the Charmed Ones and Darryl, including the give-and-take of information on cases of mutual interest. This relationship remains under the radar, as well, since Reese, at first, cannot even admit to himself that the supernatural exists, and Helena views herself as forever outside the system, even though she fights both human and superhuman crime. Likewise, in the first season of *Medium*, protagonist Allison assists District Attorney Devalos with jury selection and other duties via her ability to visualize people's thoughts and memories and to see and talk to the dead, although Devalos instructs her to keep such assistance off the record, since people will not understand (read "accept") how she is helping him ("Suspicions and Certainty"). For the male authorities on *Charmed*, *Birds of Prey*, and *Medium*, publicizing their relationships with these superpowered women would not enhance their positions within the legal system that they serve; in the by-the-book environments in which they work, an affiliation with women who are classified as "different" by that book (in terms of both their sex and their abilities) could be detrimental to their reputations.

Superpowered men, in addition to having more credibility within the legal system, are able to manipulate that system to their advantage. While on *Charmed*, it is Phoebe's future self's unauthorized use of her powers that warrants her conviction in a court of law and before the Tribunal, on *Jake 2.0*, it is Jake's unauthorized use of his powers that allows him to overturn a ruling against him. As referenced in Chapter 4, Jake faces an NSA board of inquiry following his special operations unit's return from a mission south of the border. The mission in question aligns Jake, romantically and otherwise, with Angela, the aforementioned former CIA agent, who, in an effort to avenge

5. Female Empowerment on Trial   141

her sister's death, plans to the kill the leaders of a South American country. During this mission, Jake offers Angela asylum, but his immediate superior follows protocol and turns Angela over to local authorities. After being apprised of the details of this mission, the board is not convinced that Jake's skills were necessary for the assignment in question or that his unit acted appropriately. The board members therefore announce that they will review the evidence; in the interim, the team members will be restricted to desk duty and be kept under surveillance. Such an outcome is unacceptable to Jake, and he berates the board members for their hypocrisy, accusing them of trying to cover up the fact that the American government was selling biological weapons in South America (which is how Angela's sister died). When the board declares Jake "out of line," he uses his abilities to ready the trial's transcripts for e-mailing to a national wire service (or so he tells the board — he later reveals that he was going to send the transcripts to a dummy e-mail account). The fear of exposure causes the board to reverse its decision and return Angela to U.S. soil ("The Spy Who Really Liked Me"). Although the board vows to control Jake in the future, at this point, Jake's autonomous position is assured. By using his abilities, Jake is able to assume a position of power over those who would attempt to limit his agency. In contrast, superpowered women, like Phoebe, do not emerge from their trials with the same autonomy; such trials, instead of strengthening superpowered women's agency, solidify their positions as subordinates to the authority figures in their lives. As noted previously, the gendered legal relations within these series parallel real-life trials, as men who stand accused of, for example, sexual harassment may divert attention from their alleged crimes by instead insinuating that their accusers have engaged in wrongdoing. The law fails to provide agency for superpowered and actual women alike.

Furthermore, in regard to agency within the fictional narratives of television, superpowered men rarely are under the auspices of any type of supernatural sanctioning agency, as noted earlier. There are no institutions that grant — and therefore can remove — their abilities. Superpowered men, then, rarely have any established rules to follow vis-à-vis these abilities. Hence, Johnny, Angel, and *Smallville*'s Clark use their abilities at their own discretion. Clark, as a teenager, perhaps demonstrates less autonomy than his superpowered colleagues, since he is required to comply with his parents' directives, at least initially; however, many times Clark eventually follows his own instincts and employs his powers as he sees fit. Even the life force of Clark's Kryptonian father, Jor-El, who presumably possesses powers equal to Clark's, cannot control the teenage Clark — or perhaps allows Clark to make his own rules. At the end of the second season of *Smallville*, Jor-El, who perished when Clark's home planet exploded but whose "will" remains, tests

Clark's independence. When Jor-El, who is represented as a disembodied voice, contacts Clark and commands that the Kansas teen leave Earth, Clark resists, explaining that his home is in Smallville. While the Kents assure Clark that he can make his own destiny, Jor-El insists that Clark has no choice.[5] Clark, though, finds an alternative; to avoid being controlled, Clark destroys the spaceship that links him to Jor-El, as referenced previously ("Exodus"). While this action costs Clark a future sibling, it is also the first step in establishing his autonomy; by destroying the ship, Clark defies both Jor-El and the Kents — the supernatural and mundane authorities in his life. While Clark's defiance could be seen as a typical stage of adolescence, since all teenagers must test their boundaries as they mature, it is important to note that the similarly aged Buffy does not assume the same position of independence over the Watchers' Council (at least not until she has passed her teen years).

Finally, at least one superpowered man — Angel — serves as an agent of the law in a manner not afforded superpowered women. When *Angel*'s undead protagonist gains controlling interest in the Los Angeles office of Wolfram & Hart, he integrates himself fully within the firm, complete with his name on the letterhead. In contrast, although *Medium*'s Allison uses her extraordinary abilities to consult with the district attorney's office, she does so secretly, as noted previously, and, prior to such consulting, she quit law school (an opportunity for legitimacy under the law), as she believed her abilities would prevent her from representing clients fairly (since she would not be able to reveal how she had learned undisclosed facts of a case ["Pilot"]). Moreover, Angel, who is hounded by a law firm, ends up taking it over, while *Buffy the Vampire Slayer*'s Faith is hounded by the law and then turns herself over to that institution. Therefore, Angel, in a sense, gains from the law (additional resources and influence), while Faith loses (her freedom). As Lilah, one of the Wolfram & Hart attorneys (who remains in their employ even after her demise due to a "[s]tandard perpetuity clause"), explains regarding Angel's unexpected status as the head of the Los Angeles office, "[W]e give. You win. [...] The senior partners are ceding this territory to you" ("Home"). While later in the series there is a question as to whether the senior partners provided Angel with the Los Angeles office in recognition of his authority in that city or to distract him from some larger impending evil, Angel still has "a turn-key, state-of-the-art, multi-tasking operation" ("Home") at his disposal. Angel and his team then have the ability to utilize the vast resources of Wolfram & Hart to fight the very evil that the firm represents. In such a situation, conflicts of interest and compromise are, of course, inevitable; regardless, Angel and company still manage to promote their agenda of eliminating Los Angeles' supernatural scourge. Although Angel has misgivings about crossing over to the dark side, so to speak, he assumes the mantle of authority (and the privileges that accompany such authority) with relative ease, as the Wolfram & Hart clientele apparently does not challenge Angel's management. Within series featuring superpowered characters, the law provides opportunities for male characters that are not available to their female counterparts.

(Super)Feminist Justice

Since the current legal system operates to the detriment of women, feminist legal scholars call for a restructuring of the law. As Fineman explains, there is an attempt "to open a space for women's perspective in law as distinct from men's, and to provide the occasion for unity among women over some specifics of their lives" (234). The question then arises, what would "legal feminism," to use Fineman's term (232), or feminist justice, entail? In regard to television series featuring superpowered women and their fantastic premises, the question then becomes how can feminist, or, more specifically, superfeminist, justice be imagined? According to the narratives of these series, the law is presented as a system that impedes women's agency; therefore, such characters may attempt to enact their own form of justice by subverting the system or systems that represent the law and authority in their worlds. Such attempts at subversion may be liberal — working from within legal systems — or radical — dismantling such systems or proposing different ones — in their approach; unfortunately, the liberal attempts rarely result in any lasting effects on the systems they target, and the radical ones rarely offer a more advantageous alternative for the women involved or indicate a clear break from previous systems.

On *Sabrina, the Teenage Witch*, the title character demonstrates a more subtle form of legal subversion: she finds a loophole. When Sabrina's friend Jenny accidentally crosses over into the magical world of the "Other Realm," Drell, the male leader of the Council of Witches, turns the mortal teenager into a grasshopper, per the laws of the land (rule number 714, to be precise ["Jenny's Non-Dream"]). When Sabrina laments her friend's fate, the female Rule Bearer, who reads the rules but does not write or enforce them, informs Sabrina that all rules have loopholes. Armed with such knowledge, Sabrina finds the loophole to rule 714; if she can convince Jenny that her experiences in the Other Realm are a dream, then Jenny can return to the mortal world (as a human). Drell is irritated, exclaiming "Oh toothpicks," but he has no choice but to acquiesce, as Sabrina confronts him with the inconsistencies of the system that he represents. As the Rule Bearer succinctly remarks, "Rules are rules, but loopholes are loopholes" ("Jenny's Non-Dream"). Therefore Sabrina, as she notes, "win[s] this round," but Drell, although his authority is temporarily usurped, remains the embodiment of the law in the Other Realm, writing off the experience as nothing more than an aggravation: "You tiny little witches are so annoying" ("Jenny's Non-Dream"). While loopholes perhaps provide Sabrina with a feminist strategy against the male bias of the law, such a strategy does not set any precedent for other "tiny little witches."

Like Sabrina, the Charmed Ones do their best to maneuver within the rules that they are subjected to, most often in their attempts to protect the innocents with whom they have been charged. Although Leo, as the sisters' Whitelighter, must answer to the Elders for the sisters' infractions, he still defends their actions; as Leo explains to Natalie, "That's what makes them great. They don't work by rote. They work on instinct, on passion" ("Blinded by the Whitelighter"). As noted previously, though, such instincts and passion, however great they make the Charmed Ones, do not protect them from the censure of the Elders or the Tribunal. Even the sanctioning of Piper and Leo's relationship is relatively short-lived; though the Elders allow Piper and Leo to marry, Leo later becomes an Elder himself and must abandon his marriage to fulfill what he considers a higher calling. Thus, the Elders allow the sisters to indulge in their minor flouting of the rules, since such breaches do not prevent the Charmed Ones from ultimately fulfilling their purpose within the supernatural system that governs them: to protect the innocent and not to punish the guilty. Nevertheless, checks are periodically in place, such as Phoebe's witch trial and the Tribunal's hearing, to remind the sisters of this purpose.

Witchblade's Sara, as a homicide detective, can claim more agency within the worldly system of law and order than other superpowered women, as she can, in a sense, speak — or at least speak for — the male language of the law. As noted in Chapter 2, when Gallo asks "What are you?," Sara's response is "Justice" (*Witchblade*). However, the supernatural justice of the witchblade resides decidedly outside of traditional law and order. The witchblade's justice, as discussed previously, claims the lives of Gallo's men in the abandoned theater, with no conscious action on Sara's part. While traditional law and order support an officer who shoots in self-defense, Sara's apparent killing of three of Gallo's men by a sword falls outside of the parameters of acceptable conduct. Although Greven argues that the witchblade grants Sara phallic power (148), in actuality, the witchblade counters the patriarchal legal system; the extralegal justice represented by the magical gauntlet is gynocentric. The witchblade's origin in the tree of the knowledge of good and evil forever connects it to women who break the law of the Father; just as Eve defied heavenly orders, so, too, does Sara defy worldly ones while powered by the witchblade. For Sara, as she is sworn to uphold traditional law, such extralegal justice, which seems to toe — if not cross — the line between retribution and vengeance,

5. Female Empowerment on Trial

conflicts her. As she explains to Ian, "Look, my cause is to bring criminals to justice. I don't need this thing [the witchblade]"; while Ian argues that Sara's "duty is to carry on the line of feminine power that balances this world" ("Destiny"), Sara is never fully comfortable carrying out this duty via the extralegal measures of the witchblade.

As with Sara and the witchblade, Buffy's radical approach to subverting the authorities in her universe falls outside of the law. However, in Buffy's case, the law in question regards the supernatural and not the criminal. While the Watchers' Council exerts its authority over Buffy for a number of years, by *Buffy the Vampire Slayer*'s fifth season, Buffy realizes that she is in the privileged position in the relationship; although Quentin asserts that "[t]he Council fights evil" and "the Slayer is the instrument by which [they] fight," Buffy counters with "You're Watchers. Without a Slayer, you're pretty much just watching *Masterpiece Theatre*" ("Checkpoint"). With this speech, Buffy declares her independence from the Council, but the Council remains for a time, preparing and monitoring potential Slayers to replace Buffy (or Faith, as fans argue which of the two is the "active" Slayer) upon her demise. The Council, however, is destroyed in the series' final season by the First, and the potentials gather in Sunnydale under Buffy's command to assist her in battling this ultimate evil. In preparation for this battle, Buffy uses a magical device that had been possessed by a previous Slayer to learn more about the source of her power. Through this device, Buffy learns that a group of men (who later became known as Watchers) chained a girl to the earth and released the spirit of a demon into her body, thereby creating the first Slayer. When the men offer Buffy the same option, to increase her strength by making the demon "become one with [her]," Buffy refuses and berates the men for their abuse of the girl: "You violated that girl, made her kill for you because you're weak" ("Get It Done"). The first Slayer's power, then, stems from a demonic rape, a power that then was passed from Slayer to Slayer, one Slayer at a time. In the series' final episode, Buffy dismantles this power system established by the original male Watchers. With Willow's magical assistance, Buffy activates all of the potentials, providing them with the same power that she and Faith have. This act ostensibly breaks the hold the Watchers' Council has had over Slayers for thousands of years (at least according to Buffy's accounting of the chronology), and, while Buffy provides the potentials with the choice that was denied the first Slayer, asking them, "Are you ready to be strong?" ("Chosen"), her query does not consider whether power established by a patriarchal system such as the Watchers' Council can ever be divorced fully from that system. So, while this episode may be interpreted as Buffy truly overthrowing the law dictated by "a bunch of men" all those years ago, using their very weapon against them, it can also be read as Buffy multiplying the effects of that group's

In the series' finale of *Buffy the Vampire Slayer*, the title character (center) activates the power of all potential Slayers, breaking from the "one Slayer at a time" rule that had been imposed by the patriarchal Watchers' Council (UPN/20th Century-Fox/Photofest).

first violent and invasive act against a woman. Thus, for superpowered women, disengaging themselves from the rules established by patriarchal authorities may not be possible even through radical means, as, even in the fantastic worlds inhabited by superpowered women, a feminist justice system cannot be imagined fully.

Trying Women's Cultural Empowerment

The abilities of superpowered women do not preclude them from being subject to traditional systems of authority, including school officials, police officers, and parents. Such authorities often use the law, the rules that they represent, to their own advantage — an advantage not afforded superpowered women, as they generally cannot claim the male language of the law as their own. Along with these traditional judicial systems, superpowered women on television also must answer to supernatural institutions that sanction their abilities; since superpowered women are subjugated to these institutions, they have no choice but to undergo any trials these authorities deem necessary — even when such trials result in a danger to themselves or a restricting or stripping of their powers. In addition, superpowered women may be tried by the public or sentenced publicly; such public trials often indicate to these characters that their abilities may be perceived as dangerous. While men with such abilities may also be considered dangerous, their trials result in a lesson learned by the public who stand as their accusers. Furthermore, superpowered men benefit from associations with traditional systems of law and order and often have the opportunity to manipulate such systems to their own advantage or even run them; these male characters with extraordinary abilities do not answer to supernatural sanctioning agencies as their female counterparts do. Finally, although superpowered women may be successful in their efforts to subvert either traditional or supernatural authorities, such efforts rarely have long-term effects, since the systems they oppose continue to subordinate them or the alternative systems they propose or embody do not necessarily represent an advantage over or a break from previous systems.

Hence, from 1996 to 2006, narratives featuring superpowered women's relationships to the traditional and supernatural legal authorities in their universes functioned to question these characters' right to possess their abilities in the first place. NBC's promotion of the fifth episode of *Medium* even included the following narration: "What she saw could seal a killer's fate. Now her power will be put on trial, and her gift could become a curse — with one question...." The promo then cuts to a scene from the upcoming episode that features a defense attorney asking Allison, "Who are you really, Mrs. DuBois?" ("In Sickness and Adultery"). Since superpowered women's interactions with the law metaphorically represent women's off-screen relationships with the law, such narratives indicate to viewers that women's power and influence are not sanctioned culturally — that women's worthiness to hold such power and influence in contemporary society warrants deliberation and not recognition. Therefore, on-screen and off, women experience problematic relationships with the law, as that institution questions rather than accurately represents who they really are.

As feminist legal theorists attest, the problematic nature of women's relationships with the law stems from antagonism, as women often are pitted against the legal system. Five years before the gilded age, in 1991, Anita Hill's testimony against then–Supreme Court Justice nominee Clarence Thomas is one of the most well-known and widely debated cases regarding a woman versus the law. Although Hill's allegations of Thomas's sexual harassment before an all-white and all-male Senate committee exemplifies the legal system, in the form of the committee, as a male-dominated institution, Patricia Mann, in *Micro-Politics: Agency in a Postfeminist Era*, contends that by a year after the trial, Hill's straightforwardly graphic description of Thomas's harassment was serving as a form of consciousness-raising for a number of women who had suffered similar abuse. However, at the time of the trial, polls indicated that Thomas was believed more readily than Hill (179). The African-American Hill's ethnicity, as well as her gender, compounded the complexity of her relationship with the law in the hearings, as she was objectified by many as a racial role model, or a black superwoman. As Karen Baker-Fletcher explains in "The Difference Race Makes: Sexual Harassment and the Law in the Thomas/Hill Hearings," such objectification disallows black women's status as either "fully human" or "fully women" (10). Hill's experiences before the Senate Committee indicate that in 1991, the nation was unable to accept the sworn testimony of a woman over that of a man and that a woman on trial — even when she was in the role of accuser rather than accused — faced objectification, even though it took a seemingly positive face.

During the gilded age of superpowered women on television, several real-life notable women experienced high-profile encounters with the law. Media mogul Oprah Winfrey faced legal troubles in the late 1990s when she was sued for slander by a group of Texas cattlemen after she aired an episode of her syndicated talk show that addressed the dangers of mad-cow disease. While Winfrey won her courtroom battle and, according to *The Wall Street Journal*, declared "the verdict as a victory for the First Amendment, and a triumph for blacks" ("Jury Decides"), it can be argued that Winfrey's alleged slander of the beef industry was not the only issue on trial. As Winfrey's accusers blamed a drop in cattle prices on her broadcast ("Jury Decides"), Winfrey's considerable influence — and her right to command such influence at her discretion — was perhaps the more salient concern. Should a woman — even more so, an African-American woman — be allowed to wield such cultural power? Winfrey's "triumph" in court certainly can be interpreted as an affirmative answer to that question; however, the necessity for her to defend such a right judicially and publicly cannot be separated from her gender, and, as with Hill, her ethnicity.

A few years later, in 2003, television personality Rosie O'Donnell both faced and filed charges of breach of contract when her *Rosie* magazine publishing agreement with Gruner + Jahr became unsatisfactory. During the preliminaries to the proceedings, O'Donnell, known as "The Queen of Nice" during her daytime talk show's run from 1996 to 2002 ("Rosie O'Donnell"), faced accusations of abusive behavior, instability, and media manipulation from Gruner + Jahr's representatives. O'Donnell countered that Gruner + Jahr did not allow her appropriate control over the magazine's editorial content, which caused her to pull out of the partnership — an exit that caused the downfall of the magazine (Rose B1). As with Winfrey, O'Donnell's considerable influence was at the forefront of her trial coverage alongside her alleged breach of contract, as such coverage omitted references to her "niceness" and included references to her outspoken advocacy of gun control and gay adoption (*e.g.*, see "Rosie Fights"). Although a judge ruled that neither O'Donnell nor Gruner + Jahr made their respective case, O'Donnell seemed to have been found guilty of having too much influence as a woman — moreover an openly homosexual one.

Finally, media magnate Martha Stewart and her 2004 trial for insider trading fostered debate over whether financially powerful women are afforded the same leeway that men are under the law. Although Stewart was convicted for this crime, her lawyers argued — as did others in the media — that "the founder of Martha Stewart Living Omnimedia Inc. was being prosecuted [and prosecuted more harshly] because she is a successful woman in a man's world" (Scannell C1). Marketing expert Robert Passikoff even noted that "It wasn't just that she was found guilty [of insider trading]. She was also found to be mean-spirited [throughout her defense]" (qtd. in Crawford). Interestingly, Stewart exhibited "open defiance" throughout her trial, similar to *Charmed*'s Phoebe, yet, like Phoebe, Stewart accepted her punishment, although not as readily as her fictional counterpart. After a nearly three-year legal fight, Stewart agreed to prison time (she spent five months in a minimum-security West Virginia prison nicknamed "Camp Cupcake"), even though she had an appeal pending that may have saved her from serving any time behind bars (Crawford). Stewart's brand of success at the time of her trial was especially problematic, as her then-television series and magazine, both named *Martha Stewart Living* (Syndicated, 1997–2004), featured Stewart as the self-proclaimed expert on all things tasteful and domestic, despite her lack of recognizable warmth in her instruction and carrying out of such tasks as cooking, decorating, and entertaining. Stewart, as a woman who conducted such women's work in a masculine (read "ruthlessly ambitious") manner, faced more accusations than accolades. As Jennifer Grossman wrote in *The Wall Street Journal* prior to Stewart's conviction, "[I]n the court of public opinion she stands condemned, not for what she may have done wrong, but for all she has attempted to do right."[6] Culturally, then, Stewart's greatest crime was not a legally and ethically questionable business decision (selling thousands of shares of stock before that stock's price plummeted), but her financial prowess and inability to be classified neatly along gender lines.

When powerful women encounter the law in its various manifestations — whether those women have extraordinary abilities or extraordinary publicists — their right to be recognized fully as independent agents of that power often is tried along with their alleged or actual crimes. What is really on trial, then, is a powerful woman's entitlement to her agency, influence, and/or voice — whether or not such agency, influence, and/or voice may be sanctioned under the law and, thus, result in cultural empowerment. The trials of these powerful women, then, serve as a periodic repositioning of these women from the active subjects they must be to serve as the protagonists of their series or the CEOs of their companies to the more passive — or at least defensive — objects they must become to undergo the trials and tribulations stipulated by the authorities in their lives. And while, as Matthew H. Kramer, in *Critical Legal Theory and the Challenge of Feminism: A Philosophical Reconception*, argues that critiques of the legal system that "equate the thralldom of women with inert thinghood" are problematic since such critiques deny women *any* agency (279–80), systems of authority both on- and off-screen during the gilded age almost unfailingly depicted such systems subordinating powerful women or questioning their right to have such power culturally sanctioned. According to the writers and creators of television series featuring superpowered women and feminist legal theorists, that is definitely the way the system works.

CHAPTER 6

Sacrifice and Sanctuary

ROXIE: [who has psychic visions] It was kind of cool for a minute—being all magical.—*Eastwick*, "Magic Snow and Creepy Gene"

CJ: [who has the ability to perceive the micro-emotions of others] I make sacrifices. I make them for this school. I make them for my friends—for you [her father]. I make them because they will affect people I don't even know—people who have never heard of Tower Prep [a boarding school for supernaturally gifted teens].—*Tower Prep*, "Trust"

GRETCHEN: [a "normal" college student, after visiting a carnival operated by superpowered women and men] God, this whole night just felt like a bad Fellini film. [...]
CLAIRE: [Gretchen's roommate, who has the ability to heal from any injury] I'm gonna stay. Just for a couple days. [...]
GRETCHEN: I saw your face, Claire, the way you looked at them, like you belong, like you knew them. I've never had that feeling anywhere in my whole life. I'm happy for you.—*Heroes*, "The Fifth Stage"

End of an Era

Following the Halliwell sisters' trial in "Crimes and Witch-Demeanors," Piper, Phoebe, and Paige fought demons and protected the innocent (while trying to maintain some semblance of a "normal" life) for another season and a half, with the series culminating in its 178th episode, "Forever Charmed," an episode that its writer—and *Charmed*'s show runner—Brad Kern termed, in the DVD commentary, a "valentine" for viewers. This 42-minute valentine followed Piper's efforts to travel through time (via a borrowed ring from Coop, Phoebe's love interest, a cupid) to alter the outcome of a battle that led to her sisters' death in the previous episode. Piper's journey takes her through the past to "meet" her parents when she was a toddler to 50 years in the future when she and husband Leo (who in the present is no longer with her since he has become an Elder) meet their senior-citizen selves, who are happily enjoying their golden years playing Scrabble (using demon names to score extra points), back to the past when Piper witnesses her grandmother telling her elementary-school self that "[y]ou may not know it yet, but you have gifts. The most amazing gifts. And, someday, those gifts are going to make you even more special." Finally, Piper, her mother, grandmother, and Leo arrive at the moment of the battle at which Phoebe and Paige lost their lives, and they are able to alter the event so that the sisters live. As Piper later summarizes the confusing storyline, "We changed the past to fix the future and saved the future, that's all." The series then concludes with a montage of that "fixed" future: each sister is happily married (Piper to Leo; Phoebe to Coop; and Paige to parole officer Henry), each is raising three children, and each is pursuing a calling (Piper is a chef/restaurant owner; Phoebe is an advice columnist for those seeking love; and Paige, who is half–Whitelighter, is "help[ing] the next generation of witches come into their own"). One of the final scenes shows Piper reading the story of the Charmed Ones to her granddaughter: "Although we certainly had our struggles and share of heartache over the years, we're a family of survivors, and we will always be. Which is why we have truly been charmed" ("Forever Charmed"). On that idealized love note, the longest-running of the gilded age series (*Charmed* ran for eight seasons)—and the gilded age itself—came to a close.[1]

In the five years following *Charmed*'s series' finale, superpowered female characters maintained a presence in primetime, although not as unified or memorable a one as during the gilded age. Despite this continued visibility, many series that centered on superpowered women failed to find an audience, as they lasted only a single or partial season. While elements of the supernatural and the superhuman were primarily presented as feminine phenomena in the gilded era, superpowered women were outnumbered by superpowered male protagonists and/or shared screen time as equal or lesser members of superpowered mixed-sex ensembles from 2006 to 2011. (Several of these mixed-sex superpowered series experienced the multiple-season success that eluded series with female protagonists.) Although fewer in number and with less time to develop ardent fan bases (with the notable exceptions of *Medium* and *Ghost Whisperer*, which started in the gilded age and lasted seven and five seasons, respectively), these more contemporary series featuring superpowered women thematically resembled their counterparts in the gilded age: extraordinary female characters are stigmatized as freaks, held to a high-degree of selflessness, kept under surveillance, and put on trial. For the most part, this next generation of superpowered women continued to face constraints on their abilities that served to marginalize more so than to empower them; however, variations on these themes did occur, most notably characters "choosing" to marginalize themselves, and a new theme emerged, that of finding sanctuary. In some ways during this more recent time period, though, a greater level of "equality" existed between the sexes, as superpowered men faced similar constraints, but often with fewer consequences. Ultimately, as with superpowered women from *Bewitched*'s Samantha Stephens forward, this new generation of superpowered women on television reflected actual women's challenges, frustrations, and marginalization when navigating the space between power and empowerment.

The Next Generation of Superpowered Women

After the final first-run episode of *Charmed* aired, *Medium* and *Ghost Whisperer*, with their respective communicating-with-the-dead protagonists, Allison DuBois and Melinda Gordon, continued their runs on broadcast television, and *Painkiller Jane* (SyFy, 2007) enjoyed a brief run on basic cable. Jane Vasco, the series' superhuman title character, is an agent for a secret government agency charged with finding and containing neuros ("neurological aberrants" that can influence others through mind control); on her first mission, she discovers that she can heal rapidly from any injury — even a forty-six-story fall that kills her (temporarily). She uses this ability to protect other members of her team by walking into the line of fire (literally — she gets shot multiple times in the first episode ["Pilot"], and her superior shoots through her to take down a hostile neuro in the second ["Toy Soldiers"]), since she knows she will survive (although she remarks, "I'm not sure anyone would count this as living") ("Pilot"). Jane is somewhat ambivalent about her ability, which she refers to as "my condition" ("Toy Soldiers"); when someone refers to her ability as "an amazing gift," she replies, "Some might call it a curse," but eventually implies that she does not know who she would be without her gift/curse: "Love or hate what makes us different, it really does makes us who we are ... you take that away..." ("Piece of Mind").

A few months after Jane's debut, she was joined on basic cable by *Saving Grace*'s Grace Hanadarko, a woman who communes with the divine. Grace, like Jane, is in law enforcement, although, as an Oklahoma City police officer, her version of serving and protecting is, initially, of the more mundane variety. Grace, driven by grief and guilt over her sister's death in the 1995 bombing of the Federal Building (Grace blames herself for her sister's presence at the building that day), lives hedonistically, drinking heavily and behaving promiscuously, while Earl, her "last-chance angel" ("Pilot"), attempts to redeem her. Grace, eventually, does find her path to salvation (ultimately through self-sacrifice), along the way surviving a multi-story fall, like Jane; Grace's fall, though, is more accurately described as a leap of faith and is dubbed by the media as "the miracle downtown" ("Let's Talk"). Grace's transformation from sinner to saint is not a smooth or an immediate one. In one episode, she wrestles with Earl, Jacob-like, as he laments, "You're going to fight me every step of the way, aren't you?" ("Bring It On, Earl").

Rounding out the prime-time superpowered female crimefighters debuting in 2007[2] was the twenty-first-century reimagining of Jaime Sommers in *Bionic Woman*, which dropped the "*The*" from the title of the 1970s version, because this new Jaime is not the first nor only bionic woman in her fictional world. The bioengineering of this contemporary Jaime, which included bionic legs, an arm, an eye, and an ear, perhaps due to inflation, cost fifty million ("Sisterhood"), far greater than the funds necessary to create the original Jaime's male counterpart in the 1970s—Steve Austin, *The Six Million Dollar Man*. Jaime works as an agent for the Burket Group, the organization that is responsible for making her a cyborg (a transformation that saved her life following a car accident), whose mission, according to Jaime's boss, Jonas, is to "sav[e] the world" ("Paradise Lost"). (Another character refers to the Burket Group as an organization that carries out "private sector ops" ["Trust Issues"].) Doing her part to save the world, Jaime employs her super hearing, sight, strength, and speed by tracking down airborne toxins ("Paradise Lost") and computer chips ("The Education of Jaime Sommers") and disarming those attempting to misuse or steal them, all while parenting her teenage sister.

Although 2007 introduced viewers to three female characters with supernatural or superhuman abilities (Jane, Grace, and Jaime), none of these characters had the longevity of the mainstays of the gilded age (Sabrina, Buffy, and the Halliwell sisters): *Painkiller Jane* aired one season, *Saving Grace* three seasons, and *Bionic Woman* only eight episodes. Not until *True Blood*, premiering in 2008, did a series pass the three-season mark and receive prolific media coverage and a cult following reminiscent of the gilded age.[3] *True Blood*, named for the brand of synthetic blood that the vampires in this series drink, features telepathic Louisiana barmaid Sookie Stackhouse. While *True Blood* also features several other prominent superpowered characters (both female and male), Sookie is the clear protagonist, as the series is based on Charlaine Harris's best-selling Sookie Stackhouse novels, the last of which was published in May 2013. Due to Sookie's ability to "hear people's thoughts" ("I Got a Right to Sing the Blues"), which has made her an outcast her entire life, she is often coerced into assisting the vampires in their bid for political power, which keeps her in near-constant danger. In addition to vampires finding her telepathy useful, they also find Sookie's blood irresistible—more so than the blood of "normal" humans—and valuable as a "supernatural sunscreen" that lets them walk in daylight for brief periods ("Fresh Blood"). Near the end of the third season, Sookie learns why her blood has such an effect on vampires: she has otherworldly roots, or, as she exclaims, "I'm a fairy? How fucking lame!" ("I Smell a Rat"). Despite how troublesome Sookie's superpower may be or how "lame" her supernatural identity is (technically, Sookie is a "human-fairy hybrid" ["Fresh Blood"]),[4] Sookie eventually learns to use her position amongst the vampires—that said superpower and identity led to—to her advantage; for example, she demands payment in exchange for caring for an amnesiac vampire ("If You Love Me, Why Am I Dyin'?"). Sookie, unlike most previous superpowered women, then, does not fight crime (supernatural or otherwise) or save the world and has a healthy sense of self-preservation, although she does, often, save the day by putting her own life on the line to rescue loved ones from danger.

Likewise, the three witches of *Eastwick* do not fight crime and have not been charged with saving the world, but their powers have set them apart in ways that, at times, they find burdensome. In the pilot, an artist and unmarried mother named Roxie, a nurse and beleaguered mother of five named Kat, and a reporter and socially awkward singleton named Joanna meet one another at the Eastwick town fountain, each making a wish with a coin that had "appeared" to them that day; each woman wishes that her life could change (or, as Joanna says, "I just want to be a completely different person"), and, magically, it does, as their wishes imbue them with extraordinary abilities (or perhaps activate latent powers) ("Pilot"). Roxie has premonitions (although viewers later learn she had this ability as a young child ["Tasers and Mind Erasers"]) and can read minds; Kat has control over the elements and is connected to all of nature; and Joanna has a hypnotic effect on men and later develops telekinesis. A wealthy and mysterious newcomer to town, Darryl Van Horne, interacts with each of the women and urges her to embrace and develop her abilities, despite Roxie's fear that she is cursed ("Red Ants and Black Widows"), Kat's fear that her inability to control her growing powers will hurt her family ("Tasers and Mind Erasers"), and Joanna's general misgivings ("Pilot"). Through Darryl's tutelage (he claims that he was called to Eastwick by their wishes) and their growing bond with one another, the three witches eventually choose to use their abilities actively, despite the near brushes with death each have had since they met at the fountain, and invite Darryl's continued presence in their lives ("Magic Snow and Creepy Gene").

Completing the series featuring superpowered female protagonists debuting 2006–11[5] are two teen-oriented series: the summer-premiering *The Nine Lives of Chloe King* (ABC Family, 2011) and the fall-premiering *The Secret Circle* (CW, 2011–12). *Chloe King* resembles gilded-age hallmark *Buffy the Vampire Slayer* in both its protagonist and mythology, although it lacks *Buffy*'s satirical edge and dark, fictional setting; in keeping with *Nine Lives*' family friendly basic-cable home, it offers more saccharine than satire and is set in San Francisco. The title character, Chloe, tired of being the "good girl," makes a wish over a pre-birthday cupcake to "not be [herself] for a while," reminiscent of the wish Joanna made by throwing a coin in the fountain on *Eastwick*. The next day, on her 16th birthday, Chloe discovers that she has superhuman abilities: heightened hearing and agility, along with retractable claws ("Pilot").[6] She also discovers, after being chased to and pushed from the top of Coit Tower, that death for her, at least from a fall, as for *Painkiller Jane*'s and *Saving Grace*'s title characters, is only temporary. Chloe not only is able to walk away from the fall but to continue running from her attacker; as see flees, she encounters schoolmates Alek and Jasmine, who explain to Chloe that she, like them, is Mai, a descendent "of an ancient and sacred race, not completely human, not completely god, the offspring of Bastet, the most powerful of all the goddesses."[7] All of the Mai, befitting their connection to Bastet, who is symbolized as a cat,[8] have super hearing and agility (as well as claws); however, like Buffy, Chloe is a chosen one. Her ability to survive death indicates to Jasmine and Alek that she is "the Uniter," the Mai who has been prophesied to save her people: "Only the Uniter has nine lives to live. [...] Nine lives to endure" ("Pilot"). Within the first few episodes of the series, Chloe endures threats to her friends, another assassination attempt (an organization known as "The Order" seeks to destroy the Mai, and especially the Uniter), and the mistaken belief that her first kiss (on her birthday eve) caused the death of a human[9] (Mai and humans cannot be intimate; as Jasmine remarks, "I guess you call it a curse" ["Pilot"]). As Jasmine's mother, Valentina, the leader of the Mai, explains to Chloe in the fourth episode, "Like it or not, the whole world is coming for you," to which a now resolute Chloe replies, "Let it come" ("All Apologies").

The Secret Circle, although by title an ensemble series, features teen witch Cassie Black as its protagonist. Upon her mother's death, Cassie, who never knew her father, moves to her mother's hometown of Chance Harbor to live with her grandmother. Soon after arriving, Cassie learns of her heritage as a witch (another magical teen informs her: "You're a full-blooded, 100 percent witch" ["Pilot"]), and that her powers link her to five other teens who also hail from magical families. The six form a "circle"; once their powers are bound together they will be unable to perform magic solo, but, through their connection, will be able to access their full powers. Cassie initially tries to resist involvement with the magical world, but, after finding a letter from her late mother, she learns, like *Nine Lives of Chloe King*'s title character, the "whole world" may be coming for her: "I didn't want you to have this life, but destiny's not easy to run from. I hoped that keeping the secret would keep you safe, but all I've done is left you unprotected. You have incredible

6. Sacrifice and Sanctuary

The powers of *The Nine Lives of Chloe King*'s title character prevent her from having a relationship with her true love, Brian, as a kiss from Chloe can be deadly to a human (ABC Family/Photofest).

power inside you. People will come for it. They will come for you" ("Pilot"). Cassie later learns that she, alone, can perform magic individually after the circle is bound, and that her powers are far stronger than those belonging to the other members of the group—and potentially deadly (when one of her friends is threatened, Cassie is able to kill the attacker ... seemingly setting him on fire with her thoughts ["Masked"]). She also learns that her father, long thought dead, is alive and a source of dark magic, and she fears the same darkness will consume her.

Allison, Melinda, Jane, Grace, Jaime, Sookie, the Eastwick trio, Chloe, and Cassie, then, like their predecessors, find that their powers mark them as Other (and for Chloe and Cassie, they are *the* Other among the Others), require great personal and bodily sacrifice (none can enjoy a "normal" life, and Jane, Grace, and Chloe all "die" in their efforts to protect others), cause them to look over their shoulders (all try to hamper or hide their powers at one point or another, and Chloe and Cassie must worry about people "coming for" them), and position them as the object of judgment (all question or are questioned about why they are "gifted"/"cursed" with their abilities). Furthermore, while *Medium* and *Saving Grace* each received some critical acclaim for their compelling emotional content, both were described primarily as women using their abilities in the service of others rather than an exploration of women exercising power; *Ghost Whisperer* was considered the television equivalent of a "chick flick," and the others did not last long enough to merit much media attention at all. Clearly, the "girl-power" era of television had been replaced by an eclectic array of superpowered female protagonists that caused little cultural impact; television's supernatural content from 2006 to 2011 more often aligned with the masculine domain.

It's (Mostly) a Man's World

As noted previously, several male-centered series either completed their runs or debuted from 2006 to 2011, as did several series featuring mix-sexed ensembles of superpowered characters. *Smallville*, the Clark-Kent/not-yet–Superman series, concluded its tenth and final season in 2011 (thereby lasting two seasons longer than *Bewitched* and *Charmed*, the two longest-running series featuring superpowered women), and *The Dead Zone* completed its six-season run during this time period. As with *Smallville* and *The Dead Zone*, *Supernatural* (CW, 2005–) continued a run begun in the previous era. Unlike those series, though, *Supernatural* begins with its male leads, Dean and Sam Winchester, battling the supernatural, not struggling with their own superpowered identities. "Hunters" Dean and Sam travel from town to town chasing down reports of the paranormal, finding the sources of the unusual occurrences, and killing whichever creatures are causing them, until they learn of their own mystical connection to the cosmos: Dean has been designated as the earthly vessel for archangel Michael, which will pit him against his brother Sam, designated as the earthly vessel for fallen angel Lucifer (Dean refers to this celestial connection as "Six degrees of Heaven Bacon" ["The Song Remains the Same"]). Although the brothers are able to subvert this fate (mostly — Sam is possessed by Lucifer for a time), the heavenly battle wages on, often with the Winchester brothers caught in the crossfire.

Alongside these continuing shows, a string of new series about superpowered male characters emerged: *Kyle XY*, about genetically enhanced super-teen Kyle, who is adopted by a suburban family; *Journeyman* (NBC, 2007), about time-traveling husband and father Dan; *The Dresden Files* (SyFy, 2007), about wizard-for-hire Harry Dresden; *Moonlight* (CBS, 2007–08) and *Blood Ties* (Lifetime, 2007–08), about trying-to-control-their-impulses vampires Mick and Henry, partnered with human women (a reporter in Mick's case and a private investigator in Henry's case); *Pushing Daisies*, about Ned the pie maker, who has the ability to raise the dead, but only for 60 seconds at a time, unless he wishes to bring death to another; *Chuck*, about the titular electronics-store employee who accidentally downloads a vast database (known as the intersect) into his brain and becomes a spy; *New Amsterdam* (FOX, 2008), about immortal New York City homicide detective John; *Eli Stone* (ABC, 2008–09), about the titular attorney plagued by prophetic visions (that may or may not be caused by a brain tumor); *The Listener* (NBC, 2009), about telepathic paramedic Toby; *The Vampire Diaries*, about undead brothers Stefan and Damon, who vie for the affections of human teen Elena (the keeper of the title chronicles);[10] *Teen Wolf* (MTV, 2011–), about high-school student Scott learning to control his newfound lycanthropic abilities; *A Gifted Man* (CBS, 2011–12), about skilled, yet arrogant and selfish, neurosurgeon Michael, who can see and communicate with his deceased ex-wife, Anna (although it is unclear if it is Michael who is supernaturally gifted or if it is Anna's gift reaching him from beyond the grave); and *Grimm* (NBC, 2011–), about a police detective who can recognize monsters behind their human guises. While series featuring superpowered male leads were more prolific than ones featuring female leads from 2006 to 2011, most of these series fared no better than their female-led counterparts. During this time period, ensemble shows had a greater chance of multiple-season longevity.

Ensemble series featuring female and male superpowered allies, housemates, and/or co-workers were pervasive on television from 2006 to 2011; however, in many of these series, male characters were given more prominent or more heroic roles.[11] *The 4400* (USA, 2004–07), a miniseries turned regular series, is the story of 4400 individuals who had been abducted, over the course of eighty years, by humans from the future; the abductees are simultaneously returned to earth in a flash of light, and many develop supernatural abilities. While the 4400 are not all men, teen Kyle, who had been in a coma after witnessing the abduction of his cousin Shawn, receives special status as the "messenger" of the future humans (Brooks and Marsh 494), while Shawn gains prominence with the power to either heal or take another's life force through the laying of hands. Similar to *The 4400*, the initially critically acclaimed *Heroes* follows the adventures of a group of seemingly unconnected individuals who have developed superhuman abilities. While there are female heroes featured throughout the four seasons, the characters most central to the series' mythos are male: villain Sylar and hero Peter have parallel powers (they can take on the powers of others), and Hiro, the time-traveling comic book enthusiast, embraces his hero's journey so earnestly that he serves as the heart of the show. Self-healing teen Claire (who is Peter's niece) does factor prominently in the mythos, but, as her power is a passive one, she is often in need of rescuing; for example, a season one story arc begins when a Hiro from the future tells Peter: "Save the cheerleader, save the world" ("Hiros").

Soon after *Heroes* concluded, summer series *The Gates* (ABC, 2010) premiered, offering a glimpse inside an exclusive community designed for werewolves, vampires, witches, and succubi, with "normal" security chief Nick leading his family's discovery of the community members' secret (the "outside" world is not aware of their supernatural common denominator) and attempting to broker peace between its warring factions. A few months later, fall-premiering *No Ordinary Family* (ABC, 2010–11) featured a family of four that develops superpowers after surviving a plane crash, although the patriarch has the greatest abilities: dad, Jim, has the Superman-like ability to leap tall buildings and catch bullets; mom, Stephanie, has super speed; daughter, Daphne, is telepathic; and son, J.J., has superhuman intelligence. Also that fall, *Tower Prep* (Cartoon Network, 2010) debuted and introduced viewers to a boarding school for supernaturally gifted teens. While multiple teen characters, including two girls, were featured — CJ (aka Candice) can read people "like a book" ("New Kid"); Suki can mimic any voice; and Gabe, can talk his way out of anything — storylines focused primarily on new kid Ian, who has "preflex" ("The Rooks"), *i.e.*, the ability to see things—and therefore take action—a "half step" before they occur ("New Kid"). Ian's questioning of the mysterious circumstances that brought each of them to Tower Prep starts the quartet on a journey to discover the history of the school and the agenda of its current administration. Following *Tower Prep*, early 2011 brought *Being Human*, a U.S. adaptation of a BBC series (BBC Three, 2008– ; BBC America 2009–), about a male vampire named Aidan, a male werewolf named Josh, and a female ghost named Sally who live together in the house in which Sally died. While the series is a true ensemble, with each character granted a fair share of storylines, Sally's spectral existence, at least initially, limits the narrative choices for her character, as her consciousness is bound to the house and only Aidan, Josh, and other supernatural beings can see and interact with her. Finally, the summer-premiering *Alphas* (SyFy, 2011–12) portrays the missions of a team of extraordinarily abled individuals: Rachel, whose synesthesia enhances her senses to the point that she can "read the *New York Times* from 10 blocks away" ("Pilot"); Nina, who can manipulate others through thought suggestions (an ability known as "pushing"— she once "pushed" Bill Murray to get his character's hat from *Caddyshack* (1980) ["Bill and Gary's Excellent Adventure"]); Gary, whose transduction allows him to see electromagnetic waves; Cameron, whose hyperkinesis provides him with perfect balance and aim ("*Alphas* Males and Females" 24); and Bill, who has super strength based on adrenaline spikes (and whose life is in danger when his adrenaline elevates for too long). While each of these team members plays an integral role in various cases, it is former FBI agent Bill who is the team leader in the field, serving as second in command to Dr. Lee Rosen, a psychologist contacted by the Department of Defense whenever "alphas" ("ordinary folks [that] have extraordinary abilities" ["Cause & Effect"]) pose a threat.

6. Sacrifice and Sanctuary

In contrast to the above series, several ensemble shows during this time period prominently featured superpowered women, although not always in a progressive manner.[12] Science-fiction drama *Sanctuary* details the adventures of the immortal Magnus, who, as noted earlier, is the director and protector of a safe house for supernatural creatures; Helen's team includes fellow "abnormals" (to use the vernacular of the series ["Fragments"])—a werewolf named Henry and a bigfoot-esque being affectionately called the "Big Guy"— but she holds the most physical and legitimate power. Helen's hand-picked recruit to the team, "normal" psychologist Dr. Will Zimmerman, though, serves as the viewer's de facto guide through the fantastic world she helms. On the lighter side, kid-oriented sitcom *Wizards of Waverly Place* (Disney, 2007–12), follows the magical adventures of the Russo family: former-wizard dad, Jerry; mortal mom, Theresa; and wizards-in-training teens, Justin, Alex, and Max. While Justin and Max, and, on occasion, Jerry and Theresa, are highlighted in numerous storylines, it is middle child and lone daughter, Alex, who serves as the protagonist. Alex's magical mishaps feature prominently in the series, as does her sibling rivalry with the rule-abiding Justin, her chief competition for the family wizarding title (only one member of each wizarding family may keep her/his powers for life). The darker-toned *Fringe* (FOX, 2008–13) is a supernatural procedural, recounting the cases of the "fringe division," an FBI unit that investigates supernatural occurrences. *Fringe*'s primary female character is Olivia, a fringe agent who works with civilian consultants Dr. Walter Bishop, a genius, yet mentally unstable scientist who experimented on her as a child, and Walter's equally genius son, Peter. Due to Walter's paranormal experiments, Olivia discovers she serves as a psychic link to a parallel universe; her powers, though, are unpredictable, and Peter's connection to the supernatural—he is the missing piece of a machine that can bridge the crumbling and warring multiverse—factors just as or more prominently in the series' mythos. Also dark in tone, *V* (ABC, 2009–11), a remake of a 1980s sci-fi classic (NBC, 1984–85), describes the seemingly peaceful arrival of the "V" (alien "Visitors") to earth. The V, led by Anna, can resemble beautiful humans, but, in their natural state, appear lizard-like. Anna, who is dark-haired and exotic looking (read "not white"), is the most powerful of the V, but she is depicted as a monstrous mother (*TV Guide* even ran an article about the series titled "An Out-of-this-world Mommy Dearest" [50]), stopping at nothing to populate her species (the V, like lizards, lay eggs) and maintain her power (she even imprisons and kills her mother ["Serpent's Tooth"; "Mother's Day"]), tortures her teenage daughter ["Fruition"], and makes another V's child sick to use as leverage ["Serpent's Tooth"]). In contrast, human FBI agent Erica is depicted as a model mother, as well as blonde and white, stopping at nothing to protect her son and all humans from the Visitors' attempts to take over earth. Once again on the lighter side, *Warehouse 13* (SyFy, 2009–) depicts the wacky adventures of government agents who neutralize and store supernatural "artifacts" in the title facility; while father-figure Artie heads the warehouse and field agents Myka and Pete drive most storylines, it is young Claudia, Artie's protégé, who has been named the successor to Mrs. Frederic, the warehouse's mysterious caretaker who has a visceral connection to the supernatural storage facility. Likewise, *Haven* (SyFy, 2010–) features a mysterious woman, as it details FBI agent Audrey Parker's arrival in Haven, Maine, a small town experiencing "the troubles" ("Fur"), a term used to describe the paranormal afflictions of many of its residents. Audrey and her partner, local police officer Nathan, himself a victim of the troubles (he has no sense of touch), investigate a woman who gives birth to multiple babies in a week's time ("Ball and Chain"), machines that come to life and kill their users (all repaired by the same man ["Love Machine"]), and other strange cases. Through the course of these investigations, Audrey discovers her own connection to Haven; she has been there decades before, with a different name and a different set of memories, and she may be the source of or the solution to the troubles.

Freak-Adjacent

Superpowered women in the post-gilded age, whether depicted as a source of or solution to the problems in their fictional universes, are stigmatized by their abilities with the same frequency and intensity as previous superpowered women, being downgraded to "what"s and referred to as "freaks" on a regular basis, sometimes after a display of their powers and sometimes just because of their presence. For example, Michael on *A Gifted Man*, asks Anna, his reaching-out-from-beyond-the-grave ex-wife, "What are you?," instead of wondering what *he* is/might be that is causing him to see her ("Pilot"), and Rachel from *Alphas*, explains that her own mother thinks she is a "freak"—that her abilities make her a "walking crime lab" who is good at nothing else ("Never Let Me Go"). However, in this more contemporary era, such objectifying and marginalizing rhetoric most often originates with the superpowered women themselves. In other words, superpowered women from 2006 to 2011 take for granted that their abilities make them Other, *i.e.*, freaks, and resign themselves to this outsider status with varying degrees of acceptance (some resentfully, some dutifully, and some quasi-optimistically).

True Blood's Sookie is the contemporary character most asked "What are you?" and called a "freak," since, as a telepathic human-fairy hybrid, Sookie

6. Sacrifice and Sanctuary

is not a human, neither is she a vampire, werewolf, shapeshifter, or witch — supernatural beings all common to her fictional Louisiana. The demeaning interrogatives begin in the series' premiere, when vampire Bill, who later becomes Sookie's lover, twice asks her, "What are you?," first receiving the non-quite-responsive, "I'm Sookie," and then the more-exasperated, "I told you. I'm a waitress" ("Strange Love"). Bill's queries, like many other supernatural beings who encounter Sookie, are prompted, not by a display of her powers, but by her very existence — her powers give off a type of supernatural radar that other "supes" can recognize but not readily identify. Throughout the first three seasons, Sookie often is asked, "What are you?" by vampires ("I Got a Right to Sing the Blues," "Hitting the Ground") — her reply to one: "I'm the bitch that's gonna kill you" ("Hitting the Ground") —

True Blood's protagonist, telepathic barmaid Sookie, is called upon to define *what* she is by numerous human and superhuman beings, including her vampire lover Bill (HBO/Photofest).

and, twice, by a maenad, a female follower of Dionysus ("New World in My View," "Beyond Here Lies Nothin'") — her response the second time: "I'm a waitress. What the fuck are you?" ("Beyond Here Lies Nothin'"). In fact, she is asked this question so frequently that, in season four, when Eric, the amnesiac vampire she is caring for, inquires for the second time in the same evening, "What are you?," Sookie's indignant reply is, "I'm really sick of being asked that question, is what I am" ("If You Love Me, Why Am I Dyin'?"). In addition, Sookie is often called a "freak" or some variation thereof: a werewolf addicted to vampire blood calls her a "freak" ("Hitting the Ground," "Night on the Sun"), a vampire calls her a "freaky little human" ("Fresh Blood"), and her brother, Jason, tells her he loves her "even though" he wishes she would cook for him and she was "normal with a normal boyfriend" ("I Will Rise Up"). Based on Sookie's repeated exposure to such debasing rhetoric, it is not surprising that when she and a fellow telepath, Barry, visit the land of the fairies her query to him is: "Do you realize this is the only place in the universe where we're not freaks?" ("She's Not There").

Despite the near-constant demand that Sookie categorize/objectify herself as a "what," she does present moments of self-acceptance, although such moments communicate resignation to her fate more so than an embrace of her abilities. When Jason expresses his desire for Sookie to be "normal," as noted above, she remarks, "I didn't have any say about being normal. We're born the way we are" ("I Will Rise Up"). In a later episode, Sookie and Jason have a similar conversation, prompted by his fears of becoming a werepanther (following an attack):

> JASON: I like being a regular old all–American human. I don't want to be some freak of nature.
> SOOKIE: Like me.
> JASON: That ain't what I meant. [...]
> SOOKIE: For most of my life I'd say my prayers at night and wish to God to be normal, and then I realized there ain't no such thing as normal. Everyone's got something in them they're ashamed of [...] ["I Wish I Was the Moon"].

While this scene demonstrates that Sookie has realized she is not so different from everyone else after all, she is identifying shame as the common denominator. Toward the conclusion of this scene, however, Sookie does acknowledge that no one can run from what is inside her/him, and there is a chance that "what's inside you" could be a "blessing" ("I Wish I Was the Moon").

Other superpowered women are not on the receiving end of marginalizing questions and name-calling as frequently as Sookie is, but they are, nevertheless, acutely aware of their outsider status and struggle with their own balance of shame and blessing in regard to their abilities. This struggle leads many superpowered women to self-identify as freaks (or some equivalent), often in a self-loathing or self-deprecatory manner. For example, *Bionic Woman*'s Jaime accuses Jonas of turning her into a "half-robotic freak" ("Paradise Lost") and fears telling her sister the truth about her bionic status: "I don't want her to think I'm a freak" ("Do Not Disturb"). Likewise, Claire from *Heroes* and teenage succubus Andie from *The Gates* call themselves "freak"s ("Thanksgiving"; "Dog Eat Dog"), and Sally from *Being Human* refers to herself and her kind as "monsters" ("I See Your True Colors..."). Similarly, *The Nine Lives of Chloe King*'s title character[13] self-describes as a "freak," even when others are admiring her powers. When Chloe's friend Paul notes that she is "like a superhero," her retort is "More like a superfreak" ("Redemption"), and, when Chloe learns from Jasmine that the Uniter has abilities the other Mai do not, Chloe sarcastically proclaims, "Great, so my powers came with an extra scoop of freak" ("All Apologies").

Despite Chloe's "extra scoop of freak," she does express a greater level of self-acceptance in regard to her abilities than many of her counterparts. In the premiere episode of *The Nine Lives of Chloe King*, Chloe is initially curious—not frightened—by her emerging powers and is able to joke about the situation with her lifelong best friend, Amy, even making light of Amy's use of "freak":

> AMY: Obviously there has to be some kind of explanation for this [Chloe's new abilities, which include being able to jump over dumpsters]. Other than, you know, you're a freak.
> CHLOE: And you're worthless ["Pilot"].

After Chloe learns of her connection to the Mai and her role as the Uniter, she, understandably, struggles to embrace her abilities and the sacrifices they require. She does continue, though, with a semblance of self-acceptance when she tells Amy that she, Chloe, will not apologize for who she is, and that Amy must accept her for how she is now—"faults, claws, and all" ("All Apologies").

Chloe's self-acceptance is surpassed by the *Eastwick* witches, who eventually celebrate their "freak" status. After Kat's powers develop to include healing, the three share the following exchange:

> KAT: I am potent and mighty.
> ROXIE: I'm proud of you, sweetie. You're finally embracing the fact that you're a freak. Like us.
> KAT: Wait. We're not freaks, come on ... we're...
> ROXIE: Freakish?
> JOANNA: We're freak-adjacent?
> KAT: OK, so what if we are freaks? We are freakishly awesome ["Tea and Psychopathy"].

Although still self-identifying as freaks (or, rather, freak-adjacent), *Eastwick*'s Kat, Joanna, and Roxie appropriate the derogatory term for their own purposes and simultaneously embrace their powers.

This recent generation of extraordinary women more readily self-identifies as freaks than their predecessors and, as evidenced by Chloe and the *Eastwick* witches, not always in a self-deprecatory or preemptory manner (calling themselves freaks before someone else has the chance to). Hence, the "freak discourse" of "wonder becom[ing] error" (Thomson, *Freakery* 3) displayed by male characters in the presence of female power in the gilded era shifted to "error becoming (grudging) acceptance" displayed by female characters in regard to their own power in this more contemporary era. Such acceptance, no matter how grudging, can be read as a step forward in superpowered women claiming agency; however, as their powers still are read initially as "error"—as that which is problematic for women—the empowering potential of this acceptance for the characters—and their female viewers—is diminished.

Even More Awesome

In contrast, some superpowered male characters from 2006 to 2011 followed a discursive trajectory of "error becoming wonder" or "wonder becoming more wonder" in regard to their own abilities. While there are examples of superpowered men being asked "what are you" and being called "freaks," such as when Harry on *The Dresden Files* and Henry on *Blood Ties* are both on the receiving end of this question and that appellation during the same evening of television ("The Other Dick"; "Gifted") and when Scott on *Teen Wolf* is told by his nemesis, "It's pretty obvious that you're a freak" ("Pack Mentality"), there are counter-examples of male characters espousing more self-affirming rhetoric.

Haven's Nathan, in an attempt to comfort another "troubled" man, explains, "We're different, but you know what? It doesn't make us any less than anyone else. In some ways maybe it [a special ability] makes us even more" ("Fur"). Although Nathan later admits that he is not certain he believes what he said, his word choice of "maybe it makes us even more" indicates more of a buy-in than Joanna's "freak-adjacent." More greatly self-affirming is *Tower Prep*'s Gabe's description of his classmates and himself: "We [the students at Tower Prep] can do something weird in a really awesome way" ("The Rooks").

It is *The Listener*'s Toby, though, who best exemplifies this positive discourse, as his perspective on his ability shifts throughout the first episode: "I don't tell many people about my gift. I'm not into being the freak show at the party. [...] All my life I told myself, 'Turn it off. Shut it down. Make it go away.' Today I broke the rule. I stopped looking the other way, and I saw the truth. This isn't a curse; it's a gift" ("I'm an Adult Now"). As during the gilded age, being a "freak," *i.e.*, having superhuman power, does not carry as great a stigma for superpowered men as it does for their female counterparts.

Selfless Is as Selfless Does

Just as the freak stigma continues for superpowered women in the post-gilded age, so, too, does the cultural expectation of selflessness. These more contemporary superpowered women, like their predecessors, are constantly told that they must fulfill the responsibilities that come with their abilities (which may be measured/defined as their capacity for sacrifice) and that their powers should always be used for the betterment of others. However, in more recent series, the impetus for superpowered women to impose this heightened level of selflessness often comes from internal rather than external sources; in other words, as with the labeling of "freak," it is self-imposed.

Reminiscent of the gilded age, *Saving Grace*, *Bionic Woman*, *Eastwick*, *Warehouse 13*, and *The Nine Lives of Chloe King* all offer examples of a superpowered woman being reminded by authority figures that their powers come with non-negotiable obligations. On *Saving Grace*, Grace's brother, Johnny, a priest, angrily asks Grace, "What are you doing with this responsibility? This gift?" in regard to God's granting her an angel ("Looks Like a Lesbian Attack to Me"), while on *Bionic Woman*, Jonas tells Jaime her newfound abilities are a "gift," and, even though it is not fair, her reality now consists of raising her little sister and saving the world ("Paradise Lost"). Kat on *Eastwick*, Claudia on *Warehouse 13*, and Chloe on *The Nine Lives of Chloe King* receive more specific messages about the employment of their gifts, as each are told of their calling. Darryl, the *Eastwick* witches' guide to all things supernatural, tells Kat, "You have a destiny far greater than you ever imagined possible," "You have the power to perform miracles," and "You have been given a gift." When Kat protests that she did not ask for this gift and does not want it, Darryl informs her that she has "no choice." While the scene ends with Kat telling Darryl, "Yes, I do" ("Tasers and Mind Erasers"), it is clear that Darryl has actually had the last word in the conversation. Claudia receives a similar message from Mrs. Frederic, as the ailing caretaker selects Claudia to be her replacement; when Claudia asks "Mrs. F" (as she is known) why she has been chosen, the response is, "All of us have our purpose." Although Claudia does not have to link to the warehouse until Mrs. Frederic's death (a link that will connect her fate to the warehouse's), another authority figure, Dr. Vanessa Calder, tells Claudia that "she will be ready" when that time comes ("Buried"). This time might not ever come, as, in the next episode, Artie tells Claudia that he will make sure she can control her own destiny ("Reset"); ironically, this declaration denies Claudia's agency just as Mrs. Frederic's does. Chloe's agency, too, is denied when Valentina tells her that, as the Uniter, Chloe's life is no longer her own. When Chloe asks, "What if I don't want to be the Uniter?," Valentina explains, "That's like wishing you didn't have blue eyes. Some things simply are." Perhaps as consolation, Valentina explains that Chloe is "destined for greatness"; Chloe sarcastically responds, "Why does that sound like the worst thing anyone has ever said to me?" ("Green Star").

Although *Nine Lives* was cancelled before viewers could learn whether

Chloe's destiny ultimately leads to greatness, the final episode of the series does indicate that when Chloe strays from her predestined path, even momentarily and unconsciously, the worst happens. Chloe had been growing closer to human Brian, although resisting the urge to connect with him physically. However, when Chloe is shot and presumably dies yet again, Brian finds her unconscious, declares his love, and kisses her. Chloe regains consciousness, understands what is happening, and gasps "No"; the final scene of the episode depicts Chloe cradling an unconscious Brian crying, "He's dead" ("Beautiful Day").

The worst does not happen to other superpowered women who stray from righteousness, but they, too, face repercussions when they temporarily break from their selfless paths. On *Medium*, Allison's oldest daughter, Ariel, who shares her mother's gift (as her two sisters do), is told by a ghost that if she does a favor for him (erasing a file from his former wife's computer), he can help her ace a college interview. Ariel complies, only to have the ghost's former wife, who is her interviewer, accuse her of having an affair with her deceased husband ("Sal"). On *The Secret Circle*, Cassie's circle-mate Fay longs to perform magic on her own: "What's the point of being a damn witch if I can't do any magic by myself? I might as well become a cheerleader. [...] Why can't it be fun, like that movie *The Craft*? I mean the first half, not the stuff with the snakes. The part where we put spells on boys, change our hair color, and levitate" ("Heather"). When Fay enlists the help of a less-than-reputable boy to help her gain the power to perform magic solo, she endangers the entire circle, as the boy's spell starts to drain her friends' powers ("Fire/Ice").

While declarations from authority figures or "cosmic" repercussions persuade some superpowered women to use their powers only for the betterment of others, many superpowered women impose their own restrictions on their abilities; they take it upon themselves to enact the cultural expectation of selflessness. For example, *Sanctuary*'s Magnus only takes a long weekend off every seven years, as she can't stand to do "nothing" for any longer, because her work is more important ("Next Tuesday"); *Haven*'s Audrey notes she does not "get days off," since she is in Haven to "save everyone" ("Audrey Parker's Day Off"), which is the only true thing she knows about herself ("Business as Usual"); and *Being Human*'s Sally misses her chance to move on to the afterlife when she ignores her "door" (the show's symbol for a transition to the great beyond) to assist a near-death Aiden ("A Funny Thing Happened"). *Ghost Whisperer*'s Melinda and *No Ordinary Family*'s Stephanie not only choose selflessness for themselves, but they impart that expectation to their children as well. Melinda tells son Aiden, "We call it a gift [their mutual ability to communicate with ghosts] for a reason. It allow us to be able to help people in ways that others can't, and we have to respect that, learn from it, take care of it and never hide it from each other again" ("The Children's Parade"), and Stephanie tells daughter Daphne that, even though they did not ask for their powers, they have to use them to do what is right ("No Ordinary Quake"), and what is right for Stephanie is that with her new powers she does not "have to choose anymore" between work and home ("No Ordinary Marriage"). Stephanie's portrayer, Julie Benz, described her character's application of her powers around the house: "She's been failing at being a mother and a wife, so there's some fun moments where you see her using her powers to make her life easier—like unloading the dishwasher" (Keck, "Classic Benz" 36). With her powers, Stephanie can make up for "failing" by giving "100 percent" to her family and her work ("No Ordinary Marriage")—and presumably zero percent to herself.

Saving Grace's title character, though, commits the ultimate act of selflessness when she sacrifices her life in an attempt to stop evil, as it is personified in human form. Although Grace has been directed toward redemption by Johnny, as well as Earl and her best friend, Retta, her decision to sacrifice herself comes after she wrestles with God, not Earl this time, and is reduced to crying on the floor of her closet, asking/praying, somewhat reminiscent of Jesus in the Garden of Gethsemane before the crucifixion: "Is this why I was born? Some destiny I don't want hurdling towards me? [...] Why did you choose me? I don't want this. [...] I'm asking you to take it from me because I can't do it. I can't." Meanwhile, Earl sits outside the closet crying silently ("You Think I'm Gonna Eat My Gun?"). Before Grace is killed by an explosion started by the evil entity, she declares to Earl, "You win. I'm turning my life over to God." As Earl notes, "I don't believe you" ("I'm Gonna Need a Big Night Light"), it is unclear whether Earl has foreknowledge of Grace's upcoming sacrifice, although he had previously been shown a "new page in the book of Grace" by another angel ("You Think I'm Gonna Eat My Gun?"); apparently, Grace chooses to make an offering of herself, a choice deemed heavenly by CBS News entertainment writer Devon Thomas in "'Saving Grace' Finale Lives Up to Show's Name": "So in the end, the show's title lived up to the final showdown. Grace, although taking her own life, did in fact become the 'Saving Grace' for the people around her. And that's a pretty divine way to go out."

Superpowered women from 2006 to 2011 accepted and even embraced the responsibilities (read "selflessness"), divine or otherwise, associated with their abilities, as outlined by the authority figures in their lives. Many of these more contemporary female characters even choose to enact this cultural expectation of selflessness unprompted, because they ostensibly decide it is the right thing for someone in their position to do. These characters illustrate Wood's contention that women "internalize" the "burden of selflessness" (5,

On *Saving Grace*, hard-living homicide detective Grace starts down the road to redemption with the help of "last-chance angel" Earl — a road that ultimately leads to self-sacrifice (TNT/Photofest).

33), and these extraordinary female characters internalize it to an even greater degree than their counterparts in the gilded age. Such self-imposed selflessness underscores to viewers that women's power must operate by a strict code: 100 percent used in the service of others. This all-or-nothing approach to women's power detracts from the seemingly progressive narrative shift of superpowered women choosing how and when to employ their powers. As Melinda in *Ghost Whisperer* asks about her own plight, "So that's how this works? Fate and free will working together?" ("Birthday Presence"). Free will for these characters is never truly free, as fate (or their families, bosses, or deities) requires an offering of selflessness. Grace's death, then, can be interpreted by viewers as both noble and desperate, as the burden of selflessness for Grace is so great that the only way she can carry it (noble) and lay it down (desperate) is to offer her life.

Selflessness, Now with Fornication

The selflessness of male characters rarely reaches the noble/desperate state that Grace's does; however, male characters in the post-gilded age do face a higher expectation of selflessness than their precursors. As referenced earlier in this chapter, on *Supernatural*, Dean and Sam Winchester, like Grace, are connected to a heavenly destiny, as spelled out to them by the angel Gabriel, who contends that they were born for the purpose of being earthly vessels for Michael and Lucifer ("Changing Channels"). Also, like Grace, Sam sacrifices himself to stop evil, letting Lucifer embody him as he leaps through a portal to hell ("Swan Song"). Unlike Grace, though, Sam is returned to earth, damaged at first (he is sans soul), but later returned to his pre-sacrificial state. Also unlike Grace or any superpowered woman, Dean is reminded, by the angel Zachariah, of the concrete and very human personal rewards that come along with the daily acts of selflessness being a hunter requires: "You get to change things. Save people. Maybe even the world. All the while you drive a classic car and fornicate with women. This isn't a curse, it's a gift. [...]" ("It's a Terrible Life").

For other superpowered men, those reminding them of the obligations that come with their "gift" have little power or authority over them. For example, on *Teen Wolf*, Scott's best friend, Stiles, urges Scot to take action against the alpha werewolf that is terrorizing their town: "You have something, Scott. Ok? Whether you want it or not, you can do something no one else can do. That means you don't have a choice anymore. That means you have to do something" ("Heart Monitor"). On *Heroes*, Noah, Claire's father and a former agent of the "Company" (an organization that hunts and contains individuals with superhuman abilities) makes a similar plea to telepathic Matt to assist with a rescue mission: "You're one of the good guys, Matt. You have a responsibility. You're not a coward." Matt, who is doing his best to be a stay-at-home father, sends Noah away after claiming, "You know some days, maybe you just can't save the world. Some days it's just better getting your own house in order" ("Close to You").

Finally, whether male characters are saving the world or getting their own house in order, they have more autonomy and flexibility built into their cultural expectation of selflessness. *Smallville*'s Clark Kent may lament the sadness and loneliness that accompanies his hero status, but he notes, "I do it because I want to help people. [...] Not because I have to, but because I choose to" ("Warrior"). Furthermore, Clark has the capacity to compartmentalize, to some extent, his superhero and regular guy personae and enjoy some aspects of a "normal" life; as his mother explains, "One of those lives is full of sacrifice, so I'm glad to see the other one has Lois [his girlfriend/later wife-to-be] in it"

("Hostage"), and, as Clark, himself, explains to Lois, "The only thing that's ever made me feel normal is you" ("Scion"). Likewise, Scott on *Teen Wolf* overcomes numerous challenges to build a relationship with girlfriend, Allison; in the first-season finale, Allison even kisses Scott in his wolf mode, and the episode concludes with a scene of the two of them cuddling on the roof of Scott's house ("Code Breaker"), a stark contrast from Chloe King's final scene. Overall, then, for male characters, there is a higher degree of choice in regard to if, when, and how the burden of selflessness will be picked up, and, if picked up, there may be rewards in store, fit for sinners (fornication), saints (holy matrimony), and all those in between (rooftop romance).

Here's Looking at You

Superpowered women in series that aired from 2006 to 2011 face as many spying eyes as their gilded-age predecessors, and, as in that previous era, those spying include both institutional agents and trusted loved ones (both often depicted as white men), with such surveillance leading to an internalization of the gaze (literally for one character). Also a holdover from the gilded age, many superpowered women's abilities continue to include alternate forms of vision. A few notable examples of more contemporary superpowered women, however, provide evidence of progression from the previous era in regard to this theme, while superpowered men found themselves the objects of surveillance more frequently than their gilded-age counterparts.

Institutionally bound surveillance (Bartky 143) is present in *Ghost Whisperer*, as Melinda frequently encounters her own "watcher," like Buffy before her. Melinda's watcher, Carl, appears unexpectedly to offer cryptic messages about Melinda's and Aiden's abilities. Melinda expresses her frustration over this surveillance and its seeming impracticality to Carl: "Sometimes I wish you were less of a watcher and more of a talker." Speaking on behalf of his cosmic bureaucracy, Carl replies, "It's the rules" ("Birthday Presence"), and later explains, "We're watchers, not meddlers" ("Devil's Bargain"). *Fringe* includes its own version of watchers, called "Observers," within its mythos; befitting this more clinical term, the Observers, who are depicted as white, bald men, keep watch over Olivia, Peter, and Walter throughout the series, and are revealed in a fourth-season episode as a team of scientists from the future that "travels within and outside of time" to monitor human history ("The End of All Things"). The Observers meddle more frequently and with greater impact than *Ghost Whisperer*'s Carl, such as when an Observer tells Olivia that she must die ("Back to Where You've Never Been"), and, in the final season, become overlords.

It is *Bionic Woman*'s Jaime, though, who suffers the greatest effects of institutional surveillance. Jaime learns that her cybernetic makeover includes a tracker so that the Burket Group can locate her at all times, or as Jonas explains, "Fifty million dollars and you didn't think we'd throw in a GPS?," as well as a camera that streams video from Jaime's brain. Jaime, outraged at this bodily violation, tells Jonas she wants the equipment removed. After Jonas explains that is not an option, as it would cause brain damage (the camera is grafted onto her cerebral cortex), they share the following exchange:

JAIME: This is an invasion of my privacy. It's stripping me of my dignity, and it's a little pervy.
JONAS: Pervy?
JAIME: It's perverted.
JONAS: It's for your own safety.
JAIME: That is crap. It's so you can watch me and watch your investment.
JONAS: That is also true.
JAIME: This conversation is not over.

Despite Jaime's anger, the conversation, actually, is over, as the two switch gears to discuss a case ("Sisterhood"). As Jaime's very sight has been coopted by the institution that sanctions her power, she literally has internalized the Burket Group's gaze; she cannot escape it without significant physical damage to herself.

While *Bionic Woman* provides an extreme example of institutionally bound surveillance, most series offer examples of more informal, institutionally unbound surveillance (Bartky 143). For example, on *True Blood*, Bill keeps a file on Sookie and her family ("I Got a Right to Sing the Blues"), and, on *Eastwick*, Kat notes that she is sick of being watched and judged by members of her community ("Mooning and Crooning"). Claire, on *Heroes*, is under surveillance by both friend and foe. When Claire's friend Gretchen enters Claire's dorm room uninvited, Gretchen witnesses Claire using her ability ("Jump, Push, Fall"), thus exposing Claire's "secret" before Claire is willing to share this information. In addition, Claire, who hopes to join a sorority, is monitored by rush chair Becky, who has the power of invisibility. Becky, who is working on behalf of her Uncle Samuel, uses the information she learns from this observation to help Samuel manipulate Claire into joining his traveling carnival of "specials"—the series' term for individuals with abilities ("Hysterical Blindness").

Ironically, although these more contemporary superpowered women tend to be the objects of rather than the perpetrators of surveillance, many, like their precursors, possess alternate or enhanced forms of vision. As noted previously, *Medium*'s Allison and *Ghost Whisperer*'s Melinda, carry-overs from the gilded age, can see the dead. Other examples include *Bionic Woman*'s Jaime, whose engineered body includes a bionic eye ("Sisterhood"); *Eastwick*'s Roxie, who has psychic visions ("Reaping and Sowing"); *Heroes*' Emma, a deaf woman, who can see sound ("Hysterical Blindness"); and *True Blood*'s Sookie, who can, in a sense, see into the minds of others to access their thoughts. As with similarly powered characters in the gilded age, such alternate sight is often more liability than gift, as it is perceived as unstable or frightening; for example, Allison's co-worker calls her "toxic" after word gets out about her ability ("Everything Comes to a Head"), and Roxie's mother confesses she has always been afraid of her daughter ("Tasers and Mind Erasers").

More progressively, a few superpowered women from this era exhibit the adversarial gaze employed by superpowered men during the gilded age. For example, in the later seasons of *Smallville*, Chloe, Clark's longtime best friend (who is, on occasion, superpowered—at one point, Chloe discovers she has healing abilities and, for a time, superhuman intelligence because of an encounter with supervillain Brainiac), becomes "Watchtower," command center for Green Arrow and his team, tracking team members, monitoring their actions, and supplying them with information ("Hex"). Although Chloe later abdicates this position because she feels that she has been watching life more than living it ("I can't be the eye in the sky anymore, Clark. And now that I have Ollie [aka Green Arrow, Chloe's boyfriend], I want to plug in to the real world. Virtual reality bites"), her role as "Big Sister" (as she once referred to herself ["Hostage"]) placed her in the privileged position of looking generally denied superpowered women on television. Somewhat similarly, on *Eastwick*, Roxie, Kat, and Joanna stare daggers at Gus, a teen who assaulted Roxie's daughter; Gus later dies in a freak accident, intimating that the three witches are able to channel their collective anger and abilities through their very sight ("Reaping and Sewing"). While vigilante justice is not the most admirable use of their abilities, their blatant display of power toward Gus—a public staring down/pointing out of the enemy—indicates an active and self-serving use of power more often equated with male characters. Finally, Claire on *Heroes*, tired of living life in the shadows and on the run because of her abilities, decides to reveal her name and abilities to the media, to the dismay of her father (who claims Claire is "breaking [his] heart]") and uncle Peter (who says Claire is "going to change everything"). With this step, Claire asserts her autonomy from the male authority figures in her life and exploits the traditionally masculine-based politics of visibility to her advantage; supervillain Sylar characterizes the effects of Claire's action by saying, "It's a brave new world" ("Brave New World"). Unfortunately, viewers do not learn how this "brave new world" will manifest itself, as Sylar's pronouncement closes the final episode of the series.

Narratives featuring more recent superpowered women continued to include themes related to vision, visibility, and surveillance, and how each reflect power, based on who is watching whom. These characters suffer the effects of surveillance by loved ones and enemies alike, and those who possess alternate forms of vision are marginalized. In this regard, surveillance is the theme least changed in the years following the gilded age. However, it is also the theme that offers the most extreme regressive and progressive examples. The high-tech, dystopian reality of *Bionic Woman*'s Jaime makes her body the Panopticon, as the equipment that monitors her is embedded in her brain — there is no escaping such a gaze that is "alert everywhere" (Foucault, *Discipline* 195), even in one's very thoughts. At the other end of the spectrum, *Smallville*'s Chloe-as-Watchtower storyline makes Chloe the guard tower at the center of the Panopticon; she is the "eye in the sky" ("Hostage") that knows all and sees all. It is Claire's decision to reveal her powers on her own time and in her own terms, though, that provides the most liberating note, as she confronts the gaze that has long objectified her.

Watch This!

Gilded-age superpowered men are more often watchers than the ones watched; however, more contemporary male characters are just as likely to be the object of surveillance, whether that surveillance is targeted or generalized. For example, on *The Listener*, a detective keeps a file on Toby, as she finds his actions suspicious ("A Voice in the Dark"); on *Supernatural*, Lucifer, in possession of Sam's body (and speaking to Sam through a mirror), tells Sam that he — Sam — has been watched and manipulated his whole life, by an elementary school teacher, a prom date, a friend ... ultimately leading to this moment of possession ("Swan Song"); and, on *Smallville*, Clark advises the Wonder Twins, young superheroes, that there is no room for errors when using their powers, "Not when the world is watching" ("Idol"). Male characters, too, may have alternate forms of sight, since Toby, like Sookie, can "see" into the minds of others, and Pete on *Warehouse 13* gets "bad feelings," a heightened sense of intuition that allows him to recognize when danger is near ("The New Guy"); such alternate vision, with its more unpredictable nature, may not be seen as a liability the way it is for superpowered women, but it may make these characters the object of suspicion or derision.

More recent superpowered men, despite a more frequent positioning as the object of surveillance, continue to take the privileged position of looking as well. Dean and Sam often stake out suspicious individuals or expected victims in their efforts to rid the world of supernatural evil, and Clark has Chloe put a tracker on Lois's keychain when he thinks she is keeping something from him — Chloe notes the irony ("Upgrade"). On *Chuck*, the title character, who toward the end of the series' run, has lost the intersect, becomes the surveillance expert for his spy team, coordinating the team's movements from a high-tech van, a mobile version of Chloe's Watchtower; when Chuck laments this more passive role (the intersect made him a martial arts expert, among other abilities), Sarah, Chuck's wife and a superspy, reassures him: "Chuck, you're our leader" ("Chuck Versus the Zoom"). In the fictional worlds of post-gilded-age superpowered men, placing others under an objectifying gaze frequently continued to be associated with the privileged positions of white and male described by Haraway (283).

Deserving Judgment

Superpowered women from 2006 to 2011 faced judgment as frequently as their predecessors, since, as noted previously, their powers draw criticism and the spying eyes of others. For example, on *Ghost Whisperer*, Melinda's friends discuss their concerns for her behind her back, deciding that she can no longer distinguish between her spectral visions and reality ("Dead Ringer"). However, Grace and Alex, the protagonists of *Saving Grace* and *The Wizards of Waverly Place*, are the only two characters who face formal trials that are reminiscent of those experienced by their counterparts in the gilded age, except both of these more recent characters exert some influence on the outcome, and, in Grace's case, the trial itself. Such influence, though, does not indicate greater empowerment for these characters. Male superpowered characters, on the other hand, face more formal trials, but, continuing from the gilded age, these male characters emerge from their trials with their empowerment intact, if not strengthened.

The episode featuring Grace's trial was titled "So Help You God" and characterized (via TNT's on-screen description) as "Grace has to answer for herself and face judgment for her life's deeds." These life's deeds include her violence, promiscuity, and alcoholism, with the alcoholism noted as fueling the other two. Grace's trial begins when she visits the grave of Leon Cooley, a death-row inmate with whom she shared Earl as a last-chance angel. When she lies in front of the grave and closes her eyes, she "awakens" in a crowded courtroom and is immediately called to the stand. As Grace is being sworn in, the courtroom empties except for Grace and Earl, who indicates that she is somehow controlling the trial, noting, "It's your party." The courtroom is suddenly refilled, with Earl serving as Grace's attorney and two unknown women serving as the prosecutor and judge. The prosecutor claims that

6. Sacrifice and Sanctuary 177

Grace's addiction already may have been responsible for one life (Grace had a hangover the day before her sister died — since Grace could not babysit that day, her sister made the trip to the Federal Building on the day of the bombing). As Grace's friends, family members, former lovers, and co-workers are called to testify, the prosecutor tries to prove that Grace has a self-destructive pattern of behavior; in her defense, Earl passionately argues that Grace is a "loyal, strong-willed, always-be-there-for-you friend as well as a loving aunt [Grace is close to her dead sister's son, Clay] whose passion for life is infectious and whose heart slowly carves initials into the souls of her closest friends," and, in a flashback, Earl notes he has more faith in Grace than he did in Joan of Arc ("So Help You God"). Since this trial occurs only a few episodes before the series' finale and Grace's sacrifice, the reference to Joan of Arc is significant, as Grace, too, will soon meet a fiery end. Toward the end of the trial, the courtroom again almost empties; this time, Grace, Earl, and the prosecutor remain and are joined by Ben Cooley, Leon's son. The viewer and, presumably, Grace flash back to Leon's execution, for which Grace was present; Grace then "awakens" back at Leon's grave, where she greets Ben and the rest of his family as Earl stands nearby ("So Help You God"). Grace's ambiguous role in her own proceedings, which, according to Earl's comments, may be the result of Grace putting herself on trial, and the trial's lack of a verdict can be read as Grace deciding her own judgment. However, any agency such a decision might demonstrate is undercut by Grace's continued connection to Leon, who had been on death row for murdering a prison guard. Since he was guilty and "deserved" to die, so, too, apparently, does Grace.

Alex's trial on *The Wizards of Waverly Place* is neither as dark nor ambiguous as Grace's, befitting the tween-oriented series' home network — Disney. Also, in contrast, Alex's trial is an examination that tests her knowledge and ability as well as her character and includes her two brothers, since only one Russo progeny can carry on the title of family wizard and its accompanying powers. After Alex completes a selfless act (making dinner for the family, unprompted), which was the final requirement for the family to begin the family wizard competition, the family is instantly transported to a game show setting for "Last Wizard Standing." Before the competition begins, Jerry makes the siblings promise that, regardless of who wins the competition, they will "stick together." Once the siblings are in play, Theresa roots for Justin, because he has stuck by the rules and studied the hardest to become a wizard, while Jerry roots for Alex, because of her past feats of bravery, which included defeating the angels of darkness and saving the world from an asteroid, "Plus he [Justin] can easily get a career if he doesn't win; we'd be stuck with her [Alex] for life" ("Who Will Be, Part 1"). Justin takes an early lead, and Max, surprises everyone by remaining competitive, while Alex is a distant third. Midway through the competition, Alex's friend, Harper, and Justin's friend, Zeke, are captured by a griffin, a magical creature, and Alex convinces her brothers to combine their timeouts so they can temporarily leave the competition to save them. Her brothers reluctantly agree, and it is Alex who takes the lead in saving their friends (even though Justin is a trained monster hunter). They do not make it back to the competition in time, though, and they are all disqualified ("Who Will Be, Part 1"). Justin and Max blame Alex (Justin even says, "Alex just cut down our family tree and burned it" ["Who Will Be, Part 2"]), and the three siblings fight until they learn their behavior is forcing Jerry and Theresa to close the family sandwich shop; the siblings then band together to save the business, with Justin and Max forgiving Alex in the process. Once the family is reunited, the competition is resumed; the Russos learn that the griffin adventure was a test of their sibling bond. Entering the final round, Alex and Justin are tied, with Max trailing slightly. In the final challenge, a magical obstacle course, Alex is ahead, but Justin gets caught on some branches, and Alex goes back to help him, noting, "I don't want to win this way." Justin then crosses the finish line before her. However, just before Justin is named the family wizard, he confesses that Alex truly deserved to win, and she takes his place at the podium. Professor Crumbs, the retiring headmaster of the wizard school, is so impressed by Justin's "integrity and knowledge" that he offers Justin his position; thus, Justin becomes a full wizard, too. Max, to his delight, learns he will inherit the family business, and the episode — and the series — end on an idyllic note, as Alex concludes, "Check it out! We're all happy at the same time" ("Who Will Be, Part 2"). While such as ending allows Alex to maintain her powers into adulthood and carry on the family wizarding line (a privilege generally associated with the patriarchal), she is willing to let Justin claim the prize, noting that she thinks he deserves it, and, presumably, she thinks she does not. Furthermore, Justin is rewarded for his "selfless" act of revealing Alex's help, while Alex is initially "punished" for helping others (her friends and her brother). So, even though Alex chooses to affect the outcome of her trial by assisting her brother, ultimately, her fate is in her brother's hands.

Although *Saving Grace* and *Wizards of Waverly Place* are wildly different series in terms of genre, tone, and target audience, Grace and Alex, and their trials, share commonalities. Both Grace and Alex often flout the rules, doing things their own way (in Grace's trial, her nephew Clay even testifies to this ["So Help You God"]). In this sense, they exhibit agency, countering Fineman's description of the law as a set of "coercive rules" (217); Grace and Alex resist such coercion under the "law" in their respective universes. However, their trials are a reality check that the rules do, indeed, apply to them — they can expect no special privileges. In addition, in both trials, a question arises regarding which powers and privileges female characters "deserve." Grace, apparently, deserves death to atone (in her mind), specifically, for her sister's death and, generally, for her hedonistic lifestyle, while Alex, initially, deserves to lose the competition for realizing too late the value of hard work (as embodied by Justin) and that selflessness should be its own reward (it is her act of domestic selflessness that begins the entire tournament, after all), reinforcing Wishik's contention that the law reinforces the societal status quo in regard to power (22). Therefore, even though both characters have some role in their own trials, neither exhibits true empowerment, especially Grace, since she ostensibly is being judged by her own conscience and finds herself "guilty."

Commuted Sentences

Like Grace, superpowered male characters in the post-gilded age may find themselves guilty of the crimes for which they are tried. These trials, however, have vastly different endings than Grace's. On *Heroes*, a dying Hiro, who is suffering from a brain tumor, is put on "trial" while on the operating table (like Grace, Hiro seems to be tried by his own conscience). Hiro is being charged for altering the timeline for personal gain — he tried to go back in time to prevent the death of his true love, waitress Charlie; the trial takes place in Charlie's diner with Hiro's father presiding, his best friend, Ando, serving as his attorney, and his nemesis, Adam, prosecuting. During the trial, Hiro confesses that he made a deal with Sylar: if Sylar saved Charlie, then Hiro would kill whomever Sylar designated. Hiro explains, though, that Sylar double-crossed him, and now Charlie is lost in time. While Hiro admits to errors in judgment, he defends himself, noting he has followed a code and saved the world — twice: "Yes, I used poor judgment, but despite the sometimes disastrous effects, it was to make the world a better place ... for family. And friendship. And love. And if breaking my code for these things makes me guilty.... Then, I suppose I'm guilty" ("Pass/Fail"). Hiro's father than pronounces Hiro guilty, Hiro officially changes his plea to "guilty," and Hiro has a sword fight with Adam, saying he wants to "go out with honor" (the battle scenes represent Hiro's fight for his life on the operating table, as those scenes are interspersed with images of him flatlining). After felling Adam, Hiro sees his dead mother, who tells him she is proud of him, that his destiny is stronger than the science that told him he would die from the tumor, and that she is there to heal him; the scene then changes to the operating table where Hiro has been resuscitated ("Pass/Fail"). Hiro, then, unlike Grace, is found guilty of breaking his own rules, but is able to forgive himself and continue on his heroic path instead of sacrificing himself.

Supernatural's Dean, likewise, finds himself guilty, but is able to emerge from his trial to continue his life as a hunter. In a seventh-season episode titled "Defending Your Life," Dean is put on trial by Osiris, an Egyptian god who executes the guilty; Osiris claims that people want to be judged, and, if Dean believes he — Dean — is innocent, then he is. Sam volunteers to serve as Dean's attorney, and Osiris allows it. Osiris calls two witnesses: first, Jo, a family friend who Dean had encouraged to become a hunter who later died in an explosion during a mission with the Winchester brothers; and, then, Sam. Jo and Sam are two elements of Dean's life that cause Dean the most guilt — he thinks he ended Jo's life by encouraging her to be a hunter and ruined Sam's life by pressuring him to do the same. As the trial continues, Dean fears Osiris will call Amy as a witness: Amy is a demon — one that Sam owed his life to and asked Dean to leave alone — that Dean killed. Osiris has enough evidence against Dean before that happens, and Dean is declared "guilty in [his] heart" and told to get his affairs in order. While Sam searches for a weapon that can defeat Osiris, Jo's ghost visits Dean, telling him, "It's time." As Jo turns on the gas and starts to flick a lighter (so that Dean, too, will die in an explosion), Sam stabs Osiris, and Jo lovingly touches Dean's face and fades away. Dean, unlike Grace, finds forgiveness for at least one of the lives his own destructive pattern of behavior allegedly has taken, and, like Hiro, he is able to continue on his heroic path, although without leaving his guilt behind. Superpowered men, then, in this more contemporary era, are more often held accountable for their actions than their predecessors; however, they still fare better in their trials than their female counterparts.

Symbols of Sanctuary

In addition to the carry-over themes from the gilded age, series featuring superpowered characters from 2006 to 2011 also introduced a new theme — that of finding sanctuary. The mixed-sex protagonists of these more contemporary series, unlike their female counterparts from the previous era, are not as likely to be predestined to fight evil or even crime, although, as discussed previously, they choose to employ their abilities to protect their friends, families, and communities. In this new era of supernatural television, such characters seek tolerance and may find acceptance from those they trust, as illustrated by a vampire resident of *The Gates* who challenges Nick to reconsider his perspective on his new neighbors by asking, "What if they're not monsters? What if they're just people with unique differences and difficult histories?" ("Digging the Dirt").

The search for acceptance or tolerance is what drives the superpowered characters of contemporary television. All are, in some way, seeking sanctuary ... from the hardships of their abilities, from not-so-benevolent others of their kind, or, even, from "normal" humans who fear and seek to eliminate them. This concept of seeking sanctuary has its roots in comic books; as Fingeroth explains, "And when you're freak, you need a family of freaks. [...] You need a surrogate family, one composed of those the world has abused and persecuted the way you have been all your life" (107). On *Kyle XY*, Kyle finds this sanctuary with the Trager family members, who, although "normal," take him into their home and become his surrogate family, since Kyle appears to be an amnesiac. As Kyle learns about his past and must elude capture from those who want to control his powers, the Tragers, especially mother-by-proxy Nicole, care for and protect him, offering him a haven where he is accepted, despite his superhuman attributes. Claire, on *Heroes*, longs for the sense of acceptance that Kyle finds. Even though Claire has loving, albeit complicated, "normal" parents (she is adopted), she does not feel truly at home until she glimpses what life among her own kind could be like. When Samuel, another special, introduces Claire to his traveling carnival of extraordinarily abled individuals, Claire is drawn to the idea of living out in the open with her ability amongst others who understand her plight ("The Fifth Stage"), laying the foundation for her series-finale revelation. Unfortunately for Claire, Samuel's carnival is not an option, as she learns of Samuel's murderous past. The supernatural housemates on *Being Human*, though, succeed where Claire could not, as they find sanctuary with one another; werewolf Josh, the only one of the trio who actually eats, even insists that they sit down to dinner together like a family ("A Funny Thing Happened..."). While such nontraditional "families" could be found during the gilded age, such as Buffy's "Scooby gang" who aid her in fulfilling her Slayer duties, these new families are not bound to any purpose greater than community, with *The Gates*' neighborhood as a prime example.

Sanctuary, for these characters, is more than just a safe haven — it is a family or a community that links them to something greater than themselves. This connection redefines what it means to be human in these fictional universes; it is not about whether one is "normal" or "extraordinary," it is the ability to be humane. As Annie, Sally's counterpart in the BBC version of *Being Human*, explains, "Humanity isn't a species; it's a state of mind. It can't be defeated. It moves mountains; it saves souls. We were blessed as much as we were cursed, and, in this little enclave of the lost, I witness the very best of being human. We were safe here, while outside the monsters prowled" ("Lia"). Contemporary series featuring superpowered characters, especially superpowered ensembles, explore salvation through sanctuary, redefining humanity through character and companionship rather than through categorization.

The supernatural trio on the U.S. version of *Being Human* consists of (from left) ghost Annie, werewolf Josh, and vampire Aiden; the three live together, hoping to maintain some semblance of a "normal" life (SyFy Channel/Photofest).

Although the gilded era of superpowered women on television has given way to a more contemporary era that features more male characters, women still serve a key role in these series, as they are the catalyst to achieving this new humanity. For example, on *Sanctuary*, Magnus serves as leader and protector to her team and the safe house's residents, or, as Magnus's portrayer, Amanda Tapping, described it, "[Magnus] has an overwhelming duty as the protector of the world's abnormal creatures" (Logan, "Sanctuary" 33); on *The Gates*, a vampire named Claire offers her human neighbor a lesson in tolerance by saying, "Now you know what we are, try not to forget who we are" ("Bad Moon Rising"); on *Tower Prep*, a computerized woman known as Whisper guides and protects Ian and his friends as they seek to uncover the secrets of the school; and on *Being Human*, Sally is a nearly ever-present fixture in the house who represents "home" to both Josh and Aiden. In each of these series, a superpowered woman symbolizes the character and companionship that are hallmarks of the new humanity, which can be read as a re-imagined domestic sphere. So, despite the great powers that these extraordinary female characters utilize bravely and boldly within and outside the home, they are still symbols of homemaking and caretaking.

The Power to Choose

The television narratives of superpowered women from 2006 to 2011 thematically resemble those of the gilded era in numerous ways; however, these more contemporary narratives include a recurrent rhetoric of choice. Superpowered women in the post-gilded age are more often given the opportunity to choose — to choose to call themselves freaks, to choose to sacrifice themselves for some definition of the greater good, to choose to return the gaze, to choose to affect the results of their own trials, and to choose to join communities of their "own kind." This rhetoric, while seemingly progressive, is actually paradoxical — it allows these superpowered female characters a greater degree of agency, but the "choices" of these characters are often more limiting than liberating. This on-screen rhetoric of choice paralleled an off-screen one, as the term "choice feminism" entered the lexicon in late 2005 (Hirshman), as the gilded era of superpowered women was coming to a close.

The term "choice" has long been associated with feminism. For second-wavers, "choice" has always been linked to the idea of reproductive freedom; however, for third-wavers, "choice" can apply to any number of options in their lives. As Suzanne Ferriss and Mallory Young write in "Chicks, Girls and Choice: Redefining Feminism," "[T]he right to choose is no longer singular but endlessly plural: career choices, lifestyle choices, fashion choices" (87). This plurality of choice led *The American Prospect* writer Linda Hirshman to name the phenomenon "Choice Feminism," explaining that "[t]he choice talk spilled over from people trying to avoid saying 'abortion,' and it provided an irresistible solution to feminists trying to duck the mommy wars. A woman could work, stay home, have 10 children or one, marry or stay single. It all counted as 'feminist' as long as she *chose* it." Off-screen women, then, can justify any choice as being available because of, as well as further advancing, feminism; likewise, on-screen superpowered women who choose to give 100 percent to family and career, like *No Ordinary Family*'s Stephanie and *Bionic Woman*'s Jaime, or choose to sacrifice themselves for the greater good, like the title character of *Saving Grace*, can be read as feminist texts that empower their viewers to make their own choices.

Such rhetoric is, of course, problematic, as not every choice a woman can make, extra- or intra-textually, contributes to the advancement of gender equality. Virginia McCarver discusses the conflation of "choice" and "feminism" in her article "The Rhetoric of Choice and 21st-Century Feminism: Online Conversations About Work, Family, and Sarah Palin," stating that "[t]o enact choice means to enact feminism" (21). According to McCarver, this conflation, as part of the overall rhetoric of choice, is "potentially damaging and dangerous to women" in that it "often serves to limit rather than free women in exploring alternative experiences and life paths"; in other words, the rhetoric of choice presents only a "series of narrow scripts" for women (21). In McCarver's case study of online discussions of 2000 vice presidential hopeful Palin, three main scripts present themselves: "Family First," "You Can't Have It All," and "Superwoman"; each of these scripts outlines a potential path for women to follow in regard to work and family (33). Ultimately, McCarver concludes that "choice rhetoric can be dangerous to women because it obscures a reality of limited choices [such as the three scripts], assigns blame and individual responsibility to women alone for the outcome of their choices, and packages both dangers in language heralding personal freedom and women's rights" (33–34). In Palin's case, she was both lauded and vilified for her "choices," as women on both ends of the political spectrum judged her for decisions made in both her personal and professional lives. For example, Palin's "embrace of the hockey-mom label" and her return to work only days after the birth of her youngest child were cheered and defended by some women (Baird et al.), while her characterization of herself and her followers as "mama grizzlies" and her anti-abortion stance were deemed examples of "faux-feminism" and a "lead[ing] us back to a Bronze Age" mentality by others (Stiehm, "Sarah Palin's"). For superpowerful women off screen, such as Palin, and for superpowered women on screen, such as Jaime, their "choices" are scrutinized harshly, whether self-proclaimed hockey moms or freaks or balancing motherhood and politics or sisterhood and covert ops.

The theme of sanctuary in the post-gilded-age narratives of superpowered women represents a specific subset of the rhetoric of choice — that of women choosing to embrace aspects of traditional domesticity. Superpowered women representing sanctuary — home and humanity — in the face of danger can be interpreted as a continuation of what Susan Faludi refers to in *The Terror Dream: Fear and Fantasy in Post-9/11 America* as the "sanctioned fantasy" (118) of a "Nesting Nation," as her chapter on this subject is titled (116). This fantasy was perpetuated by the media following 9/11 and "maintained in pop[ular] culture" for several years after (139). Faludi describes television's take on this nesting fantasy as "a domestic idyll where men wore all the badges and women wielded all the roasting pans" (139). As a specific example, Carol A. Stabile, in "'Sweetheart, This Ain't Gender Studies': Sexism and Superheroes," describes *Heroes* in terms similar to Faludi's: "Indeed, *Heroes* underscores that in the post–9/11 landscape, the gendered lines of protection remain inviolable: men are heroes and women are victims, perpetually in need of protection" (89). While all of the more contemporary series featuring superpowered characters do not follow this fantasy as closely as *Heroes* does, since the female characters certainly wield more than roasting pans, the increased number of male characters and the female characters' roles as surrogate mother figures reflects a variation of this fantasy.

Off-screen, this fantasy plays out as the "new domesticity," a "pseudo-retro trend" that includes a "pastoral vision of 'reclaiming' women's work at home" (Stiehm, "New Domesticity"). This new domesticity, apparently, is the result of feminism, as the achievements of the women's movement allow modern women to enjoy domestic activities, such as cooking, knitting, and ironing (Hilgenberg 44). While some argue that third-wave feminists approach the new domesticity ironically, detaching activities, such as knitting, from gender (Groeneveld 274), others contend that those who espouse the new domesticity are rewriting the Superwoman script. In "Better Homes & Bloggers," Holly Hilgenberg describes lifestyle bloggers who are emblematic of the new domesticity: "These women don't just maintain squeaky-clean, camera-ready homes and adorable families, they also run independent businesses, wear perfect outfits, rock exquisitely styled hair — and find the time to blog about it" (43). Furthermore, the image of domesticity painted within these blogs "can't help but underscore that, while we're all free to choose our choices, a clear and privileged path to happiness and achievement runs through the kitchen, the garden, and the nursery" (45), even the choice to relive one's pain. For example, a 2012 Advil print advertisement exemplifies a woman giving her all for home and family; it features a smiling woman named Sunshine, pictured with a child's hands over her eyes, who is described in the copy as a "mother of three." Sunshine is quoted as saying, "I take Advil because my kids deserve a mom without a headache"; this testimonial is followed by the tagline "Take Action. Take Advil" (Advil). Sunshine, it seems, is choosing to take the right action for the right reason: relieving her pain so that she can be a more devoted mother. Women who read such blogs, view such ads, and watch series featuring superpowered women may feel that they, too, should choose to use (read: "employ") all of their power and energy toward a prescribed model of domestic perfection, despite Hirshman's warning that "[t]he real glass ceiling is at home."

Overall, the rhetoric of choice, as it associates empowerment with any choice a woman can make, is, more accurately, a rhetoric of false choice, as the choices available to women may be limited or inconsequential in relation to gender equality. Such limited choices for women may stem from their power being labeled an anomaly (if not a defect), from the cultural expectation of selflessness placed upon them, from their internalization of the persistent gaze of others, from their lack of voice in regard to the law, and from their association with the domestic sphere. Television series from 2006 to 2011 represented superpowered women facing such limited choices, while simultaneously representing those fictional women as making those choices willingly, at times even contentedly. Such narratives, therefore, failed to represent or deconstruct the actual causes of these characters' limited empowerment. As McCarver writes, "Choice rhetoric not only dilutes the meaning of feminism and its relevancy to women's lives, it diverts attention from oppressive social systems and focuses on the individual, avoiding the more difficult to tackle and achieve systemic change necessary in struggles for gender equality" (22)—both off- and on-screen.

Conclusion

"It's only, like, one of my favorite old television shows"

When *Bewitched* debuted in 1964, alongside other "fantastic sitcoms" (Spigel 119), its appeal was obvious: What woman would not want, like Samantha, to "twitch [her] nose and make the laundry fold itself" to borrow *Charmed*'s Phoebe's description of Samantha's powers, when she notes that "It's [*Bewitched*'s] only, like, one of my favorite old television shows" ("Lost and Bound")? *Bewitched*, which introduced television's first superpowered female protagonist, became, like, one of a lot of people's favorite television shows. So, even though Phoebe acknowledges that Samantha could not "twitch [her] nose" unrestrictedly, since mortal husband Darrin "completely repressed Samantha's magic" ("Lost and Bound"), the show became a near-instant ratings hit for its network home, ABC (Brooks and Marsh 134). *Bewitched*'s debut, therefore, also established a power + repression narrative formula for series featuring superpowered women. Although *Bewitched* certainly did not pass along its ratings success to all subsequent series featuring this character type, superpowered women have continued to hold appeal for (especially female) viewers, decade after decade, despite — or perhaps because of — the limitations placed on their abilities.

Following *Bewitched*, in the 1960s and the early 1970s, fantastic sitcoms featuring a feminine supernatural element disrupting the serenity (read: homogeneity) of suburbia persisted (Spigel 124–25) with varying success; the short-lived *My Living Doll*, *My Mother the Car*, and *The Girl with Something Extra* took their places alongside the more popular *I Dream of Jeannie* and *The Flying Nun*. The problematizing of the domestic sphere was fitting, as these series premiered on television as second-wave feminism gained momentum. Traditional gender roles, particularly those within the home, were being challenged by Friedan and others, and fantastic sitcoms like *Bewitched* explored such "threats to patriarchy" (Case 197) as Samantha using her abilities to fool Darrin's boss or entertain her children in the safe environs of half-hour episodes complete with laugh tracks.

By the late 1970s, however, the appeal of the fantastic sitcom had waned, as ABC's attempt at reviving *Bewitched*'s ratings success with a spin-off about Samantha and Darrin's daughter, *Tabitha*, failed to find an audience (Brooks and Marsh 1351). Viewers instead embraced *The Bionic Woman* and *Wonder Woman*, two action-oriented superpowered series with protagonists who employed their abilities outside the home, reflecting the advancements made by second-wave feminism, as women by now had protested for unbiased hiring practices, equal access to federally funded educational opportunities, and reproductive rights, and otherwise made the personal political. While *The Bionic Woman*'s Jaime and *Wonder Woman*'s title character are influenced by the men in their lives (Jaime was indebted to the male-run organization that saved her life by making her bionic, and Wonder Woman left her Paradise Island home to care and work for Army Major Steve Trevor), they do represent women living independently and demonstrating more agency than Samantha.

The dearth of iconic superpowered women in the 1980s and early 1990s paralleled the backlash to the feminist movement present during that time period. Both sitcoms (such as *Jennifer Slept Here* and *Free Spirit*) and dramas (such as *Tucker's Witch* and *Something is Out There*) featuring superpowered women lasted no more than a season; only the heavenly premised *Touched by an Angel* found longevity. However, kid-oriented series featuring superpowered girls fared much better, as *Small Wonder*, *Out of This World*, *Mighty Morphin Power Rangers*, and *The Secret World of Alex Mack* each aired for multiple seasons. The somewhat forgettable array of series featuring adult characters and the eclectic array of series featuring child characters seemed regressive after *The Bionic Woman* and *Wonder Woman*, as these 1980s and early–1990s characters faced constraints from authority figures, surveillance by neighbors and family members, and repercussions if their powers were revealed. Thirty years after *Bewitched*'s debut, its narrative formula of power + repression held fast.

The Limitations of Girl Power

Over the next ten years that narrative formula was explored in more ways and with more attention from the popular and academic presses than ever before, as representations of superpowered women experienced an influx from 1996 to 2006 in live-action and animated series, including sitcoms and dramas aimed at both children and adults. During this seeming golden age of superpowered women on television, characters named Sabrina (of *Sabrina, the Teenage Witch*), Phoebe, Piper, Prue, and Paige (of *Charmed*), Buffy (of *Buffy the Vampire Slayer*), Max (of *Dark Angel*), Sara (of *Witchblade*), and Helena (of *Birds of Prey*), among others, protected innocents, staved off the apocalypse, and fought both human and superhuman crime — all while managing to hold down their day jobs, whether as students or professionals. These extraordinary, albeit fictional, women offered (and continue to offer via a syndicated, DVD, and/or online presence) female viewers much to admire: powerful women who drive their storylines, who hold important positions, and who are considered, if not heroes, women who make a difference. Just as *Bewitched* and *I Dream of Jeannie* debuted on television as second-wave feminism gained momentum in the 1960s, *The Bionic Woman* and *Wonder Woman* found popularity following the height of that movement in the following decade, and the lower-profile and less-successful series featuring superpowered women in the 1980s and early 1990s paralleled the backlash to second-wave feminism, the influx of series centering on this character type from 1996 to 2006 reflected yet another era of feminism, the third wave: "a movement that contains elements of second wave critique of beauty culture, sexual abuse, and power structures while it also acknowledges and makes use of the pleasure, danger, and defining power of those structures" (Heywood and Drake 3).

Specifically, television's superpowered women from 1996 to 2006 exemplified an incarnation of third-wave feminism associated with "girl power." Tringali describes this third-wave/girl-power connection: "Despite initial skepticism, third-wavers eventually did adopt Girl Power — if not in name, then in practice — as the philosophy of supporting young girls and teenagers of varying interests and identities" (29). While this modified version of girl power is certainly a worthwhile philosophy to adopt, girl power, at its core, while rhetorically empowering, has failed to live up to its potential. As Fudge explains, "Girl power tricks us all into believing that girls are naturally powerful and therefore ignores the many ways their power is contingent on adhering to cultural expectations of female behavior" ("Girl, Unreconstructed" 160). Television's superpowered women during this time period depicted the tension between "natural power" and "cultural expectations of female behavior" over and over again in series after series, as demonstrated when Buffy saves a teenage boy from a vampire: his bewildered response is, "But you're just a girl," and her world-weary reply is, "That's what I keep saying" ("The Gift"). While the superpowered women named previously possess an array of extraordinary abilities any female viewer could envy, the empowering potential of these characters remains unfulfilled, as they face any number of constraints on their supernatural and superhuman abilities. Regardless of the feminist theoretical lens employed to read these television texts, whether it is based in applications of freakery, psychoanalytic theory, panopticism, or critical legal studies, the limitations of these mid-1990s to mid-2000s characters are apparent, as their agency is diminished in a number of ways.

The first time male television characters unexpectedly witness superpowered women using their supernatural or superhuman abilities, the male characters' stammered responses are often "What are you?" or some variation thereof. This interrogatory subordination of superpowered women from individuals ("who"s) to objects ("what"s) reflects an underlying discourse of normalcy versus ab-normalcy present in series featuring these extraordinary female characters. Television's superpowered women, since their abilities are innate, *i.e.*, physically embodied, are often labeled freaks for falling outside of the bodily bounds of normalcy for women. This labeling, although paradoxical since these characters also are considered beautiful, stigmatizes superpowered women; their physical prowess is deemed a gender transgression that renders them the object of rejection, prejudice, misguided sympathy, and/or physical violence. In an effort to manage the repercussions of such stigma, superpowered women often try to conceal their abilities. These characters who attempt to pass as normal may privilege their non-superpowered personae, failing to admit even to themselves who they truly are, and, while some superpowered women self-identify as freaks, those women do so preemptively, knowing that they will never fully be accepted by society. In contrast, superpowered men and their abilities are accepted more readily than their female counterparts, and these male characters have the opportunity to separate who they are from what they do in a manner not afforded superpowered women.

To compensate for their alleged gender transgression, for claiming power that traditionally has been allocated for the masculine domain, television's superpowered women enact a high degree of selflessness. For superpowered women, such self-sacrifice fulfills a cultural expectation; thus, self-abnegation provides another way for superpowered women to manage the stigma of being deemed freaks, to attempt to avoid rejection or censure from others. The assumption of this masquerade of selflessness then becomes a sign of maturity for superpowered women, of the necessary putting aside of the impulses of girlhood in order to fulfill the heroic destinies dictated by their powers. For some superpowered women, this inordinate selflessness is their most extraordinary gift, as they are not equipped with additional abilities to assist them with their self-sacrificing missions, which may include both caring for siblings and saving the world. When such characters attempt to remove this masquerade or use their powers for their own purposes, they face repercussions

Conclusion 191

from others or self-imposed guilt. Additionally, when superpowered women don some other, less-philanthropic and, therefore, less-burdensome guise, they may expose themselves to danger or, at the very least, reproach. This expectation of selflessness is so ingrained in these characters' personae that, when they consider forgoing their self-sacrificing missions, they may suffer emotional breakdowns. While superpowered men also may exhibit selfless behavior, as heroism requires a degree of sacrifice, such behavior for these male characters may be considered noble, but not required. Since the cultural expectation of selflessness is much lower for men, superpowered men who act selfishly are more readily forgiven for such transgressions than their female counterparts.

This cultural expectation of selflessness for television's superpowered women often may be enforced — or at least underscored — by the near-constant surveillance to which they are subjected. Such surveillance may be conducted formally by an institution that may institute compulsory examinations to test these characters' abilities and/or systems of registrations to mark these women's bodies physically and permanently as objects of the gaze. Likewise, superpowered women may be surveyed by individuals; while such surveillance is less formal than that done by institutions, it is no less intrusive. Regardless of the formality of the surveillance trained upon them, superpowered women eventually internalize the gaze of others, becoming self-policing. These extraordinary characters then learn to preempt their own behavior; the gaze of others, therefore, becomes inescapable, as even when it is not physically present its effects are still felt. Therefore, for superpowered women, visibility is a trap, and vision is a position of privilege that they are denied or for which they are punished for assuming. Within these series, those who gaze are almost always male, while those whom they gaze upon are almost always female. Perhaps in compensation for superpowered women's lack of traditional vision, these characters often possess alternate forms of sight, such as clairvoyance. Similarly to superpowered women, superpowered men may also be kept under surveillance; however, the gaze under which they fall is an adversarial versus an objectifying or admonishing one. Thus, superpowered men often are surveyed as worthy opponents by their surveyors rather than as malleable instruments the way that superpowered women are.

The surveillance of superpowered women illustrates one way in which these characters are subject to the judicial authorities in their lives. Within television series featuring superpowered women, such authorities, like those who gaze, are predominantly male, whether representatives of traditional systems of law and order or supernatural ones. Within mundane legal systems, superpowered women are denied access to the voice of the law; therefore, those authorities who speak the language of the law may use the rules to serve their own purposes, to the detriment of superpowered women. Otherworldly judicial systems are biased against superpowered women as well; supernatural adjudicators impose rules that infringe upon superpowered women's use of their abilities by testing or questioning their worthiness to hold or use such powers. Also, both traditional and supernatural systems of authority may subject superpowered women to public trials that reinforce societal power structures and/or situate superpowered women as cautionary examples to deter others who would challenge the law's authority and, more specifically, its classification of the norm. Such public trials for superpowered women are designed to teach these characters a lesson, *i.e.*, that their abilities make them dangerous. While superpowered men may experience similar trials, these trials instead teach the accusers a lesson, *i.e.*, that superpowered men are misunderstood, not dangerous. Furthermore, superpowered men are afforded more agency under the law than their female counterparts, since they have publicly recognized relationships with legal authorities, are able to manipulate the system to their advantage, and are even able to assume the voice of the law rather than answering to a sanctioning institution. On the contrary, when superpowered women attempt to subvert existing legal systems, the results may be successful but short-lived, and, when they attempt to embody or propose alternative systems, such systems may not represent improvement or a break from the ones they replace.

From 1996 to 2006, then, *Bewitched*'s narrative formula morphed into power + multiple repressions, as the protagonists of *Sabrina, the Teenage Witch*, *Buffy the Vampire Slayer*, and *Charmed*, just to name a few, were marginalized as freaks, coerced into selflessness, kept under perpetual surveillance, and subjected to biased legal systems. Thus, these characters reflected the limits of the girl power movement in general. As Phoebe asks in a third-season episode of *Charmed*, "What good is this power if I can't use it when I need it?" ("Once Upon a Time"). While television could find a place for powerful — moreover superpowerful — women during this era, it could not, apparently, make room for empowered women, as these characters could not use their abilities when or how they wanted. Therefore, for television's superpowered women, 1996–2006 was a gilded age, at best.

Bad Choices

The end of the gilded age of television's superpowered women and the associated girl-power movement can be marked with the final episode of *Charmed* in 2006; however, its death knell surely had rung the year before with the release of the *Girls Gone Wild: Girl Power* installment of the video series featuring college-aged women exposing their breasts.[1] In this post-gilded age, the third wave continues, but the rhetoric of girl power has been replaced by the rhetoric of choice. "Choice feminism," the term proposed by Hirshman in 2005, refers to the U.S. ideology that the gains made by the feminist movement have now liberated women to such an extent that they can make any choices they want; since women are the ones making choices, then any choice must be perceived as feminist (Hirshman). As Michaele L. Ferguson writes in "Choice Feminism and the Fear of Politics":

> While Hirshman focuses on choices women make about wage work and unpaid labor in the home, choice feminism is a much broader phenomenon. The view that today all choices are feminist can be invoked to support decisions to wear lipstick and high heels, to participate in *Girls Gone Wild!*, to sleep with men, to enjoy pornography, to not have children, to hire a maid, or to adopt a gendered division of labor [247].

Ferguson also notes that choice feminism is the "creed" of certain third-wave feminists, although she notes that Hirshman names second-wave icon Steinem's brand of 1970s feminism as its origin (247–48). Regardless of its decade of genesis, choice feminism and its accompanying rhetoric have been evident in the narratives of television's superpowered women in the post-gilded age.

From 2006 to 2011, despite a growing number of series featuring superpowered men and mixed-sex superpowered ensembles, superpowered women maintained a presence on television, offering an eclectic array of characters, including Grace (of *Saving Grace*), Jaime (of *Bionic Woman*), Sookie (of *True Blood*), Roxie, Kat, and Joanna (of *Eastwick*), Chloe (of *The Nine Lives of Chloe King*), and Cassie (of *The Secret Circle*), along with Allison (of *Medium*) and Melinda (of *Ghost Whisperer*), carry-overs from the gilded age. Many of these characters have passive abilities, *e.g.*, Grace, like Joan (of *Joan of Arcadia*) and Jaye (of *Wonderfalls*) before her, has the "power" to be selfless, rather than an active ability, although Jaime, Chloe, and Cassie can defend themselves and be aggressors. Regardless of whether they can read minds or "kick ass" (*Dark Angel*, "Pilot"), these more contemporary female characters face similar constraints on their power as their counterparts in the gilded age; they, too, are called freaks, held to a cultural expectation of selflessness, kept under surveillance, and put on trial. In contrast to previous series featuring superpowered women, though, superpowered women beginning or continuing their runs from 2006 to 2011 seemingly exhibited a greater degree of agency.

Grace, Jaime, and company are more likely to have the opportunity to choose, whether to choose to call themselves freaks, to choose to be self-sacrificing, to choose to turn the gaze on their surveyors, and/or to choose to affect the outcome of their own trials. While, superficially, this rhetoric of choice indicates greater agency, the result is often more limiting than liberating, as only a narrow array of choices may be available — or perceived to be available. *The Secret Circle*'s Cassie, one of television's most recent superpowered women, faces such a non-choice when her father tells her that she most stop using magic altogether lest she be lost to the dark side. He then amends this pronouncement with, "You have a choice, Cassie" ("Lucky"). For Cassie, the choice becomes power or no power, hardly liberating and not so different from the choice that Samantha faced — continue to use her powers unrestrained or grant Darrin his "repression" and enjoy home and family.

Post-gilded-age superpowered women, likewise, made choices for home and family, even though their homes and families were often far from traditional ones. Since *Charmed*'s finale, several series, including *Heroes*, *Sanctuary*, and *Being Human*, have featured premises or story arcs in which superpowered characters seek sanctuary with surrogate families, families generally composed of other superpowered characters. Superpowered women serve as symbols of these sanctuaries, *i.e.*, the center of these re-imagined domestic spheres in which a superpowered woman brings together or provides a haven for other superpowered characters. In this regard, these series featuring superpowered women in the post-gilded age resemble the fantastic sitcoms of the 1960s and 1970s; thus, these sixty-minute series without laugh tracks from 2006 to 2011 can be termed "fantastic dramas." As noted in Chapter 1, while Samantha's ability "to choose" Darrin's "safe restriction of her powers" can be read as "a small but important evolutionary step above earlier situation comedy heroines" (Bryant 136), given the time frame, 1964–72, similar choices made in 2006–11 cannot be read as evolutionary. It seems, instead, that superpowered women on television have come full circle.

Catch the (Fourth) Wave?

Alternately, television's new era of superpowered characters and their quest for sanctuary may be read through the framework of an emergent fourth wave of feminism, which, like Faludi's concept of the "nesting nation" (116), is described as a post–9/11 phenomenon. Although little has been published about this next wave of feminism, Pythia Peay, in "Feminism's Fourth Wave," describes it as "a fusion of spirituality and social justice reminiscent of the American civil rights movement and Gandhi's call for nonviolent change," and Diana Diamond, in "The Fourth Wave of Feminism: Psychoanalytic Perspectives," characterizes it as "combin[ing] politics, psychology, and spirituality in an overarching vision of change" (213). Therefore, spirituality seems to be the defining characteristic of fourth-wave feminism. While the spiritual aspect of contemporary series featuring superpowered characters is not overt, the seeking of some type of sanctuary — whether from a tortured soul, isolation, or persecution — indicates a yearning for the sacred, or at least a thread of the divine that runs through the mundane. The BBC version of *Being Human* most directly addresses this aspect of the divine when a dying werewolf, who has lived most of his life with a female ghost and male vampire as a supernatural family (just like the main characters of the series), tells his housemates: "Together, we did the impossible. A werewolf, a vampire, and a ghost. But this doesn't have to be the end for you. Remember this moment. Remember what we had. We were on the outside of humanity so we could guard it. You understand? So we could guard it" ("Eve of the War"). While these words come from a male character, it is Annie, the ghost of the main trio of housemates in the series, who embodies them, as, after her original roommates, Mitchell and George, die, it is Annie who is left to lead the charge to guard humanity, as she assembles a new surrogate family and cares for George's orphaned daughter.

The increased presence of men and the mixed-sex ensembles of contemporary series also align with fourth-wave feminism, as, according to scholar E. Ann Kaplan in "Feminist Futures: Trauma, The Post-9/11 World and a Fourth Feminism?," this new feminism will enlist men in its cause (54). Furthermore, Peay refers to the work of V-Day founder Eve Ensler, who calls for a new paradigm of power that embraces collaboration. The community, or communion, that the superpowered characters find in their sanctuaries can be read as a reflection of this collaboration.

Taken together, these two interpretations—choice feminism and the fourth wave — of the contemporary era of superpowered characters represent cultural ambiguity in regard to women and power. Viewers can perceive the female characters as emblematic of a rhetoric of (false) choice or as the leaders of a new era of feminism that is distinguished by spiritual collaboration in its quest for change. Such ambiguity, however, seems to serve a purpose, as superpowered characters continue to function as a site of negotiation for cultural perceptions of women and power.

Power vs. Empowerment

Television's superpowered women from 1996 to 2011 certainly were depicted as powerful characters, as they physically embody any number of extraordinary abilities. However, narratively, these characters struggle with externally imposed restrictions on their powers or blame such powers for the difficulties in their lives just as readily as they may celebrate or find satisfaction in the use or conferral of their abilities. Hence, these depictions of *powerful* women do not translate into *empowering* images for female viewers, as the empowerment that would logically accompany these characters' abilities — the cultural recognition of their right and competency to use their powers as they deem appropriate — is curtailed in a number of ways. Hegemonic power structures, whether representative of patriarchy, matriarchy (as in Wonder Woman's case), or some other institution, are at work within these characters' universes. Although the terms "power" and "empowerment" are often conflated, an analysis of series featuring superpowered women during the gilded age and beyond indicates a distinction between the two.

Feminists and feminist scholars, alike, regardless of the specific camp with which they identify, seek to increase women's agency by exposing social institutions that limit that agency. In other words, they seek to empower women — to have women's power, their abilities and contributions, culturally recognized, valued, and compensated. Such efforts are, of course, necessary for practical reasons, as equal pay, equal rights, and equal opportunities cannot be possible unless those who exert influence on key social institutions (the dominant groups in the hegemonic model of power) acknowledge and appreciate women's cultural roles. Rhetorically speaking, though, such efforts perhaps suggest that women's power is only valid when it receives such a stamp of approval. Designating who gets to decide whether to grant such validation complicates this scenario, as illustrated by numerous series from 1996 to 2011. Milly Williamson, in her *The Essential Cult TV Reader* entry on *Buffy the Vampire Slayer*, addresses the tension between power and empowerment present in that series, noting that *Buffy* engages with the concept of empowerment in a complex manner both narratively and generically: "Buffy may be the 'chosen one' and powerful, but she still has little control over her destiny. This supernatural dilemma mirrors the experience of many women in Anglo-American culture, which tells us that equality has been achieved while hiding the fetters of continued female subordination" (61). Therefore, even though a print ad for *The Secret Circle* included the tagline "Discover your power" (*The Secret Circle*), when Cassie, that series' protagonist, begins to experience the extent of her abilities, she is afraid and questions the appropriateness of using those abilities, even to save her own life: "I liked it. [...] The feeling of power. Destroying the box that was sucking the life out of me. [...] I know that it isn't right, but it felt really good" ("Darkness"). Power? Yes. Empowerment? Not quite.

The term "empowerment," denotatively, refers to the sanctioning, allowance, or bestowal of power by some individual, institution, or authority, thereby implying that power cannot be inherent (earned, developed, or claimed) — it must be granted or, at least, permitted. Connotatively, though,

Conclusion 197

according to third-wave ideology, as discussed previously, power can be chosen. Helene A. Shugart, Catherine Egley Waggoner, and D. Lynn O'Brien Hallstein discuss the third-wave perspective on power and empowerment in "Mediating Third-Wave Feminism: Appropriation as Postmodern Media Practice": "Empowerment takes on a different meaning in this new feminism in other ways, as well — not in collective terms, as with the second wave, but in very individualistic terms. Being empowered in the third-wave sense is about feeling good about oneself and having the power to make choices, regardless of what those choices are" (195).[2] By this definition, superpowered women on television meet one of the criteria for empowerment — they do have the power to make choices — but they fail to meet the second — they generally do not feel good about themselves. Their superhuman abilities come with superhuman problems, such as ancient curses, imposed secrecy, physical and mental breakdowns, and potentially fatal examinations, to name a few, which impede upon their self-worth.

Despite television's superpowered women's ability to meet even this loose interpretation of empowerment, these characters' continuing narrative of power + repression (or power + lack of empowerment) has struck a chord with viewers, as even the shortest-lived series like *Wonderfalls* have garnered cult followings. Female viewers, who likely have been influenced by the third-wave's rhetoric of girl power and empowerment by choice, were not deterred by the contradictory nature of superpowered women from 1996 to 2011, since third wavers embrace a postmodern perspective.[3] Valerie R. Renegar and Stacey K. Sowards, in "Contradiction as Agency: Self-Determination, Transcendence, and Counter-Imagination in Third Wave Feminism," even argue that some third-wave feminists "complicate their consumption of popular culture through their recognition of the empowering and objectifying principles they encounter because they are able to see past initial feminist or social objections to such popular culture artifacts and appreciate the value or entertainment in both kinds of images" (13). In other words, for third wavers, *Sabrina, the Teenage Witch* or *True Blood* could still be their favorite show, because, just like Phoebe with *Bewitched*, they could set aside any troubling ideology that might come along with Sabrina's or Sookie's contradictory entertainment value (*i.e.*, their version of Phoebe's "not that part" ["Lost and Bound"]). Further complicating the consumption of these characters is the fact that the greatest contradiction within these series does not stem from the superpowered women themselves. Instead, it lies in the depictions of the infrastructures inherent in superpowered women's universes, infrastructures that cannot reconcile the concepts of "women" and "power." In other words, television's superpowered women from 1996 to 2011 represent the fantastic, while the cultural institutions that they encounter indicate closer ties to reality, perhaps the true appeal of these series: Power + repression = fantasy + reality. Television series featuring superpowered women during the gilded age and beyond offered viewers a foot in two worlds: a fantastic one in which women could be the most powerful beings in their universe and a realistic one in which that same universe limits that power. In other words, such series present the fusion of one world that is only imaginable and another that is relatable. Thus, women who are athletes, politicians, business owners, celebrities, parents, etc., can all recognize some aspects of their own lives—the frustrations and obstacles they face as women—mirrored by superpowered women on television.

Failure of Imagination

The 2011-12 television season marked nearly five decades of superpowered women on television; however, it also indicated that women's empowerment had not been realized any more fully than it was with *Bewitched*'s debut in 1964. In fact, several subsequent series have been heralded as the next *Bewitched* or claimed it as an inspiration. For example *Sabrina, the Teenage Witch*, the series that initiated the gilded age, was called "a *Bewitched*, for the '90s" (Brooks and Marsh 1186). Likewise, *TV Guide* critic Matt Roush once noted that "Allison DuBois [*Medium*'s protagonist] could be this generation's Samantha Stephens" (22), and Jennifer Love Hewitt, who portrayed *Ghost Whisperer*'s protagonist and served as an executive producer for the series, "grew up idolizing Elizabeth Montgomery" and, when describing a nanny character she planned to add to her show, noted, "Think Endora" (Keck, "*Ghost Whisperer's*" 12). While these series from the gilded age and beyond did not replicate *Bewitched*'s magical housewife in suburbia premise (although *Medium* comes close, as show creator Glen Gordon Caron saw the series as depicting the "complicated, often stressful life of a woman who sees dead people for a living, then goes home to her aerospace engineer husband and three kids" [Charkalis]), the superpowered women that followed face many of the same repressive forces that Samantha does. Even though Phoebe "never actually wanted to become" Samantha ("Lost and Bound"), the two characters—and their superpowered sisters of television past and present—have much in common.

The re-visioning of Samantha, to varying degrees, via Sabrina, Buffy, Phoebe, Allison, Sookie, and Cassie, illustrates Whelehan's assertion that "[r]epresentations of women, from the banal to the downright offensive, have a way of replicating themselves across the decades as if they tell us some fundamental 'truths' about femininity" (11). So what does the representation of

Conclusion 199

superpowered women on television express about American culture vis-à-vis femininity, or, more appropriately in this case, female power? Despite the gains made by second- and third-wave feminists, hegemonic power structures continue to be fueled, in large part, by cultural power differentials based on gender (along with ethnicity and sexuality), and the representation of superpowered women on television is one way that this unfortunate truth continues to be disseminated.

As *Joan of Arcadia*'s title character remarks of her own short-sightedness in one episode, there has been "a failure of imagination" ("The Devil Made Me Do It"). Culturally, the on-screen failure of imagination from 1996 to 2011 paralleled the off-screen one, as these superpowered female characters served as metaphors for real-life powerful women: women who, despite their talents and abilities, still were classified as freaks, socially expected to be selfless, harassed via surveillance, objectified or penalized unfairly under the law, and/or assumed to have an instinctive connection to the domestic sphere (although in many cases a reimagined one). Stabile describes this phenomenon in relation to *Heroes*, noting how that series "compellingly illustrates the limits on how we imagine the gendered nature of power and the role of women as protectors" and that "[i]f the popular culture of our time is any indication, U.S. culture remains unable to imagine femininity absent vulnerability" (88, 91). The pervasiveness of such failed imagination on screen reinforces the status quo for female television viewers and women in general, as no one yet has envisioned fully what women's empowerment would look like or how it would operate.[4]

"We're like Wonder Woman or something"

Despite the lack of empowerment of superpowered women on television from 1996 to 2011, the character type remains a metaphor for women's potential both on screen and off. In the first episode of the *Bionic Woman* remake, the post-operative Jaime Sommers, on foot, dashes past a car carrying a young girl. The girl says to her mother, who is driving, "Mommy, there's a lady out there running really fast, like as fast as the car." Although her mother, who missed Jaime's appearance, replies, "Sweetie, what did I tell you about making things up?," the young girl notes, "I just thought it was cool that a girl could do that, that's all" ("Pilot"). Likewise, Sonia Luna, one of the teen subjects of the Rachel Simmons–hosted PBS documentary *A Girl's Life*, smiles into the camera when she explains, "The best thing about being a girl is that we can do anything, like I feel nobody can stop us; we're like Wonder Woman or something, I don't know" ("Sonia"). The superwoman then, including its often high-profile television manifestations, remains a symbol of women's limitless potential.

Hopefully the next generation of television's superpowered women will offer a version of this character type that comes closer to fulfilling its symbolic potential. Perhaps a remake of *Bewitched* (and, as of January 2012, one was in development at CBS ["More Hot Projects"]), the series that introduced the superpowered woman to television, will provide a more empowered incarnation of the character type. Stark muses that the original *Bewitched* (and its fellow fantastic sitcoms) perhaps communicated "something about who we were and might yet become" (118); since television's superpowered women from 1996 to 2011 have covered "who we are," maybe a *Bewitched* remake or a reimagining of *Charmed* will focus on "who we might become." Phoebe — and all female viewers — can only hope.

Chapter Notes

Introduction

1. Ironically, later in this episode, Phoebe actually becomes Samantha, or at least Samantha-like, as she fades to black and white and becomes obsessed with and delighted by domestic chores after putting on her late grandmother's cursed wedding ring. Likewise, teen alien Isabel in *Roswell* (WB and UPN, 1999–2002) becomes Samantha-like, at least in a daydream, as she imagines what life would be like if her husband, Jesse, knew about her otherworldly origin and supernatural abilities ("I Married an Alien").

2. Although *Topper* (CBS, ABC, and NBC, 1953–56), included husband-and-wife ghosts among its primary characters (Brooks and Marsh 1411–12), *Bewitched* was the first — and most popular and long-lived — series in the 1960s to revolve around a superpowered female character. *Bewitched* beat *My Living Doll* (CBS, 1964–65) to the air by ten days (Brooks and Marsh 134, 943).

3. While *Xena: Warrior Princess* and *La Femme Nikita* both feature ultra-strong female protagonists with superior fighting abilities, neither character is included in this study (although Xena is referenced briefly in Chapter 1), since neither is depicted with supernatural or superhuman abilities, although Xena often encounters gods and other immortal beings.

4. The 2007 *Bionic Woman* was a remake of the 1970s *The Bionic Woman*, which is discussed in Chapter 1.

5. Although the "wave" terminology has been contested by feminist scholars because it indicates bursts of action on the part of feminists rather than highlighting their continuous efforts toward eradicating inequality, such terminology continues to be used to categorize eras of U.S. feminism. The first wave refers to the work of suffragettes to establish women's right to vote as well as other legal rights, while the second wave refers to the work of feminists in the 1960s through the 1980s to gain greater personal, professional, and sexual equity. Third-wave feminism, which emerges in the 1990s, "valorizes women's agency and female sexuality as forms of power" as well as emphasizes multiculturalism (Lorber, *Gender Inequality* 283). A fourth wave, associated with the post-9/11 United States, has been identified by a few feminist scholars; this nascent wave will be addressed in the conclusion.

6. In contrast to Whelehan, however, Karlyn offers a more positive analysis of the Spice Girls and the girl power phenomenon, arguing that the band members, as well as characters such as Buffy and Xena, "challenge familiar representations of femininity by affirming female friendship, agency and physical power."

7. Gaye Tuchman discusses symbolic annihilation in her introduction to *Hearth and Home: Images of Women in the Mass Media*. Tuchman, drawing on the work of George Gerbner and others, argues that women are subject to what Gerbner terms "symbolic annihilation" (Tuchman, Daniels, and Benét 8) in the mass media, as women are underrepresented on television, for example, or, when represented, they are deni-

grated, victimized, and/or trivialized within that medium's programming (9–17).

8. For examples of articles that address issues of ethnicity and sexuality within series such as *Buffy the Vampire Slayer*, see Kent A. Ono's "To Be a Vampire on *Buffy the Vampire Slayer*: Race and ('Other') Socially Marginalizing Positions on Horror TV" (in Helford's *Fantasy Girls*, 163–86) or Farah Mendlesohn's "Surpassing the Love of Vampires; Or, Why (and How) a Queer Reading of the Buffy/Willow Relationship Is Denied" (in Wilcox and Lavery's *Fighting the Forces*, 45–60).

9. *Witchblade*'s protagonist, Sara, a homicide detective, is a notable exception, as she does benefit from an association with a traditional system of law and order; however, as discussed in Chapter 5, this association conflicts with the supernatural authority of her powers.

10. Ellen Riordan addresses the association of "empowerment" with such popular culture texts as the Spice Girls and *Buffy the Vampire Slayer* in "Commodified Agents and Empowered Girls: Consuming and Producing Feminism," noting there are "serious implications for the popularization of the term 'empowerment,' and this needs to be situated in a discussion of feminist agency." Riordan's argument goes beyond the concept of simple agency, as she considers whether the individual empowerment promoted by popular culture can foster collective agency or merely encourages women to focus on their own immediate needs. Ultimately, she argues that this commodified version of empowerment "can come at the expense of actual change" (295).

Chapter 1

1. Chapter 2 of *The Feminine Mystique* is titled "The Happy Housewife Heroine" (Friedan 33).

2. There have been a number of series since the fantastic sitcoms of the 1960s and 1970s through the gilded age that have featured male characters with supernatural or superhuman powers as well, including *The Six Million Dollar Man* (ABC, 1974–78), *The Amazing Spider-Man* (CBS, 1978), *The Incredible Hulk* (CBS, 1978–82), *Mork & Mindy* (ABC, 1978–82), *The Powers of Matthew Star* (NBC, 1982–83), *Manimal* (NBC, 1983), *Highway to Heaven* (NBC, 1984–89), *Starman* (ABC, 1986–87), *Beauty and the Beast* (CBS, 1987–90), *Superboy* (Syndicated, 1988–91), *My Secret Identity* (Syndicated, 1988–91), *The Flash* (CBS, 1990–91), *Forever Knight* (CBS, Syndicated, and USA 1992–96), *Highlander* (Syndicated, 1992–98), *Lois & Clark — The New Adventures of Superman* (ABC, 1993–97), *Hercules: The Legendary Journeys* (Syndicated, 1995–99), *Early Edition* (CBS, 1996–2000), *Millennium* (FOX, 1996–99), *Angel*, *The Invisible Man* (Sci-Fi, 2000–02; two other similarly premised series titled *The Invisible Man* had aired previously [CBS, 1958–60; NBC, 1975–76]), *Static Shock* (WB and Cartoon Network, 2000–04), *The Tick* (FOX, 2001–02), *Smallville* (WB and CW, 2001–11), *The Dead Zone* (USA, 2002–07), and *Jake 2.0* (UPN, 2003–04). Therefore, superpowered men, like their female counterparts, have maintained a steady presence on television since the 1960s (and even before with *The Adventures of Superman* [Syndicated, 1952–57]). The y-chromosome version of this character type, though, has not experienced the television proliferation — or overall media saturation — that superpowered women did beginning in the mid–1990s. Superpower on television from 1996 to 2006 was predominantly a female — or feminine — phenomenon.

3. Segments featuring these characters aired as part of *The Krofft Supershow* (1976–78).

4. This series originally aired as part of *The Shazam!/Isis Hour* for two seasons; beginning in 1977, it remained on the air, sans *Shazam!*, as *The Secrets of Isis* (McNeil 413).

5. Although Wonder Woman debuted in *All-Star Comics* in 1941 and had appeared in the animated *SuperFriends* (1973) along with Superman, Aquaman, et al., this was the character's first solo television series. The pilot for this series aired on ABC as a telefilm in 1975.

6. Diana's mother, the Amazon Queen, presents Wonder Woman's "uniform," which has a detachable skirt, to the princess after she wins the tournament. The queen explains that she made the uniform herself and that the red-white-and-blue color scheme represents allegiance to "freedom and democracy"

(even though earlier in the telefilm another Amazon had asked Major Trevor, "What's the U.S.?" [*The New Original Wonder Woman*]).

7. There was also an ensemble network series during the 1980s that included a female cast member with superhuman abilities: the telekinetic Gloria of *Misfits of Science* (NBC, 1985–86) (Brooks and Marsh 900).

8. Likewise, one syndicated ensemble series featured a superpowered woman among its regular cast members: alien empath Deanna Troi of *Star Trek: The Next Generation* (Syndicated, 1987–94) (Brooks and Marsh 1295–96).

9. *Mighty Morphin Power Rangers* has continued in some form, whether through series or movies and under various names, since its inception in 1993.

10. *Poltergeist: The Legacy* (Showtime and SyFy, 1995–99) also debuted during this time period, featuring a mixed-sex society of psychics that battles "the unspeakable evil of the supernatural world" (Brooks and Marsh 1093–94).

11. The pilot for this series aired on TNT as a telefilm in 2000. *Witchblade*'s protagonist, Sara, was portrayed by Yancy Butler, who also portrayed Eve in *Mann & Machine*.

12. This series aired as *Justice League* for its first two seasons.

13. This series aired as *1–800 Missing* in its first season.

14. David Greven discusses the metahuman status of *Alias*'s Sydney and other contemporary female television protagonists in "Throwing Down the Gauntlet: Defiant Women, Decadent Men, Objects of Power, and *Witchblade*."

Chapter 2

1. Foucault's reference to this type of discourse is in regard to homosexuals' use of medical terminology as a rhetorical strategy, as homosexuality previously was classified as a mental illness.

2. Melinda has a son named Aiden in the first episode of the fifth and final season of the series; Aiden does, indeed, have abilities—he is an "empath" ("Birthday Presence").

3. It takes Clark Kent ten seasons on *Smallville* to embrace fully his superhero identity.

4. Within Rome's columns, he regularly names individuals "freaks" and may even, on occasion, have used the term in an admiring manner. For example, he referred to professional baseball player Barry Bonds as both "this generation's best player, possibly the greatest player of all time" and "freaky" in the same paragraph (27 Nov. 2003). Rome may, therefore, be referring to Wie in a similarly complimentary fashion; in fact, in another column, he even defended Wie's right to compete in men's PGA tour events (25 June 2003). More often than not, however, the use of the term "freak" in Rome's columns is employed in a derogatory way, as when he referred to pop star Michael Jackson as the "King of Freaks" (in the same column that named Wie "a freak" [1 Dec. 2004]), actress Angelina Jolie as "the freakiest" in a "town of freaks" (22 Oct. 2003), and Liza Minelli's ex-husband David Gest as a "broadway producer and all around freak" (24 Dec. 2003).

Chapter 3

1. In Bordo's discussion of how women are socialized to feed others, she notes that such socialization may have literal—bodily—effects in addition to the more symbolic—intellectual, emotional, and spiritual—effects noted above. Bordo proposes that such a need to feed others and deny the self can lead women to anorexia (171).

2. In "Sabrina, the Teenage...? Girls, Witches, Mortals, and the Limitations of Prime-Time Feminism," Sarah Projansky and Leah R. Vande Berg discuss, by drawing on the work of Wood, how *Sabrina, the Teenage Witch*'s recurrent narrative incorporation of the "cultural notion that caring and taking responsibility for others is expected of females" is one way that the series' feminist potential is undermined (31).

3. When comparing *Early Edition* and *Tru Calling*, it is also interesting to note that, although Gary is the recipient of the prescient paper, others (like his friend Chuck) can see and read it, while Tru, alone, can hear the call of the dead.

4. Although the titular superpowered woman—or girl—of *Sabrina, the Teenage Witch* often uses her powers to her own ad-

vantage (many times in a frivolous manner, as early episodes open with her standing in front of a mirror to consider a series of fashion choices that she magically zaps into appearance), older and more mature superpowered women realize the folly and risk of such self-serving acts.

5. While George's role as a grim reaper ostensibly is similar to Jack's on *Tru Calling*, as described previously, George takes no pleasure in—and, as noted above, even suffers from—her role at the end of the life cycle, while Jack seems to delight—or at least take a smug satisfaction—in his contribution to maintaining the balance between life and death. Additionally, George's reaper duties include the pre-death taking of the soul—"as a courtesy"—of those fated for violent death and assisting souls in their journeys to their "final destinations" ("Pilot, Part 2"). Jack, in contrast, does not intervene in even the most violent deaths, and, when a doomed individual manages to elude fate, Jack sets events in motion to take another life to meet his quota; for Jack, then, compassion is not a consideration.

6. While Doane views the masquerade as an opportunity for increased agency, she does note that such a concept has its "drawbacks," particularly that this framework presupposes femininity's reliance on masculinity "for its very definition," ultimately subordinating women's cultural roles to men's (38).

7. Phelan notes that visibility, while politically appealing, is "a trap" (6); such benefits and consequences of visibility are discussed in the following chapter on the surveillance of superpowered women. In accordance with Phelan's contention that visibility is a detriment for women, invisibility is considered a superpower (albeit a "wimpy" one, according to Bukatman [112]) for many female comic-book superheroes. Thus the Fantastic Four's lone female member is Invisible Girl (who, coincidentally was portrayed by Jessica Alba—*Dark Angel*'s Max—in the 2005 film version of the comic book). On television, invisibility may also be an ability of superpowered men, as in the various incarnations of *The Invisible Man*; however, this lack of visibility for men, while perhaps advantageous in certain situations, is more often seen as a handicap (as with the 1950s and 1970s versions of *The Invisible Man* [Brooks and Marsh 671–72]) or associated with madness (as with the 2000–02 version [Brooks and Marsh 672]).

8. Masquerade as an expression of hyperfemininity is the central premise of *Alias*, a series that, as noted in the Introduction, features a woman named Sydney who may have ties to the supernatural. As an undercover CIA operative, Sydney's role in her missions often includes wearing hypersexualized/fetishized clothing (the title sequence of the 2005 episodes even presents a rapid-fire succession of images of Sydney in such attire, MTV-style, as the theme song plays; see chapter 3 of Brown's *Dangerous Curves: Action Heroines, Gender, Fetishism, and Popular Culture* for a discussion of fetishism and masquerade within *Alias*); for Sydney, then, in contrast to the superpowered women discussed above, such costuming represents the burden of her responsibilities to her government rather than a pleasurable release from such burdens.

9. While Peter Parker's Uncle Ben gives Peter an almost-identical speech—"With great power, comes great responsibility"—in the big-screen version of *Spider-Man* (2002), the distinction between "power" for a superpowered male and "gift" for a superpowered female is not inadvertent. Superpowers for men are indeed powers and, therefore, can be possessed and used autonomously; superpowers for women are gifts and, therefore, must be granted or sanctioned by others.

10. In the final episode of *Smallville*, Clark accepts the iconic Superman costume from both of his fathers; Jor-El reveals the suit to Clark, and Jonathan holds it out to him. Jor-El urges Clark to "seize"—not accept—his destiny. The episode is framed with a flash forward of Chloe reading a graphic novel titled "Smallville" to her son; when she gets to the part that describes Clark's heroic act after "seizing" his destiny, she reads "And that was the day the boy turned into Superman" ("Finale").

11. On *Angel*, vampire Darla, Angel's sire and sometimes lover, does indeed sacrifice herself for the sake of her and Angel's unborn (and miraculously conceived) child, staking herself in the heart so that he can be born ("Lullaby"). Joyce Millman references Darla's

sacrifice and discusses Angel's subsequent role as a single parent (and the series' recurrent theme of family), in her chapter on *Angel* in *The Essential Cult TV Reader*, edited by David Lavery (32–33).

12. While Wenegrat's article does not address depression per se, he does note that depression can fulfill the function of the illness roles he describes.

Chapter 4

1. Buffy's examination by the Council as well as examinations undergone by other women with extraordinary powers are discussed in more detail in the following chapter on superpowered women's relationships with the legal systems and authorities within their universes.

2. As with Buffy's examination by the Watchers' Council, Sara's examination by the witchblade — the embodiment of her powers themselves — is discussed in further detail in the following chapter.

3. Zeisler discusses the possibility of a "corresponding female gaze that informs how women see images of both themselves and of men and affects the images they themselves create," noting that this concept was not addressed by Mulvey since, at the time her *Screen* article was published, there were few female writers and directors (which, Zeisler observes, is still true in many cases [9] ... it can certainly be observed that the majority of writers and directors of television series depicting superpowered women are male). Since Mulvey's mid-1970s work on this subject, however, the concept of a "female gaze" and its "confrontation of the looker" has been addressed by feminist and cultural scholars as well as by filmmakers, musicians, and other artists (9).

4. The subject of invisibility is also addressed in the first-season episode of *Buffy the Vampire Slayer* titled "Out of Mind, Out of Sight," when one of Buffy's classmates, a girl named Marcie, literally disappears from lack of attention. In the Buffyverse, then, women's existence is contingent upon being seen.

5. It is interesting to note that, while all of Max's X5 siblings are under surveillance by Manticore, all of Max's sisters are women of color (Tinga, Brin, and Jace) except one (Syl), while her brothers (Zach, Ben, and Krit) are all white.

6. At the start of the series, Buffy is, indeed, the "one girl" who serves as the Slayer; however, during the minutes that she spends dead at the end of season one (friend Xander revives her after a fatal encounter with a master vampire), Kendra becomes a Slayer, too. Likewise, upon Kendra's death, Faith's Slayer powers are activated.

7. Although Buffy is under surveillance by Professor Maggie Walsh in a number of season four episodes, Professor Walsh is depicted as masculinized, as she holds a leadership position within the Initiative, an institution that, due to its affiliation with the military, is decidedly patriarchal.

8. In the 2007 *Bionic Woman* remake, the more contemporary Jaime Sommers now has both a bionic ear and eye (along with a bionic arm and two bionic legs).

9. Out of frustration with her passive power of premonition, Phoebe learns martial arts so that she can have an active physical ability in contrast to her unpredictable supernatural one.

10. Johnny's relationship with the authorities is discussed in further detail in the following chapter.

11. The trial carried out by the board of inquiry to evaluate Jake's performance is discussed in further detail in the following chapter.

12. In regard to Jake, it is also interesting to note that when he uses his ability to interface with technology, the camera focuses on his eyes, which remain unchanged in appearance, as if his powers emanate from his vision. In contrast, for Helena on *Birds of Prey* and Shalamar on *Mutant X* (Syndicated, 2001–04), their eyes change in color and appearance when they activate their powers.

13. One of Gardner's interviewees even noted that a man has a "right to sit back and just enjoy the show [women] put on, the same as if [he] was at a museum" (135).

Chapter 5

1. Portions of Chapter 5 were published as "The Wonder Woman Precedent: Female (Super)Heroism on Trial" in *The Journal of American Culture* 28 (2005): 273–83.

2. As Phoebe's powers develop through-

out the course of the series, she is able to use her power of premonition in a more active manner — at times summoning visions at will.

3. Catriona Miller discusses the hegemonic and resistant elements in the Charmed Ones' relationship to the Elders in "'I Just Want to Be Normal Again': Power and Gender in *Charmed*," a chapter in Karin and Stan Beeler's edited volume *Investigating Charmed: The Magic Power of TV*. Miller contends that there are "a number of discourses of power at work in *Charmed*, all of which are competing with each other, and so the Elders circumscribe the power of the Charmed Ones, while at the same time the sisters resist that control" (70). For Miller, then, "possibilities of both resistance and perhaps surrender are suggested" in the series (71).

4. Levine notes in her article that this episode of *Charmed* curbs the sisters' powers "more severely (not to say violently) than ever before." She also notes that the line between "punishing the guilty" and "protecting the innocent" within the series is an ambiguous one (60).

5. In the 2011 *Smallville* series' finale, Jor-El reminds Clark of the many acts of heroism he — Clark — carried out, beginning with his teen years through his early adulthood. Clark notes "Those were my trials" ("Finale"); in this sense, Clark did experience trials similar to his female counterparts, although they were self-selected and only acknowledged (and, therefore, experienced) retroactively. However, during this finale, Jor-El tells Clark to "Seize [not accept] his destiny," as noted, and, in contrast to Jor-El's earlier perspective on Smallville, he tells Clark, "Your abilities may be of my blood, but it is your time in Smallville with Jonathan and Martha Kent and all the people there that made you a hero, Kal-El [Kal-El is Clark's Kryptonian name]" ("Finale"). As mentioned previously, Clark's adoptive father, Jonathan, joins Kal-El in this scene to support Clark's choice to "seize his destiny." Thus, Clark's choice to utilize his powers is supported — and not thwarted, like many of his female counterparts — by both the supernatural and mundane systems of familial authority in his life.

6. Grossman also opined that Stewart, pre-conviction, had not been embraced by feminists as she "clash[es] [...] with the cult of feminine victimization" necessary to be considered a feminist icon. In contrast, Passikioff, writing after Stewart's release from prison, contended that Stewart's decision to accept jail time with an appeal pending gave her the opportunity to transform her image from "villain to victim" (qtd. in Crawford). Despite such difficulty in the early to mid–2000s, Stewart, post-incarceration and perhaps with a more sympathetic public persona, was able to maintain her franchise, finding a more permanent home for her programming on the Hallmark Channel (in 2010, Martha Stewart Omnimedia signed a five-year deal with Hallmark), offering her greater ease in marketing her programming than when it ran in syndication (Boorstin). However, in January 2012, the Hallmark Channel cancelled *The Martha Stewart Show*, due to low ratings, but a Hallmark spokesperson said that the channel plans to maintain a partnership with Stewart (Logan, "Martha Canned" 5).

Chapter 6

1. *Charmed*'s final episode echoed the "happily ever after" tone of *Sabrina, the Teenage Witch*'s series' finale, which aired in April 2003. In *Sabrina*'s two-part conclusion, the title character, who is no longer a teen, plans to marry boyfriend Aaron and move to Los Angeles, but, on her wedding day, wakes up with cold feet, literally — her feet are encased in blocks of ice. After lamenting that "the only reason this happened to me is that I'm a witch — magic is always messing up my life," she meets a magical entity named Doubt who helps her learn that Aaron is not her soul mate (because their "soul stones" do not quite fit together). The episode ends with Sabrina leaving the church in her wedding gown, finding first love Harvey waiting outside, kissing said first love, then riding off with him on his motorcycle into the proverbial sunset as viewers see that their soul stones are a perfect fit ("Soul Mates, Parts 1 and 2"). Unlike Sabrina and the Charmed Ones, Buffy, the other longstanding (seven-season) character from the gilded era, does not get a romantic happy ending. The final episode of *Buffy the Vampire Slayer* (which

aired a month after *Sabrina*'s in May 2003) ends with Buffy and friends defeating a great evil and closing the hellmouth below Sunnydale, destroying the town in the process — after evacuating its residents, of course. While this is a happy occasion, and the episode ends with Buffy smiling, although somewhat cryptically, at what the future has in store, it is clear she still has much work to do, even if she is no longer the "one and only chosen anymore" (as discussed in the previous chapter). Sunnydale was but one hellmouth (as Giles says, "There is another in Cleveland. Not to spoil the moment"), and Willow senses that "Slayers are awakening everywhere" who will need to be found and trained ("Chosen"). Buffy's story, unlike the Haliwell sisters' and Sabrina's, does not end on an idealized note.

2. Educational series *WordGirl* (PBS, 2007–) also debuted during this time period, introducing another superpowered female crime fighter. However, this series airs in the late afternoon and caters to a young audience, in contrast to the prime-time, more adult-oriented television fare described. In this series, WordGirl, aka fifth grader Becky Botsford, battles evildoers using super strength and an impressive vocabulary.

3. *True Blood*'s popularity has been, no doubt, bolstered by the vampire craze started by Stephenie Meyer's four-book *Twilight* series (2005, 2006, 2007, 2008) and the subsequent film adaptations (2008, 2009, 2010, 2011, 2012). The so-called "Twilight effect" has been so pervasive that it has been named the cause of a troubling, vampire-inspired teen trend — amorous pubescents biting one another to show affection (Chang, Clarke, and Pereira).

4. Sookie's fairy blood also allows her to shoot light/electricity from her fingers, an ability which, according to series creator (and sometimes director and writer), Alan Ball, the *True Blood* writers refer to as "microwave fingers" (Stack 45); likewise, a character within the series lists Sookie's powers as "the mindreading, the microwave fingers" ("And When I Die").

5. *Unforgettable*, features a female protagonist with an extraordinary ability — she can "[p]ick any day of [her] life" and "tell you what [she] saw or heard" ("Heroes"). In other words, she can remember everything.

While this ability is remarkable, it has a real-world precedent; the rare condition, referred to as "highly superior autobiographical memory," actually is experienced by six people in the world, including actress Marilu Henner, who serves as a consultant on the series (Eng).

6. Chloe later learns that she is empathic, too — but only with humans ("All Apologies").

7. Chloe was born in the Ukraine and adopted by Americans; she knows nothing about her birth family, and she has not had contact with her adoptive father in ten years ... until she receives an e-mail from him that reads, "Trust no one," at the end of the first episode ("Pilot").

8. Bastet, although unexplained in the series, most likely refers to the feline Egyptian goddess of the same name, as the series is based on the *Nine Lives of Chloe King* (2004) book trilogy, by Liz Braswell (writing as Celia Thomson), who majored in Egyptology at Brown University (Braswell).

9. The Order killed the boy to make Chloe think it was her fault.

10. It is interesting to note that the show's title, which is based on an L.J. Smith book series, references a female observer of the supernatural world, offering the reverse of a series such as *Bewitched*, the title of which references Darrin being "bewitched" both magically and romantically by wife-witch Samantha. However, as episodes of *The Vampire Diaries* unfold, viewers learn that Elena, herself, has a connection to the supernatural.

11. Series that included elements of the supernatural also were present during this time period, with many of those series depicting male characters who channeled or were connected to the supernatural. Media phenomenon *Lost* (ABC, 2004–2010), with its revolving cast of plane-crash survivors, "Others," and hatch dwellers, often incorporated seemingly inexplicable occurrences, including time travel. By the series' finale, it is "explained" (although some *Lost* fans still debate interpretations of the final episode) that Jack, a doctor and one of the original crash survivors, has a cosmic link to the island itself (he is the island's protector), one that, moments before his imminent death (he knows he will not survive a heroic act to save the island), he passes on to friend and

fellow crash survivor Hurley ("The End"), keeping the protection in male hands, as previous protector Jacob had done. Lower-profile series that touched on the supernatural followed on both broadcast and basic cable networks: *Reaper* (CW, 2007–09), about the exploits of twenty-something Sam, who is conscripted into service by the devil himself after Sam learns his parents sold his soul before he was even born; and *Life on Mars* (ABC 2008–09), a U.S. remake of a BBC series (BBC One, 2006–07) about "time-traveling" police detective Sam (viewers learn in the final episode that Sam is actually an astronaut who had dreamed his visit to 1970s New York).

12. *Once Upon a Time* (ABC, 2011–), as its main characters are derived from well-known fairy tales such as Snow White, features prominent female characters, such as the Evil Queen/Mayor Regina, who perform acts of magic; however, such magic often is performed via spells received from others, so it is unclear whether a character such as the Evil Queen holds any power herself.

13. Coincidentally, Andie on *The Gates* and Chloe on *The Nine Lives of Chloe King* are both portrayed by Skyler Samuels.

Conclusion

1. The DVD description for the series reads: "You'll be amazed by just how far [these girls] will go to prove they have POWER" (qtd. in Tringali 31).

2. Riordan "argues for an examination of the rhetoric of feminist empowerment," as noted previously, noting that "there are serious implications for the popularization of the term 'empowerment'" (295). Riordan cautions that cultural production can either serve the feminist agenda or become commodified (*i.e.*, "packaged and sold by media industries") to the detriment of that agenda; she contends, therefore, that empowerment for women must occur collectively (*i.e.*, as a movement) and not merely individually (295). A recent example of the popularization of "empowerment" feared by Riordan is NBC's short-lived *The Playboy Club* (2011) being marketed as about "female empowerment" (Holmes). *The Onion* even once satirized the overuse of "empowerment" with an article titled "Women Now Empowered By Everything A Woman Does."

3. Such a postmodern perspective includes the embracing of style over substance, the desegregation of high and popular culture, and a skepticism about metanarratives (see, for example, Strinati 221–45.) In regard to third-wave feminists and postmodernism, Melissa Klein argues in "Duality and Redefinition: Young Feminism and the Alternative Music Community" that "feminism has moved away from a struggle for equality toward an engagement with difference, an assertion that girls can have the best of both worlds (that they, for example, can be both violently angry and vampily glamorous). This feminism owes much to the struggles of the second wave, yet it differs in many ways, especially in the way it is defined by contradiction" (207–08). Heywood and Drake also emphasize the paradoxical nature of the third wave, noting that "we [third-wave feminists] are products of the contradictory definitions of and differences within feminism, beasts of such a hybrid kind that perhaps we need a different name altogether" (3).

4. As mainstream network television remains male- and white-dominated in terms of producers, directors, and writers, new media outlets may provide for more imaginative depictions of powerful women. For example, Aymar Jean Christian, in "Out of This World: How Web Sci-Fi Is Bucking Whitewashed Hollywood," describes how online science fiction is providing alternatives to contemporary film and television, meeting the needs of niche audiences through "conceptually ambitious series" (15–16).

Bibliography

"About AskMen." *AskMen.com*. AskMen, 2009. Web. 25 Mar. 2012.
Adam, Alison. *Artificial Knowing: Gender and the Thinking Machine*. London: Routledge, 1998. Print.
Advil. Advertisement. *Entertainment Weekly* 20 Apr. 2012: 41. Print.
"*Alphas* Males and Females." *TV Guide* 11 July 2011: 24. Print.
"Anna Kournikova." *AskMen.com*. AskMen, 2009. Web. 25 Mar. 2012.
Baer, Judith A. "Nasty Law or Nice Ladies? Jurisprudence, Feminism, and Gender Difference." *Feminist Legal Theories*. Ed. Karen J. Maschke. New York: Garland, 1997. 159–89. Print.
Baird, Julia, et al. "From Seneca Falls to ... Sarah Palin?" *Newsweek* 152.12 (2008): 30–36. *Academic Search Complete*. Web. 25 Mar. 2012.
Baker-Fletcher, Karen. "The Difference Race Makes: Sexual Harassment and the Law in the Thomas/Hill Hearings." *Journal of Feminist Studies in Religion* 10.1 (1994): 7–15. Print.
Balsamo, Anne. *Technologies of the Gendered Body: Reading Cyborg Women*. Durham: Duke University Press, 1996. Print.
Bartky, Sandra Lee. "Foucault, Femininity, and the Modernization of Patriarchal Power." *Writing on the Body: Female Embodiment and Feminist Theory*. Eds. Katie Conboy, Nadia Medina, and Sarah Stanbury. New York: Columbia University Press, 1997. 129–54. Print.
Bartlett, Katharine T. "Feminist Legal Methods." *Feminist Legal Theory: Foundations*. Ed. D. Kelly Weisberg. Philadelphia: Temple University Press, 1993. 550–70. Print.
Beeler, Karin. *Seers, Witches and Psychics on Screen: An Analysis of Women Visionary Characters in Recent Television and Film*. Jefferson, NC: McFarland, 2008. Print.
"Best of Fall Preview: 2000s." *TV Guide* 14 Sept. 2002: 72. Print.
Birmingham, Elizabeth. "Fearing the Freak: How Talk TV Articulates Women and Class [Part 2 of 2]." *Journal of Popular Film and Television* 28.3 (2000): 133–39. *Contemporary Women's Issues 1992–Present*. Web. 4 Apr. 2003.
Bogdan, Robert. "The Social Construction of Freaks." *Freakery: Cultural Spectacles of the Extraordinary Body*. Ed. Rosemarie Garland Thomson. New York: New York University Press, 1996. 23–37. Print.
Boorstin, Julia. "Cable's New Queen: Martha Stewart Starts Hallmark Channel Partnership." *CNBC.com*. CNBC, 13 Sept. 2010. Web. 23 Nov. 2011.

Bordo, Susan. *Unbearable Weight: Feminism, Western Culture, and the Body.* Berkeley: University of California Press, 1993. Print.
Braswell, Liz. "Bio/FAQ." *The Messy Desk.com.* The Messy Desk, n.d. Web. 25 Mar. 2012.
Brooks, Tim, and Earle Marsh. *The Complete Directory to Prime Time Network and Cable TV Shows: 1946–Present.* 9th ed. New York: Ballantine Books, 2007. Print.
Brown, Jeffrey A. *Dangerous Curves: Action Heroines, Gender, Fetishism, and Popular Culture.* Jackson: University of Mississippi Press, 2011. Print.
Bryant, John. "Situation Comedy of the Sixties: The Evolution of a Popular Genre." *Studies in American Humor* 7 (1989): 118–39. *Compedit.com.* Compedit, n.d. Web. 10 June 2003.
Bukatman, Scott. "X-Bodies (The Torment of the Mutant Superhero)." *Uncontrollable Bodies: Testimonies of Identity and Culture.* Eds. Rodney Sappington and Tyler Stallings. Seattle: Bay Press, 1994. 93–129. Print.
Case, David Allen. "Domesticating the Enemy: *Bewitched* and the Seventies Sitcom." *The Seventies: The Age of Glitter in Popular Culture.* Ed. Shelton Waldrep. New York: Routledge, 2000. 195–202. Print.
Castelnuovo, Shirley, and Sharon R. Guthrie. *Feminism and the Female Body: Liberating the Amazon Within.* Boulder: Lynn Rienner, 1998. Print.
Chaney, Lillian H., and Julie R. Lyden. "Putting the 'Business' in Business Casual." *Office Pro* 59.4 (1999): 15. *Business Source Premier.* Web. 1 August 2003.
Chang, Juju, Suzan Clarke, and Jennifer Pereira. "'Twilight' Effect: Are Teens Biting One Another Because of On-Screen Vampires?" *Good Morning America.* ABC News, 9 July 2010. Web. 20 Nov. 2005.
Charkalis, Diana McKeon. "The Mother in the 'Medium.'" *USA Today.* USATODAY.com, 20 Nov. 2005. Web. 22 Nov. 2005.
Chesler, Phyllis. "The Amazon Legacy: An Interpretive Essay." *Wonder Woman.* New York: Holt, Rinehart and Winston and Warner Books, 1972. N. pag. Print.
Christian, Aymar Jean. "Out of This World: How Web Sci-Fi Is Bucking Whitewashed Hollywood." *Bitch: Feminist Response to Pop Culture* (Spring 2012): 15–16, 21. Print.
Cirksena, Kathryn, and Lisa Cuklanz. "Male Is to Female As ____ Is to ____: A Guided Tour of Five Feminist Frameworks for Communication Studies." *Women Making Meaning: New Feminist Directions in Communication.* Ed. Lana F. Rakow. New York: Routledge, 1992. 18–44. Print.
Cixous, Hélène, and Catherine Clément. *The Newly Born Woman.* Trans. Betsy Wing. Minneapolis: University of Minnesota Press, 1975. Print.
Coles, Fen. "Feminine Charms and Outrageous Arms." *Feminist Theory and the Body: A Reader.* Eds. Janet Price and Margrit Shildrick. New York: Routledge, 1999. 445–53. Print.
Collins, Patricia Hill. *Black Feminist Thought: Knowledge, Consciousness, and the Politics of Empowerment.* 2nd ed. New York: Routledge, 2000. Print.
Cox, Steve. *Dreaming of Jeannie: TV's Prime Time in a Bottle.* New York: St. Martin's Griffin, 2000. Print.
Crawford, Krysten. "Martha, Out and About: Celebrity Leaves Prison, Gets Settled at Home; A Morning Walk to Feed the Horses." *CNNMoney.com.* CNN, Fortune & Money, 4 Mar. 2005. Web. 23 Nov. 2011.
Davis, Kathy. "'My Body Is My Art': Cosmetic Surgery as Feminist Utopia?" *Feminist*

Theory and the Body: A Reader. Eds. Janet Price and Margrit Shildrick. New York: Routledge, 1999. 454–65. Print.
de Beauvoir, Simone. "The Second Sex: Introduction." *Feminist Theory Reader: Local and Global Perspectives.* Eds. Carole R. McCann and Seung-Kyung Kim. New York: Routledge, 2003. 32–40. Print.
Diamond, Diana. "The Fourth Wave of Feminism: Psychoanalytic Perspectives." *Studies in Gender & Sexuality* 10.4 (2009): 213–223. *Academic Search Complete.* Web. 31 Mar. 2012.
Doane, Mary Ann. *Femmes Fatales: Feminism, Film, Psychoanalysis.* New York: Routledge, 1991. Print.
Dodge Caravan. Advertisement. *Entertainment Weekly* 28 Feb. 2003: back cover. Print.
Douglas, Susan J. *Where the Girls Are: Growing Up Female with the Mass Media.* New York: Three Rivers, 1994. Print.
Early, Frances, and Kathleen Kennedy, eds. *Athena's Daughters: Television's New Women Warriors.* Syracuse: Syracuse University Press, 2003. Print.
Efron, Edith. "He's Almost Invisible in the Glare of Success." *TV Guide* 29 May 1965: 19–22. Print.
Electrolux. Advertisement. ABC. 19 May 2011. Television.
Eng, Joyce. "Marilu Henner on Her *Unforgettable* New Gig and Her Infallible Memory." *TV Guide.com.* TV Guide, 16 Sept. 2011. Web. 5 March 2012.
Faludi, Susan. *Backlash: The Undeclared War Against American Women.* New York: Doubleday, 1991. Print.
_____. *The Terror Dream: Fear and Fantasy in Post-9/11 America.* New York: Metropolitan Books, 2007. Print.
Ferguson, Michaele L. "Choice Feminism and the Fear of Politics." *Perspectives on Politics* 8.1 (2010): 247–254. *International Political Science Abstracts.* Web. 31 Mar. 2012.
Ferriss, Suzanne, and Mallory Young. "Chicks, Girls and Choice: Redefining Feminism." *Junctures: The Journal for Thematic Dialogue* 6 (2006): 87–97. *Academic Search Complete.* Web. 31 Mar. 2012.
Fiedler, Leslie. *Freaks: Myths and Images of the Secret Self.* New York: Simon & Schuster, 1978. Print.
Field, Eunice. "You Know Her as a Witch ... Now Meet Her as a Woman." *TV Radio Mirror* Jan. 1965: 40–45, 81–83. Print.
Field, Susan, and Ros Bramwell. "An Investigation into the Relationship Between Caring Responsibilities and the Levels of Perceived Pressure Reported by Female Employees." *Journal of Occupational and Organizational Psychology* 71.2 (1998): 165–70. *Sociological Collection.* Web. 31 Mar. 2012.
Fineman, Martha Albertson. "Feminist Theory in Law: The Difference It Makes." *Feminist Legal Theories.* Ed. Karen J. Maschke. New York: Garland, 1997. 213–35. Print.
Fingeroth, Danny. *Superman on the Couch: What Superheroes Really Tell Us About Ourselves and Our Society.* New York: Continuum, 2004. Print.
Finley, Lucinda M. "Breaking Women's Silence in Law: The Dilemma of the Gendered Nature of Legal Reasoning." *Feminist Legal Theory: Foundations.* Ed. D. Kelly Weisberg. Philadelphia: Temple University Press, 1993. 571–81. Print.
Foucault, Michel. *Discipline and Punish: The Birth of the Prison.* Trans. Alan Sheridan. New York: Vintage Books, 1979. Print.

_____. *The History of Sexuality*. Vol. 1. Trans. Robert Hurley. New York: Pantheon, 1978. Print.

Friedan, Betty. *The Feminine Mystique*. New York: Norton, 1997, 1991, 1974, 1963. Print.

"From Racket-Wielding Warrior Princesses to Designing Women." *E! online*. E! Entertainment Television, 2005. Web. 6 Feb. 2005.

Fudge, Rachel. "The Buffy Effect: Or, A Tale of Cleavage and Marketing." *Bitch: Feminist Response to Pop Culture*. bitch media, 1999. Web. 31 Mar. 2012.

_____. "Girl, Unreconstructed: Why Girl Power Is Bad for Feminism." *Bitchfest*. Eds. Lisa Jervis and Andi Zeisler. New York: Farrar, Straus and Giroux, 2006. 155–61. Print.

Gardner, Carol Brooks. *Passing By: Gender and Public Harassment*. Berkeley: University of California Press, 1995. Print.

Germov, John, and Lauren Williams. "Dieting Women: Self-Surveillance and the Body Panopticon." *Weighty Issues: Fatness and Thinness as Social Problems*. Eds. Jeffery Sobal and Donna Maurer. New York: Aldine de Gruyter, 1999. 117–32. Print.

Gliatto, Tom. "Rev. of *Birds of Prey*." *People* 4 Nov. 2002: 33. *Academic Search Premier*. Web. 4 Apr. 2003.

Golden, Christopher, Stephen R. Bissette, and Thomas E. Sniegoski. *Buffy the Vampire Slayer: The Monster Book*. New York: Pocket Books, 2000. Print.

"Great Scott!" *People* 9 Dec. 2002: 188. *Academic Search Premier*. Web. 4 Apr. 2003.

Greven, David. "Throwing Down the Gauntlet: Defiant Women, Decadent Men, Objects of Power, and *Witchblade*." *Action Chicks: New Images of Tough Women in Popular Culture*. Ed. Sherrie A. Inness. New York: Palgrave Macmillan, 2004. 123–51. Print.

Groeneveld, Elizabeth. "'Join the Knitting Revolution': Third-Wave Feminist Magazines and the Politics of Domesticity." *Canadian Review of American Studies* 40.2 (2010): 259. *MasterFILE Premier*. Web. 31 Mar. 2012.

Grossman, Jennifer. "Martha Envy." Editorial. *The Wall Street Journal* 21 June 2002, Eastern ed.: A8. Proquest. Web. 10 Dec. 2004.

Grosz, Elizabeth. "Intolerable Ambiguity: Freaks as/at the Limit." *Freakery: Cultural Spectacles of the Extraordinary Body*. Ed. Rosemarie Garland Thomson. New York: New York University Press, 1996. 55–66. Print.

Guisewite, Cathy. "Cathy." Comic strip. *GoComics.com*. Universal Uclick. 24 June 2002. Web. 27 June 2012.

Hall, Stuart. "Cultural Studies and Its Theoretical Legacies." *The Cultural Studies Reader*. 2nd ed. Ed. Simon During. London: Routledge, 1999. 97–109. Print.

Hano, Arnold. "Rough, Tough, and Delightful." *TV Guide* 13 May 1967: 19–22. Print.

Haraway, Donna. "The Persistence of Vision." *Writing on the Body: Female Embodiment and Feminist Theory*. Eds. Katie Conboy, Nadia Medina, and Sarah Stanbury. New York: Columbia University Press, 1997. 283–95. Print.

Heath, Stephen. "Joan Riviere and the Masquerade." *Gender*. Ed. Anna Tripp. New York: Palgrave, 2000. 139–53. Print.

Heinecken, Dawn. *The Warrior Women of Television: A Feminist Cultural Analysis of the New Female Body in Popular Media*. New York: Peter Lang, 2003. Print.

Helford, Elyce Rae, ed. *Fantasy Girls: Gender in the New Universe of Science Fiction and Fantasy Television*. Lanham, MD: Rowman & Littlefield, 2000. Print.

Helms, Dorothea. "Iron Jane: Chopping Down the Muscle Myth." *Herizons* 9.1 (1995): 29–30. *Contemporary Women's Issues 1992–Present.* Web. 4 Apr. 2003.
Heywood, Leslie, and Jennifer Drake, eds. *Third Wave Agenda: Being Feminist, Doing Feminism.* Minneapolis: University of Minnesota Press, 1997. Print.
Hilgenberg, Holly. "Better Homes & Bloggers." *Bitch: Feminist Response to Pop Culture* (Spring 2012): 42–45. Print.
Hills, Elizabeth. "From 'Figurative Males' to Action Heroines: Further Thoughts on Active Women in the Cinema." *Screen* 40.1 (1999): 38–50. Print.
Hirshman, Linda. "Homeward Bound." prospect.org. *The American Prospect,* 21 Nov. 2005. Web. 14 Mar. 2012.
Holmes, Linda. "The Bizarre Pitch For 'The Playboy Club': It's All About Female Empowerment?" *npr.org.* NPR, 2 Aug. 2011. Web. 10 Aug. 2011.
"Home-Model Witch." *Look* 26 Jan. 1965: 75–79. Print.
Hutchinson, Allan C., ed. *Critical Legal Studies.* Totowa, NJ: Rowman & Littlefield, 1989. Print.
Hyams, Joe. "Samantha Gets Her Way." *The Saturday Evening Post* 13 Mar. 1965: 32–33. Print.
Inness, Sherrie A., ed. *Action Chicks: New Images of Tough Women in Popular Culture.* New York: Palgrave Macmillan, 2004. Print.
_____. *Tough Girls: Women Warriors and Wonder Women in Popular Culture.* Philadelphia: University of Pennsylvania Press, 1999. Print.
Jenkins, Henry. "Television Fans, Poachers, Nomads [1992]." *The Subcultures Reader.* Eds. Ken Gelder and Sarah Thornton. London: Routledge, 1997. 506–22. Print.
Jenkins, Tricia. "Nationalism and Gender: The 1970s, *The Six Million Dollar Man,* and *The Bionic Woman.*" *Journal of Popular Culture* 44.1 (2011): 93–113. Print.
"Jury Decides in Favor of TV Star Winfrey in Suit by Cattlemen." *The Wall Street Journal* 27 Feb. 1998, Eastern ed.: 1. Proquest. Web. 10 Dec. 2004.
Kaplan, E. Ann. "Feminist Futures: Trauma, The Post-9/11 World and a Fourth Feminism?" *Journal of International Women's Studies* 4.2 (2003): 46–59. *MLA International Bibliography.* Web. 31 Mar. 2012.
Karlsen, Carol F. "The Devil in the Shape of a Woman: The Economic Basis of Witchcraft." *Women's America: Refocusing the Past.* 5th ed. Eds. Linda K. Kerber and Jane Sherron De Hart. New York: Oxford University Press, 2000. 76–89. Print.
Karlyn, Kathleen Rowe. "*Scream,* Popular Culture, and Feminism's Third Wave: 'I'm Not My Mother.'" *Genders* 38 (2003): n. pag. Web. 5 Nov. 2004
Keck, William. "Classic Benz." *TV Guide* 27 Sept. 2010: 36. Print.
_____. "*Ghost Whisperer*'s Bewitching New Season." *TV Guide* 27 July 2009: 12. Print.
Kirby-Diaz, Mary, ed. *Buffy and Angel Conquer the Internet: Essays on Online Fandom.* Jefferson, NC: McFarland, 2009. Print.
Klein, Melissa. "Duality and Redefinition: Young Feminism and the Alternative Music Community." *Third Wave Agenda: Being Feminist, Doing Feminism.* Eds. Leslie Heywood and Jennifer Drake. Minneapolis: University of Minnesota Press, 1997. 207–25. Print.
Koerner, Brendan I. "Disorders Made to Order." *Mother Jones* July/Aug. 2002: 58. *Academic Search Premier.* Web. 5 Aug. 2003.
Kramer, Matthew H. *Critical Legal Theory and the Challenge of Feminism: A Philosophical Reconception.* Lanham, MD: Rowman & Littlefield, 1995. Print.

Kreider, Jodie A., and Meghan K. Winchell, eds. *Buffy in the Classroom: Essays on Teaching with the Vampire Slayer*. Jefferson, NC: McFarland, 2010. Print.

Leonard, Kendra Preston, ed. *Buffy, Ballads, and Bad Guys Who Sing: Music in the Worlds of Joss Whedon*. Lanham, MD: The Scarecrow Press, Inc., 2011. Print.

Levine, Melissa. "Charmed and Dangerous: The So-Called Power of Celluloid Witches." *Bitch: Feminist Response to Pop Culture* (Summer 2000): 58–63, 80. Print.

Lewis, Richard Warren. "'Double, Double Toil and Trouble.'" *TV Guide* 28 Nov. 1964: 20–23. Print.

Lorber, Judith, ed. *Gender Inequality: Feminist Theories and Politics*. 4th ed. New York: Oxford University Press, 2010. Print.

_____. *Paradoxes of Gender*. New Haven: Yale University Press, 1994. Print.

Logan, Michael. "Martha Canned." *TV Guide* 16 Jan. 2012: 5. Print.

_____. "Sanctuary." *TV Guide* 27 July 2009: 33. Print.

Lotz, Amanda D. "Postfeminist Television Criticism: Rehabilitating Critical Terms and Identifying Postfeminist Attributes." *Feminist Media Studies* 1.1 (2001): 105–21. *Communication & Mass Media Complete*. Web. 6 Apr. 2012.

Lyon, David. *The Electronic Eye: The Rise of Surveillance Society*. Minneapolis: University of Minnesota Press, 1994. Print.

Machelidon, Véronique. "Masquerade: A Feminine or Feminist Strategy?" *Psychoanalyses/Feminisms*. Eds. Peter L. Rudnytsky and Andrew M. Gordon. Albany: State University of New York Press, 2000. 103–20. Print.

MacKinnon, Catharine. "Difference and Domination: On Sex Discrimination." *Feminist Legal Theory: Foundations*. Ed. D. Kelly Weisberg. Philadelphia: Temple University Press, 1993. 276–87. Print.

_____. "Feminism, Marxism, Method, and the State: Toward Feminist Jurisprudence." *Critical Legal Studies*. Ed. Allan C. Hutchinson. Totowa, NJ: Rowman & Littlefield, 1989. 56–76. Print.

Magoulick, Mary. "Frustrating Female Heroism: Mixed Messages in *Xena, Nikita*, and *Buffy*." *The Journal of Popular Culture*. 39.5 (2006): 729–55. Print.

Maguire, Kerry. "The Cloak of Definition: Fantasies of Feminine Identity." *Literature and Psychology* 46.3 (2000): 43–64. Print.

Mann, Patricia S. *Micro-Politics: Agency in a Postfeminist Era*. Minneapolis: University of Minnesota Press, 1994. Print.

Maschke, Karen J., ed. *Feminist Legal Theories*. New York: Garland, 1997. Print.

McCarver, Virginia. "The Rhetoric of Choice and 21st-Century Feminism: Online Conversations About Work, Family, and Sarah Palin." *Women's Studies in Communication* 34.1 (2011): 20–41. *Biography Reference Bank (H.W. Wilson)*. Web. 6 Apr. 2012.

McFadden, Patricia. "Why Women's Spaces Are Critical to Feminist Autonomy." *Women in Action* 31 Mar. 2001: 49. *GenderWatch*. Web. 5 Nov. 2004.

McLean, Candis. "The Best of Both Worlds." *Alberta Report/Newsmagazine* 26.23: 34. *Academic Search Premier*. Web. 5 Aug. 2003.

McNeil, Alex. *Total Television: The Comprehensive Guide to Programming from 1948 to the Present*. 4th ed. New York: Penguin, 1996. Print.

Mendlesohn, Farah. "Surpassing the Love of Vampires; or, Why (and How) a Queer Reading of the Buffy/Willow Relationship Is Denied." *Fighting the Forces: What's at Stake in Buffy the Vampire Slayer*. Eds. Rhonda V. Wilcox and David Lavery. Lanham, MD: Rowman & Littlefield, 2002. 45–60. Print.

Miller, Catriona. "'I Just Want to Be Normal Again': Power and Gender in *Charmed*." *Investigating Charmed: The Magic Power of TV*. Eds. Karin Beeler and Stan Beeler. London: I.B. Tauris, 2007. 67–78. Print.
Millman, Joyce. "*Angel*." *The Essential Cult TV Reader*. Ed. David Lavery. Lexington: University Press of Kentucky, 2010. 28–35. Print.
Mitchell, Maria. "Ambitious Women and Strange Monsters: Simone de Beauvoir and Germaine Greer." *Hecate* 26.1 (2000): 98. *ProQuest*. Web. 21 Mar. 2003.
"More Hot Projects in the Works." *Entertainment Weekly*. 20 Jan. 2012: 47. Print.
Moseley, Rachel. "Glamorous Witchcraft: Gender and Magic in Teen Film and Television." *Screen* 43.4 (2002): 403–22. *Film & Television Literature Index with Full Text*. Web. 6 Apr. 2012.
Moy, Suelain. "Girls Who Fight Back." *Good Housekeeping* Apr. 1999: 86. *Vocational and Career Collection*. Web. 6 Apr. 2012.
Muir, John Kenneth. *Terror Television: American Series, 1970–1999*. Jefferson, NC: McFarland, 2001. Print.
Mulvey, Laura. "Visual Pleasure and Narrative Cinema." *The Sexual Subject: A Screen Reader in Sexuality*. London: Routledge, 1992. 22–34. Print.
"The 1990s in Review: What the 90s Mean to..." *independent.co.uk*. The Independent, 28 Nov. 1999. Web. 6 Apr. 2012.
Ono, Kent A. "To Be a Vampire on *Buffy the Vampire Slayer*: Race and ('Other') Socially Marginalizing Positions on Horror TV." *Fantasy Girls: Gender in the New Universe of Science Fiction and Fantasy Television*. Ed. Elyce Rae Helford. Lanham, MD: Rowman & Littlefield, 2000. 163–86. Print.
"An Out-of-this-world Mommy Dearest." *TV Guide* 3 Jan. 2011: 50. Print.
Oxman, Steven. "Television Reviews: Witchblade." *Daily Variety* 25 Aug. 2000: 6. *MasterFILE Premier*. Web. 6 Apr. 2012.
Parenti, Christian. *The Soft Cage: Surveillance in America from Slavery to the War on Terror*. New York: Basic Books, 2003. Print.
Paxil CR Controlled-Release Tablets. Advertisement. *TV Guide* 2 Aug. 2003: 35–38. Print.
Peay, Pythia. "Feminism's Fourth Wave." *Utne Reader*, March/April 2005. Web. 14 Apr. 2011.
Phelan, Peggy. *Unmarked: The Politics of Performance*. London: Routledge, 1993. Print.
Pilato, Herbie J. *Bewitched Forever: The Immortal Companion to Television's Most Magical Supernatural Situation Comedy*. 2nd ed. Irving, TX: Summit, 2001. Print.
Projansky, Sarah, and Leah R. Vande Berg. "Sabrina, the Teenage...? Girls, Witches, Mortals, and the Limitations of Prime-Time Feminism." *Fantasy Girls: Gender in the New Universe of Science Fiction and Fantasy Television*. Ed. Elyce Rae Helford. Lanham, MD: Rowman & Littlefield, 2000. 13–40. Print.
Radway, Janice. "Reception Study: Ethnography and the Problems of Dispersed Audiences and Nomadic Subjects." *Cultural Studies* 2.3 (1988): 359–76. Print.
Renegar, Valerie R., and Stacey K. Sowards. "Contradiction as Agency: Self-Determination, Transcendence, and Counter-Imagination in Third Wave Feminism." *Hypatia* 24.2 (2009): 1–20. *Art Full Text (H.W. Wilson)*. Web. 6 Apr. 2012.
Riess, Jana. *What Would Buffy Do?: The Vampire Slayer as Spiritual Guide*. San Francisco: Jossey-Bass, 2004. Print.

Rifkin, Janet. "Toward a Theory of Law and Patriarchy." *Feminist Legal Theory: Foundations.* Ed. D. Kelly Weisberg. Philadelphia: Temple University Press, 1993. 412–18. Print.

Riordan, Ellen. "Commodified Agents and Empowered Girls: Consuming and Producing Feminism." *Journal of Communication Inquiry.* 25.3 (2001): 279–97. Electronic Journal Center. Web. 6 Apr. 2012.

Riviere, Joan. "Womanliness as Masquerade." *Gender.* Ed. Anna Tripp. New York: Palgrave, 2000. 130–138. Print.

Rogers, Adam. "Hey, Ally, Ever Slain a Vampire?" *Newsweek* 2 Mar. 1998: 60. *LexisNexis Academic.* Web. 6 Apr. 2012.

Rome, Jim. "Rome is Burning." *ESPN.com.* ESPN, 25 June 2003. Web. 20 Mar. 2005.

———. "Rome is Burning." *ESPN.com.* ESPN, 22 Oct. 2003. Web. 20 Mar. 2005.

———. "Rome is Burning." *ESPN.com.* ESPN, 27 Nov. 2003. Web. 20 Mar. 2005.

———. "Rome is Burning." *ESPN.com.* ESPN, 24 Dec. 2003. Web. 20 Mar. 2005.

———. "Rome is Burning." *ESPN.com.* ESPN, 1 Dec. 2004. Web. 5 Feb. 2005.

Rose, Matthew. "Fireworks Are Likely at Start of Rosie Magazine Trial." *The Wall Street Journal.* 27 Oct. 2003, Eastern ed.: B1. *ProQuest.* Web. 10 Dec. 2004.

"Rosie Fights for Rosie." *The Advocate.* 3 Sept. 2002: 16. *ProQuest.* Web. 10 Dec. 2004.

"Rosie O'Donnell." *People.com.* People, n.d. Web. 6 Apr. 2012.

Rothenberg, Paula S., ed. *Race, Class, and Gender in the United States: An Integrated Study.* 2nd ed. New York: St. Martin's, 1992. Print.

Roush, Matt. "Psychic Housewife: The Mother of All TV Sleuths." *TV Guide* 27 Feb. 2005: 22. Print.

Russo, Mary. "Female Grotesques: Carnival and Theory." *Writing on the Body: Female Embodiment and Feminist Theory.* Eds. Katie Conboy, Nadia Medina, and Sarah Stanbury. New York: Columbia University Press, 1997. 318–36. Print.

Scannell, Kara. "Executives on Trial: Battle Lines Drawn for Martha Stewart Trial." *The Wall Street Journal.* 26 Jan. 2004, Eastern ed.: C1. *ProQuest.* Web. 10 Dec. 2004.

Scott, Joan W. "Deconstructing Equality-Versus-Difference: Or, the Uses of Poststructuralist Theory for Feminism." *Feminist Theory Reader: Local and Global Perspectives.* Eds. Carole R. McMann and Seung-Kyung Kim. New York: Routledge, 2003. 378–90.

The Secret Circle. Advertisement. *TV Guide* 29 Aug. 2011: 6. Print.

Shields, Vickie Rutledge, with Dawn Heinecken. *Measuring Up: How Advertising Affects Self-Image.* Philadelphia: University of Pennsylvania Press, 2002. Print.

Shoemaker, Pamela J., and Stephen D. Reese. *Mediating the Message: Theories of Influences on Mass Media Content.* 2nd ed. White Plains, NY: Longman, 1996. Print.

Shugart, Helene A., Catherine Egley Waggoner, and D. Lynn O'Brien Hallstein. "Mediating Third-Wave Feminism: Appropriation as Postmodern Media Practice." *Critical Studies in Media Communication* 18.2 (2001): 194–210. *ERIC.* Web. 6 Apr. 2012.

South, James B., ed. *Buffy the Vampire Slayer and Philosophy: Fear and Trembling in Sunnydale.* Chicago: Open Court, 2003. Print.

Spain, Daphne. "Spatial Segregation and Gender Stratification in the Workplace." *Signs of Life in the USA: Readings on Popular Culture for Writers.* 4th ed. Eds. Sonia Maasik and Jack Solomon. Boston: Bedford/St. Martin's, 2003. 443–50. Print.

Spigel, Lynn. *Welcome to the Dreamhouse: Popular Media and Postwar Suburbs*. Durham: Duke University Press, 2001. Print.
Stabile, Carole A. "'Sweetheart, This Ain't Gender Studies': Sexism and Superheroes." *Communication and Critical/Cultural Studies* 6.1 (2009): 86–92. *Communications & Mass Media Complete*. Web. 7 Apr. 2012.
Stack, Tim. "There Will Be Blood." *Entertainment Weekly* 18 June 2010: 42–47. Print.
Stanley, Alessandra. "In Search of Our Next Big Topic of Conversation." *The New York Times* 12 Sept. 2004, late ed.: 1. *LexisNexis Academic*. Web. 7 Apr. 2012.
Star, Susan Leigh. "From Hestia to Home Page: Feminism and the Concept of Home in Cyberspace." *Feminism & Cultural Studies*. Ed. Morag Shiach. New York: Oxford University Press, 1999. 565–82. Print.
Stark, Steven D. *Glued to the Set: The 60 Television Shows and Events That Made Us Who We Are Today*. New York: The Free Press, 1997. Print.
Steinem, Gloria. "Foreword." *To Be Real*. Ed. Rebecca Walker. New York: Anchor, 1995. xiii–xxviii. Print.
Stiehm, Jaime. "New Domesticity A Step Backwards for Women." *U.S. News Digital Weekly* 3.49 (2011): 20. *Academic Search Complete*. Web. 7 Apr. 2012.
_____. "Sarah Palin's Anti-Feminist Politics." *U.S. News Digital Weekly* 2.48 (2010): 14. *Academic Search Complete*. Web. 7 Apr. 2012.
Storey, John. *An Introduction to Cultural Theory and Popular Culture*. 2nd ed. Athens: University of Georgia Press, 1998. Print.
Strinati, Dominic. *An Introduction to Theories of Popular Culture*. London: Routledge, 1995. Print.
Taub, Nadine, and Elizabeth M. Schneider. "Women's Subordination and the Role of Law." *Feminist Legal Theory: Foundations*. Ed. D. Kelly Weisberg. Philadelphia: Temple University Press, 1993. 9–21. Print.
Thomas, Devon. "'Saving Grace' Finale Lives Up to Show's Name." *cbsnews.com*. CBS News, 22 June 2010. Web. 28 June 2010.
Thomson, Rosemarie Garland, ed. *Freakery: Cultural Spectacles of the Extraordinary Body*. New York: New York University Press, 1996. Print.
_____. "The Beauty and the Freak." *Michigan Quarterly Review* 37.3 (1998): 459–74. Print.
Tringali, Juliana. "Remembering the Spice Wars: Can the Spice Girls Live Up to Their Girl Power Legacy?" *Bitch: Feminist Response to Pop Culture* (Winter 2008): 29–31. Print.
Tuchman, Gaye, Arlene Kaplan Daniels, and James Benét, eds. *Hearth and Home: Images of Women in the Mass Media*. New York: Oxford University Press, 1978. Print.
Tucker, Ken. "Ask the Critic: Angel Ayes." *Entertainment Weekly* 12 Mar. 2004: 102. Print.
_____. "Guided by Voices." *Entertainment Weekly* 19 Mar. 2004: 55–56. Print.
Ventura, Michael. "Warrior Women." *Psychology Today* 31.6 (1998): 58–59+. *Academic Search Complete*. Web. 25 Mar. 2012.
Wenegrat, Brant. "Illness and Power: Women's Mental Disorders as Illness Roles." *Illness and Power* 31 Jan. 1995: 47+. *GenderWatch*. Web. 4 August 2004.
Whelehan, Imelda. *OverLoaded: Popular Culture and the Future of Feminism*. London: The Women's Press, 2000. Print.
Wiegman, Robyn. *American Anatomies: Theorizing Race and Gender*. Durham: Duke University Press, 1995. Print.

Wilcox, Rhonda V., and David Lavery, eds. *Fighting the Forces: What's at Stake in Buffy the Vampire Slayer*. Lanham, MD: Rowman & Littlefield, 2002. Print.

Wilkie, Jane. "The Secret Magic of Elizabeth Montgomery." *Good Housekeeping* Oct. 1969: 54–56+. Print.

Williams, Raymond. *Marxism and Literature*. Oxford: Oxford University Press, 1977.

Williamson, Milly. "*Buffy the Vampire Slayer.*" *The Essential Cult TV Reader*. Ed. David Lavery. Lexington: University Press of Kentucky, 2010. 60–67. Print.

Wishik, Heather Ruth. "To Question Everything: The Inquiries of Feminist Jurisprudence." *Feminist Legal Theory: Foundations*. Ed. D. Kelly Weisberg. Philadelphia: Temple University Press, 1993. 22–31. Print.

Wolf, Naomi. *The Beauty Myth: How Images of Beauty Are Used Against Women*. New York: Perennial, 2002, 1991. Print.

"Women Now Empowered by Everything a Woman Does." *theonion.com*. The Onion, 19 Feb. 2003. Web. 9 March 2012.

Wood, Julia T. *Who Cares? Women, Care, and Culture*. Carbondale: Southern Illinois University Press, 1994. Print.

Zeisler, Andi. *Feminism and Pop Culture*. Berkeley: Seal, 2008. Print.

Television Episodes, Telefilms, and Feature Films Cited

Original airdates of episodes and telefilms have been included for consistency; airdates taken from tv.com unless otherwise indicated; episodes viewed via broadcast, re-broadcast, Netflix, or DVD unless otherwise indicated.

The Adventures of Superman
"The Mind Machine." *The Adventures of Superman*. Syndicated. 7 Nov. 1952. Television.

Alphas
"Bill and Gary's Excellent Adventure." *Alphas*. SyFy. 15 Aug. 2011. Television.
"Cause & Effect." *Alphas*. SyFy. 18 July 2011. Television.
"Never Let Me Go." *Alphas*. SyFy. 8 Aug. 2011. Television.
"Pilot." *Alphas*. SyFy. 11 July 2011. Television.

Angel
"City of." *Angel*. WB. 5 Oct. 1999. Television.
"Ground State." *Angel*. WB. 13 Oct. 2002. Television.
"Home." *Angel*. WB. 7 May 2003. Television.
"Lullaby." *Angel*. WB. 19 Nov. 2001. Television.
"Not Fade Away." *Angel*. WB. 19 May 2004. Television.
"Players." *Angel*. WB. 26 Mar. 2003. Television.
"Sanctuary." *Angel*. WB. 2 May 2000. Television.
"Somnambulist." *Angel*. WB. 18 Jan. 2000. Television

Being Human (SyFy version)
"A Funny Thing Happened on the Way to Me Killing You." *Being Human*. SyFy. 11 Apr. 2011. Television.
"I See Your True Colors ... and That's Why I Hate You." *Being Human*. SyFy. 28 Feb. 2011. Television.

Being Human (BBC version; airdates from bbcamerica.com)
"Eve of the War." *Being Human*. BBC America. 25 Feb. 2012. Television.
"Lia." *Being Human*. BBC America. 19 Feb. 2011. Television.

Bewitched
"I, Darrin, Take This Witch, Samantha." *Bewitched*. ABC. 17 Sept. 1964. Television.
"Mother Meet What's His Name." *Bewitched*. ABC. 1 Oct. 1964. Television.
"The No-Harm Charm." *Bewitched*. ABC. 25 Apr. 1968. Television.
"Samantha's Power Failure." *Bewitched*. ABC. 20 Mar. 1969. Television.
"Witch or Wife?" *Bewitched*. ABC. 12 Nov. 1964. Television.
"Witches and Warlocks Are My Favorite Things." *Bewitched*. ABC. 29 Sept. 1966. Television.

Bionic Woman
"Do Not Disturb." *Bionic Woman*. NBC. 28 Nov. 2007. Television.
"The Education of Jaime Sommers." *Bionic Woman*. NBC. 24 Oct. 2007. Television.
"Paradise Lost." *Bionic Woman*. NBC. 3 Oct. 2007. Television.
"Pilot." *Bionic Woman*. NBC. 26 Sept. 2007. Television.
"Sisterhood." *Bionic Woman*. NBC. 10 Oct. 2007. Television.
"Trust Issues." *Bionic Woman*. NBC. 14 Nov. 2007. Television.

Birds of Prey
"Lady Shiva." *Birds of Prey*. WB. 27 Nov. 2002. Television.
"Prey for the Hunter." *Birds of Prey*. WB. 23 Oct. 2002. Television.
"Reunion." *Birds of Prey*. WB. 8 Jan. 2003. Television.
"Slick." *Birds of Prey*. WB. 16 Oct. 2002. Television.

Blood Ties
"Gifted." *Blood Ties*. Lifetime. 25 Mar. 2007. Television.

Buffy the Vampire Slayer
"Anne." *Buffy the Vampire Slayer*. WB. 29 Sept. 1998. Television.
"Bring on the Night." *Buffy the Vampire Slayer*. UPN. 17 Dec. 2002. Television.
"Checkpoint." *Buffy the Vampire Slayer*. WB. 23 Jan. 2001. Television.
"Chosen." *Buffy the Vampire Slayer*. UPN. 20 May 2003. Television.
"Consequences." *Buffy the Vampire Slayer*. WB. 16 Feb. 1999. Television.
"Dead Man's Party." *Buffy the Vampire Slayer*. WB. 6 Oct. 1998. Television.
"Doomed." *Buffy the Vampire Slayer*. WB. 18 Jan. 2000. Television.
"End of Days." *Buffy the Vampire Slayer*. UPN. 13 May 2003. Television.
"Get It Done." *Buffy the Vampire Slayer*. UPN. 18 Feb. 2003. Television.
"The Gift." *Buffy the Vampire Slayer*. WB. 22 May 2001. Television.
"Gingerbread." *Buffy the Vampire Slayer*. WB. 12 Jan. 1999. Television.
"Gone." *Buffy the Vampire Slayer*. UPN. 8 Jan. 2002. Television.
"Graduation Day, Part 1." *Buffy the Vampire Slayer*. WB. 18 May 1999. Television.
"Halloween." *Buffy the Vampire Slayer*. WB. 27 Oct. 1997. Television.
"Helpless." *Buffy the Vampire Slayer*. WB. 19 Jan. 1999. Television.
"Homecoming." *Buffy the Vampire Slayer*. WB. 3 Nov. 1998. Television.

"Life Serial." *Buffy the Vampire Slayer*. UPN. 23 Oct. 2001. Television.
"Never Kill a Boy on the First Date." *Buffy the Vampire Slayer*. WB. 31 Mar. 1997. Television.
"Normal Again." *Buffy the Vampire Slayer*. UPN. 12 Mar. 2002. Television.
"Out of Mind, Out of Sight." *Buffy the Vampire Slayer*. WB. 19 May 1997. Television.
"Welcome to the Hellmouth." *Buffy the Vampire Slayer*. WB. 10 March 1997. Television.
"What's My Line? Part 2." *Buffy the Vampire Slayer*. WB. 24 Nov. 1997. Television.
"Witch." *Buffy the Vampire Slayer*. WB. 17 Mar. 1997. Television.

Charmed

"All Halliwell's Eve." *Charmed*. WB. 26 Oct. 2000. Television.
"Blinded by the Whitelighter." *Charmed*. WB. 25 Jan. 2001. Television.
"Brain Drain." *Charmed*. WB. 8 Nov. 2001. Television.
"Crimes and Witch-Demeanors." *Charmed*. WB. 25 Apr. 2004. Television.
"Dream Sorcerer." *Charmed*. WB. 4 Nov. 1998. Television.
"Forever Charmed." *Charmed*. WB. 21 May 2006. Television.
"Forever Charmed." *Charmed*. Audio Commentary. The WB Television Network, 2007. DVD.
"I've Got You Under My Skin." *Charmed*. WB. 14 Oct. 1998. Television.
"Lost and Bound." *Charmed*. WB. 31 Jan. 2002. Television.
"Magic Hour." *Charmed*. WB. 12 Oct. 2000. Television.
"Morality Bites." *Charmed*. WB. 7 Oct. 1999. Television.
"Once Upon a Time." *Charmed*. WB. 19 October 2000. Television.
"Sight Unseen." *Charmed*. WB. 2 Nov. 2000. Television.
"Trial by Magic." *Charmed*. WB. 24 Jan. 2002. Television.
"The Truth Is Out There ... and It Hurts." *Charmed*. WB. 25 Nov. 1998. Television.
"Witches in Tights." *Charmed*. WB. 13 Oct. 2002. Television.

Chuck

"Chuck Versus the Zoom." *Chuck*. NBC. 28 Oct. 2011. Television.

Dark Angel

"The Berrisford Agenda." *Dark Angel*. FOX. 18 Jan. 2002. Television.
"Boo." *Dark Angel*. FOX. 2 Nov. 2001. Television.
"Flushed." *Dark Angel*. FOX. 17 Oct. 2000. Television.
"411 on the DL." *Dark Angel*. FOX. 14 Nov. 2000. Television.
"Freak Nation." *Dark Angel*. FOX. 3 May 2002. Television.
"Haven." *Dark Angel*. FOX. 27 Mar. 2001. Television.
"I and I Am a Camera." *Dark Angel*. FOX. 1 May 2001. Television.
"Meow." *Dark Angel*. FOX. 15 May 2001. Television.
"Pilot." *Dark Angel*. FOX. 3 Oct. 2000. Television.
"Pollo Loco." *Dark Angel*. FOX. 24 Apr. 2001. Television.
"Rising." *Dark Angel*. FOX. 13 Feb. 2001. Television.

Dead Like Me

"Last Call." *Dead Like Me*. Showtime. 17 Oct. 2004. Television.

222   Television Episodes, Telefilms, and Feature Films Cited

"Pilot, Part 2." *Dead Like Me*. Showtime. 27 June 2003. Television.
"Reapercussions." *Dead Like Me*. Showtime. 18 July 2003. Television.

The Dead Zone
"Collision." *The Dead Zone*. USA. 20 June 2004. Television.
"Here There Be Monsters." *The Dead Zone*. USA. 18 Aug. 2002. Television.
"Total Awareness." *The Dead Zone*. USA. 4 July 2004. Television.

The Dresden Files
"The Other Dick." *The Dresden Files*. SyFy. 25 Mar. 2007. Television.

Eastwick
"Magic Snow and Creepy Gene." *Eastwick*. ABC. 30 Dec. 2009. Television.
"Mooning and Crooning." *Eastwick*. ABC. 21 Oct. 2009. Television.
"Pilot." *Eastwick*. ABC. 23 Sept. 2009. Television.
"Reaping and Sewing." *Eastwick*. ABC. 30 Sept. 2009. Television.
"Red Ants and Black Widows." *Eastwick*. ABC. 4 Nov. 2009. Television.
"Tasers and Mind Erasers." *Eastwick*. ABC. 2 Dec. 2009. Television.
"Tea and Psychopathy." *Eastwick*. ABC. 16 Dec. 2009.

Firefly
"Safe." *Firefly*. FOX. 8 Nov. 2002. Television.

Free Spirit
"Pilot." *Free Spirit*. ABC. 22 Sept. 1989. [VideoSurferClassic. "Free Spirit: The Pilot Episode." *YouTube*. 4 Jan. 2011. Web. 8 Apr. 2012.]

Fringe
"Back to Where You've Never Been." *Fringe*. FOX. 13 Jan. 2012. Television.
"The End of All Things." *Fringe*. FOX. 24 Feb. 2012. Television.

The Gates
"Bad Moon Rising." *The Gates*. ABC. 19 Sept. 2010. Television.
"Digging the Dirt." *The Gates*. ABC. 8 Aug. 2010. Television.
"Dog Eat Dog." *The Gates*. ABC. 15 Aug. 2010. Television.

Ghost Whisperer
"Birthday Presence." *Ghost Whisperer*. CBS. 25 Sept. 2009. Television.
"The Children's Parade." *Ghost Whisperer*. CBS. 21 May 2010. Television.
"Dead Ringer" *Ghost Whisperer*. CBS. 14 May 2010. Television.
"Demon Child." *Ghost Whisperer*. CBS. 3 Mar. 2006. Television.
"Devil's Bargain." *Ghost Whisperer*. CBS. 6 Nov. 2009. Television.
"On the Wings of a Dove." *Ghost Whisperer*. CBS. 11 Nov. 2005. Television.
"Undead Comic." *Ghost Whisperer*. CBS. 16 Dec. 2005. Television.

A Gifted Man
"Pilot." *A Gifted Man*. CBS. 23 Sept. 2011. Television.

A Girl's Life [documentary]

"Sonia." Narr. Rachel Simmons. *A Girl's Life*. PBS. 30 Dec. 2009. Television.

Haven

"Audrey Parker's Day Off." *Haven*. SyFy. 19 Aug. 2011. Television.
"Ball and Chain." *Haven*. SyFy. 6 Aug. 2010. Television.
"Business as Usual." *Haven*. SyFy. 23 Sept. 2011. Television.
"Fur." *Haven*. SyFy. 13 Aug. 2010. Television.
"Love Machine." *Haven*. SyFy. 29 July 2011. Television.

Heroes

"Brave New World." *Heroes*. NBC. 8 Feb. 2010. Television.
"Close to You." *Heroes*. NBC. 11 Jan. 2010. Television.
"The Fifth Stage." *Heroes*. NBC. 30 Nov. 2009. Television.
"Hiros." *Heroes*. NBC. 23 Oct. 2006. Television.
"Hysterical Blindness." *Heroes*. NBC. 12 Oct. 2009. Television.
"Jump, Push, Fall." *Heroes*. NBC. 28 Sept. 2009. Television.
"Pass/Fail." *Heroes*. NBC. 18 Jan. 2010. Television.
"Thanksgiving." *Heroes*. NBC. 23 Nov. 2009. Television.

Jake 2.0

"The Spy Who Really Liked Me." *Jake 2.0*. UPN. 19 Nov. 2003. Television.
"The Tech." *Jake 2.0*. UPN. 9 Sept. 2003. Television.

Jennifer Slept Here

"Pilot." *Jennifer Slept Here*. NBC. 21 Oct. 1983. [imstillstuckinthe80s. "Jennifer Slept Here: Pilot (episode 1) 1/3–3/3." *YouTube*. 29 Jan. 2009. Web. 8 Apr. 2012.]

Joan of Arcadia

"The Devil Made Me Do It." *Joan of Arcadia*. CBS. 14 Nov. 2003. Television.
"Requiem for a Third Grade Ashtray." *Joan of Arcadia*. CBS. 12 Mar. 2004. Television.
"Silence." *Joan of Arcadia*. CBS. 21 May 2004. Television.

Justice League Unlimited

"Paradise Lost, Part 1." *Justice League Unlimited*. Cartoon Network. 21 Jan. 2002. Television.
"Paradise Lost, Part 2." *Justice League Unlimited*. Cartoon Network. 28 Jan. 2002. Television.

The Listener

"I'm an Adult Now." *The Listener*. NBC. 4 June 2009. Television.
"A Voice in the Dark." *The Listener*. NBC. 18 June 2009. Television.

Lost

"The End." *Lost*. ABC. 23 May 2010. Television.

Mann & Machine

"Prototype." *Mann & Machine.* NBC. 5 Apr. 1992. [imstillstuckinthe80s. "Mann & Machine: Pilot (episode 1) 1/5–5/5" *YouTube.* 19 Aug. 2008. Web. 8 Apr. 2012.]

Medium

"Everything Comes to a Head." *Medium.* NBC. 16 May 2007. Television.
"In Sickness and Adultery." *Medium.* NBC. 31 Jan. 2005. Television.
"Pilot." *Medium.* NBC. 3 Jan. 2005. Television.
"Sal." *Medium.* CBS. 30 Apr. 2010. Television.
"Suspicions and Certainties." *Medium.* NBC. 10 Jan. 2005. Television.

Mighty Morphin Power Rangers

"Day of the Dumpster." *Mighty Morphin Power Rangers.* Syndicated. 28 Aug. 1993. Television.

Missing

"Pilot." *Missing.* Lifetime. 2 Aug. 2003. Television.

My Life as a Teenage Robot

"It Came from Next Door." *My Life as a Teenage Robot.* Nickelodeon. 1 Aug. 2003. Television.
"The Return of the Raggedy Android." *My Life as a Teenage Robot.* Nickelodeon. 19 Sept. 2003. Television.

The Nine Lives of Chloe King

"All Apologies." *The Nine Lives of Chloe King.* ABC Family. 7 July 2011. Television.
"Beautiful Day." *The Nine Lives of Chloe King.* ABC Family. 16 Aug. 2011. Television.
"Green Star." *The Nine Lives of Chloe King.* ABC Family. 28 June 2011. Television.
"Pilot." *The Nine Lives of Chloe King.* ABC Family. 14 June 2011. Television.
"Redemption." *The Nine Lives of Chloe King.* ABC Family. 21 June 2011. Television.

No Ordinary Family

"No Ordinary Marriage." *No Ordinary Family.* ABC. 5 Oct. 2010. Television.
"No Ordinary Quake." *No Ordinary Family.* ABC. 26 Oct. 2010. Television.

Out of This World

"Evie's Thirteenth Birthday." *Out of This World.* Syndicated. 19 Sept. 1987. [OutofthisWorldSeries. "1x01—Evie's Thirteenth Birthday." *YouTube.* 7 July 2011. Web. 8 Apr. 2012.]
"Playing with the Power." *Out of This World.* Syndicated. 26 Sept. 1987. [OutofthisWorldSeries. "1x02—Playing with the Power." *YouTube.* 7 July 2011. Web. 8 Apr. 2012.]

Painkiller Jane

"Piece of Mind." *Painkiller Jane.* SyFy. 27 Apr. 2007. Television.

"Pilot." *Painkiller Jane*. SyFy. 13 Apr., 2007. Television.
"Toy Soldiers." *Painkiller Jane*. SyFy. 20 Apr. 2007. Television.

Roswell

"Chant Down Babylon." *Roswell*. UPN. 26 Feb. 2002. Television.
"Crash." *Roswell*. UPN. 30 Apr. 2002. Television.
"Four Aliens and a Baby." *Roswell*. UPN. 7 May 2002. Television.
"I Married an Alien." *Roswell*. UPN. 29 Jan. 2002. Television.
"Panacea." *Roswell*. UPN. 12 Feb. 2002. Television.

Sabrina, the Teenage Witch

"The Crucible." *Sabrina, the Teenage Witch*. ABC. 9 May 1997. Television.
"Dummy for Love." *Sabrina, the Teenage Witch*. ABC. 3 Oct. 1997. Television.
"Jenny's Non-Dream." *Sabrina, the Teenage Witch*. ABC. 10 Jan. 1997. Television.
"Sabrina Gets Her License, Parts 1 and 2." *Sabrina, the Teenage Witch*. ABC. 26 Sept. 1997. Television.
"Soul Mates, Parts 1 and 2." *Sabrina, the Teenage Witch*. WB. 24 Apr. 2003. Television.

Sanctuary

"Fragments." *Sanctuary*. SyFy. 13 Nov. 2009. Television.
"Next Tuesday." *Sanctuary*. SyFy. 4 Dec. 2009. Television.

Saving Grace

"Bring it on, Earl." *Saving Grace*. TNT. 30 July 2007. Television.
"I'm Gonna Need a Big Night Light." *Saving Grace*. TNT. 21 June 2010. Television.
"Let's Talk." *Saving Grace*. TNT. 29 Mar. 2010. Television.
"Looks Like a Lesbian Attack to Me." *Saving Grace*. TNT. 11 Aug. 2009. Television.
"Pilot." *Saving Grace*. TNT. 23 July 2007. Television.
"So Help You God." *Saving Grace*. TNT. 31 May 2010. Television.
"You Think I'm Gonna Eat My Gun?" *Saving Grace*. TNT. 14 June 2010. Television.

The Secret Circle

"Darkness." *The Secret Circle*. CW. 5 Jan. 2012. Television.
"Fire/Ice." *The Secret Circle*. CW. 12 Jan. 2012. Television.
"Heather." *The Secret Circle*. CW. 6 Oct. 2011. Television.
"Lucky." *The Secret Circle*. CW. 15 Mar. 2012. Television.
"Masked." *The Secret Circle*. CW. 27 Oct. 2011. Television.
"Pilot." *The Secret Circle*. CW. 15 Sept. 2011. Television.

The Secret World of Alex Mack

"The Accident." *The Secret World of Alex Mack*. Nickelodeon. 8 Oct. 1984. Television.
"Hoop War." *The Secret World of Alex Mack*. Nickelodeon. 15 Oct. 1984. Television.

The Secrets of Isis

"The Lights of Mystery Mountain." *The Secrets of Isis*. CBS. 7 Sept. 1975. Television.

The Six Million Dollar Man

"The Bionic Woman, Part 1." *The Six Million Dollar Man*. ABC. 16 Mar. 1975. Television.

"The Bionic Woman, Part 2." *The Six Million Dollar Man*. ABC. 23 Mar. 1975. Television.

"Welcome Home, Jaime." *The Six Million Dollar Man*. ABC. 11 Jan. 1976. Television.

Small Wonder

"The Neighbors." *Small Wonder*. Syndicated. 14 Sept. 1985. Television.

"Vicki's Homecoming." *Small Wonder*. Syndicated. 7 Sept. 1985. Television.

Smallville

"Duplicity." *Smallville*. WB. 8 Oct. 2002. Television.
"Exodus." *Smallville*. WB. 20 May 2003. Television.
"Façade." *Smallville*. WB. 6 Oct. 2004. Television.
"Finale." *Smallville*. CW. 13 May 2011. Television.
"Hex." *Smallville*. CW. 26 Mar. 2009. Television.
"Hostage." *Smallville*. CW. 7 May 2010. Television.
"Idol." *Smallville*. CW. 13 Nov. 2009. Television.
"Phoenix." *Smallville*. WB. 8 Oct. 2003. Television.
"Rush." *Smallville*. WB. 4 Feb. 2003. Television.
"Scion." *Smallville*. CW. 4 Mar. 2011. Television.
"Upgrade." *Smallville*. CW. 16 Apr. 2010. Television.
"Warrior." *Smallville*. CW. 12 Feb. 2010. Television.

Something Is Out There

"Gladiator." *Something Is Out There*. NBC. 21 Oct. 1988. [imstillstuckinthe80s. "Something Is Out There: Gladiator episode 1 1/5–5/5" *YouTube*. 1 Sept. 2008. Web. 8 Apr. 2012.]

Spider-Man [Feature Film]

Spider-Man. Dir. Sam Raimi. Perf. Tobey Maguire et al. Columbia Pictures, 2002. DVD.

Supernatural

"Changing Channels." *Supernatural*. CW. 5 Nov. 2009. Television.
"Defending Your Life." *Supernatural*. CW. 14 Oct. 2011. Television.
"It's a Terrible Life." *Supernatural*. CW. 26 Mar. 2009. Television.
"The Song Remains the Same." *Supernatural*. CW. 4 Feb. 2010. Television.
"Swan Song." *Supernatural*. CW. 13 May 2010. Television.

Tattooed Teenage Alien Fighters from Beverly Hills

"In the Beginning." *Tattooed Teenage Alien Fighters From Beverly Hills*. USA. 3 Oct. 1994. [jpatterson22. "In the Beginning Part 1–3." *Daily motion*. 14 Dec. 2008. Web. 8 Apr. 2012.]

Teen Wolf

"Code Breaker." *Teen Wolf*. MTV. 15 Aug. 2011. Television.
"Heart Monitor." *Teen Wolf*. MTV. 4 July 2011. Television.
"Pack Mentality." *Teen Wolf*. MTV. 13 June 2011. Television.

That's So Raven

"He's Got the Power." *That's So Raven*. Disney. 9 July 2004. Television.
"Saving Psychic Raven." *That's So Raven*. Disney. 21 Feb. 2003. Television.
"To See or Not to See." *That's So Raven*. Disney. 5 Mar. 2004. Television.

Tower Prep

"New Kid." *Tower Prep*. Cartoon Network. 16 Oct. 2010. Television.
"The Rooks." *Tower Prep*. Cartoon Network. 16 Nov. 2010. Television.
"Trust." *Tower Prep*. Cartoon Network. 21 Dec. 2010. Television.

Tru Calling

"Daddy's Girl." *Tru Calling*. FOX. 25 Mar. 2004. Television.
"Morning After." *Tru Calling*. FOX. 18 Dec. 2003. Television.
"Murder in the Morgue." *Tru Calling*. FOX. 15 Jan. 2004. Television.
"Pilot." *Tru Calling*. FOX. 30 Oct. 2003. Television.
"Star Crossed." *Tru Calling*. FOX. 11 Dec. 2003. Television.
"Valentine." *Tru Calling*. FOX. 12 Feb. 2004. Television

True Blood

"And When I Die." *True Blood*. HBO. 11 Sept. 2011. Television.
"Beyond Here Lies Nothin.'" *True Blood*. HBO. 13 Sept. 2009. Television.
"Fresh Blood." *True Blood*. HBO. 29 Aug. 2010. Television.
"Hitting the Ground." *True Blood*. HBO. 1 Aug. 2010. Television.
"I Got a Right to Sing the Blues." *True Blood*. HBO. 25 July 2010. Television.
"I Smell a Rat." *True Blood*. HBO. 22 Aug. 2010. Television.
"I Will Rise Up." *True Blood*. HBO. 16 Aug. 2009. Television.
"I Wish I Was the Moon." *True Blood*. HBO. 31 July 2011. Television.
"If You Love Me, Why Am I Dyin'?" *True Blood*. HBO. 10 July 2011. Television.
"New World in My View." *True Blood*. HBO. 23 Aug. 2009. Television.
"Night on the Sun." *True Blood*. HBO. 8 Aug. 2010. Television.
"She's Not There." *True Blood*. HBO. 26 June 2011. Television.
"Strange Love." *True Blood*. HBO. 7 Sept. 2008. Television.

Unforgettable

"Heroes." *Unforgettable*. CBS. 27 Sept. 2011. Television.

V

"Fruition." *V*. ABC. 11 May 2010. Television.
"Mother's Day." *V*. ABC. 15 Mar. 2011. Television.
"Serpent's Tooth." *V*. ABC. 11 Jan. 2011. Television.

Warehouse 13

"Buried." *Warehouse 13*. SyFy. 14 Sept. 2010. Television.
"The New Guy." *Warehouse 13*. SyFy. 11 July 2011. Television.
"Reset." *Warehouse 13*. SyFy. 21 Sept. 2010. Television.

Weird Science

"She's Alive." *Weird Science*. USA. 5 March 1994. ["She's Alive." *Hulu*. n.d. Web. 8 Apr. 2012.]

Witchblade

"Destiny." *Witchblade*. TNT. 16 June 2002. Television.
"Periculum." *Witchblade*. TNT. 24 July 2001. Television.
Witchblade [Telefilm]. Dir. Ralph Hemecker. Perf. Yancy Butler et al. TNT. 27 Aug. 2000. Television.

The Wizards of Waverly Place

"Who Will Be the Family Wizard? Parts 1 and 2." *The Wizards of Waverly Place*. Disney Channel. 6 Jan. 2012. Television.

Wonder Woman

The New Original Wonder Woman [Telefilm]. Dir. Leonard Horn. Perf. Lynda Carter et al. ABC. 7 Nov. 1975. Television.
"Wonder Woman Meets Baroness Von Gunther." *Wonder Woman*. ABC. 21 Apr. 1976. Television.

Index

Numbers in ***bold italics*** indicate pages with photographs.

Adam, Alison 120
The Addams Family 24
The Adventures of Superman 51, 202
advertising 13, 91, 93, 185
Advil 185
Aeon Flux 8
Alba, Jessica 11, 204*n*8
Alias 43, 203*n*14, 204*n*9
alien 2, 37–41, 50, 53, *56*, 97, 106, 161, 201*n*1, 203*n*8
Alien 7
All-Star Comics 202*n*5
Alphas 160, 162
The Amazing Spider-Man 202*n*2
Amazon 2, 12, 32, 34–36, 50, 125, 130, 202–3*n*6
angel 4, 40–41, 84, 153, 158, 167, 169, ***170–71***, 176–77
Angel 8–9, 44–45, 48, 50–51, 56–***59***, 66, 115, 129, 141–43, 202*n*2, 204–5*ch*3*n*12; title character on *Buffy the Vampire Slayer* 63, 81, 115
Animorphs 42
Asher, William (Bill) 25–28
AskMen.com 64
The Avengers 7

Baer, Judith A. 126
Baird, Julia 184
Baker-Fletcher, Karen 148
Ball, Alan 207*n*4
Balsamo, Anne 20, 118
Barnum, P.T. 46–47, 66
Bartky, Sandra Lee 16, 20, 99–100, 107, 109, 112, 114–16, 118–20, 172–73
Bartlett, Katharine T. 127
Bastet 156, 207*n*8

Beauty and the Beast 202*n*2
Beeler, Karin 9, 112–14, 206*n*3
Being Human (BBC version) 160, 181, 195
Being Human (SyFy version) 4, 160, 164, 168, 181–***82***, 194
Benét, James 201*n*7
Bentham, Jeremy 97, 99, 107
Benz, Julie 169
Bewitched 1, 11, 13, 17–20, 22–32, ***31***, 34, 37–38, 43, 48, 52, 54, 57, 72, 75–76, 79, 100, 103–4, 128, 131, 135, 153, 158, 187–89, 192, 194, 197–98, 200, 201*n*2, 207*n*10
The Bionic Woman (1976–78 version) 2, 7, 18, 32–34, 36–37, 112, 188–89, 201*n*4; title character on *The Six Million Dollar Man* 32–34
Bionic Woman (2007 version) 4, 154, 157, 164, 167, 173–75, 183, 193, 199, 201*n*4, 205*n*8
Birds of Prey 43–46, 48–51, ***49***, 55, 58, 61–62, 69, 72, 74, 77, 82–83, 90, 140, 189, 205*n*12
Birmingham, Elizabeth 66
Bissette, Stephen R. 132
Black Scorpion 43
Blood Ties 158, 166
bodybuilding 64
Bogdan, Robert 46, 52, 57, 66
Bonds, Barry 203*n*4
Boorstin, Julia 206*n*6
Bordo, Susan 71, 80, 118–19, 203*ch*3*n*1
Bramwell, Ros 92
Braswell, Liz (aka Celia Thomson) 207*n*8
Brooks, Tim 25, 31, 37–38, 41, 159, 187–88, 198, 201*n*1, 203*n*7, 203*n*8, 203*n*10, 204*n*8
Brown, Jeffrey A. 9, 204*n*9

230 Index

Bryant, John 30, 194
Buffy the Vampire Slayer 2–3, 8–12, 17, 42–45, 48–49, 51, 55, 58–60, 62–63, 66, 76–77, 81–90, 95, 97, 99–103, 109–12, 115–16, 122, 125, 128–30, 132–34, 137–38, 142, 145–*46*, 154–56, 172, 181, 189, 192, 196, 198, 201n6, 202n8, 205ch4n1, 205n2, 205n4, 205n6, 205n7, 206–7ch6n1
Buffy/Whedon Studies 8, 10
Bukatman, Scott 50, 52–54, 73, 81, 204n8
Butler, Yancy 48, 203n11

Cammann, Freddie 26
canonical body 47–48
Caron, Glen Gordon 198
Case, David Allen 29–30, 188
Castelnuovo, Shirley 50–51, 55, 63
"Cathy" (comic strip) 13
Chaney, Lillian H. 92
Chang, Juju 207n3
Charkalis, Diana McKeon 198
Charlie's Angels 32–33
Charmed 1–4, 11, 18, 22, 42–43, 45, 48, 50–51, 53–55, 58, 60–62, 66, 68–69, 72–74, 77, 79, 82, 84–89, 108–9, 113, 120, 122–25, *124*, 131–33, 136–38, 140–41, 144, 149, 151–53, 158, 187, 189, 192, 194, 197–98, 200, 201n1, 205n9, 206n2, 206n3, 206n4, 206–7ch6n1
Chesler, Phyllis 12
Christian, Aymar Jean 208n4
Chuck 4, 158, 176
Cirksena, Kathryn 16
Cixous, Hélène 86
clairvoyance 10, 114, 191
Clarke, Suzan 207n3
Clément, Catherine 86
Coles, Fen 64
Collins, Patricia Hill 15–16
cosmetic surgery 52, 65, 118
costume 19, 35–*36*, 41, 69, 74, 81–83, 90, 120, 204n9, 204n11
Cox, Steve 28
Crawford, Krysten 149, 206n6
critical legal studies 16, 125, 190
Cuklanz, Lisa 16
cyborg 4, 9, 32–33, 118, 154; cybernetic 34, 173

Daniels, Arlene Kaplan 201n7
Dark Angel 11, 42, 54–55, 62, 66, 68–69, 72–74, 77–79, 95–97, 99–103, *100*, 107, 109–11, 120, 189, 193, 204n8, 205n5
Davis, Kathy 118
DC Comics 50

Dead Last 42
Dead Like Me 35, 43, 79–80, 88, 205n5
The Dead Zone 79, 88–89, 114, 138–41, *139*, 158, 202n2, 205n10
de Beauvoir, Simone 47, 58, 66, 81
Diamond, Diana 194
disability studies 16, 47
Doane, Mary Ann 72, 81, 204n6
Dodge Caravan 13, 91
Dollhouse 8
Doolittle, Eliza 81
Douglas, Mary 52
Douglas, Susan J. 23, 29–30, 33, 35–36
Dr. Horrible's Sing-Along Blog 8
Drake, Jennifer 189, 208n3
The Dresden Files 158, 166

Early, Frances 9
Early Edition 75, 203ch3n3
Eastwick 4, 151, 155–57, 165, 166–67, 173–74, 193
Efron, Edith 28
Electra-Woman and Dynagirl 31, 202n3
Electrolux 13
Eli Stone 159
empowerment 3, 6, 8–10, 12, 14, 20, 22, 32, 36–37, 40–43, 62, 65, 67, 89, 111, 118, 122, 125, 127, 129, 134, 146, 149, 152–53, 166, 176, 179, 183, 185–86, 189, 192, 195–97, 199–200, 202n10, 208n2
Eng, Joyce 207n5
Ensler, Eve 195
Entertainment Weekly 17

The Fairly OddParents 42
Faludi, Susan 12, 40, 184, 194
"fantastic dramas" 194
fantastic sitcom 18, 23–24, 28–29, 31, 36, 38, 187–88, 194, 200, 202n1
father 27, 29, 33, 38–40, 70, 74, 87, 116, 138, 141, 151, 156–58, 162, 171, 174, 179, 194, 204n11, 206n5, 207n7; Father 144
Father Knows Best 24
The Feminine Mystique 18, 23, 202n1
femininity 2, 5, 7, 9, 18, 19, 22, 25, 34, 36, 46, 49–51, 54, 60, 63–65, 69–72, 74, 77–78, 81, 83, 90, 93–94, 107, 114, 116, 145, 152, 187, 198–99, 201n6, 202n2, 204n6, 206n6; hyperfemininity 46, 52, 72, 81, 83, 204n9
feminism 3, 6, 8, 12–16, 19, 22, 29, 35–36, 40, 50, 63, 66, 71, 77, 93, 94, 97, 99, 113, 118, 120, 143–44, 146, 188, 190, 196, 202n10, 203ch3n2, 205n3, 206n6, 208n2; choice 183–84, 186, 193, 195; first-wave 201n5; fourth-wave 194–95, 201n5; lib-

eral 16, 34; Marxist 16; post- 9, 147; post-structuralist 13, 16; psychoanalytic 81, 86; radical 16, 33–34; second-wave 12, 36, 187–89, 201*n*5; theory; third-wave 5–6, 14, 185, 189, 197, 199, 201*n*5, 208*n*3
feminist legal theory 125–28, 132, 136, 139, 147, 150
La Femme Nikita 3, 8–9, 201*n*3
Ferguson, Michaele L. 193
Ferriss, Suzanne 183
Fiedler, Leslie 47
Field, Eunice 27
Field, Susan 92
Fineman, Martha Albertson 126, 131–32, 143
Fingeroth, Danny 3, 12, 35, 90, 181
Finley, Lucinda M. 126, 128–29
Firefly 8, 137–38
The Flash 202*n*2
The Flying Nun 24–25, 30, 187
Forever Knight 202*n*2
The 4400 159
Foster, Jodie 7
Foucault, Michel 56, 97–99, 101, 109, 135, 175, 203*ch2n*1
freak 3, 5, 19, 21–22, 33, 39, 43–52, 54–58, 62–66, 152, 162–67, 174, 181, 183–84, 190, 192–93, 199, 203*n*4
Free Spirit 37–38, 188
Freud, Sigmund 3, 70, 86
Friedan, Betty 18, 23, 188, 202*n*1
Fringe 161, 172
Fudge, Rachel 5–6, 48, 189

Gardner, Carol Brooks 107, 120, 205*ch4n*13
The Gates 159, 164, 180–82, 208*n*13
gaze 20, 35, 97–120, 172–76, 183, 185, 191, 193, 205*n*3
Gellar, Sarah Michelle 48
gender roles 3, 7, 19, 27, 63, 72, 187
genre 7, 10, 24, 30, 42, 52, 94, 178
Gerbner, George 201–2*n*7
Germov, John 97, 99, 119
Gest, David 203*n*4
ghost 5, 37–38, 138, 160, 168, 180, **182**, 195, 201*n*2
Ghost Whisperer 4, 43, 54–55, 61–62, 66, 152–53, 157–58, 168, 170, 172–73, 176, 193, 198, 203*ch2n*2
A Gifted Man 159, 162
Gilligan, Carol 126
girl power 5–6, 42, 54, 57, 158, 188–89, 192–93, 197, 201*n*6
The Girl with Something Extra 24–25, 187

Girls Gone Wild 192–93, 208*n*1
A Girl's Life 199
Give Me Liberty: An American Dream 7
Gliatto, Tom 48
Goffman, Erving 55
Golden, Christopher 132
Good Housekeeping 7, 26–27
Good Samaritan 77, 86
Gramsci, Antonio 15
grandmother 62, 73, 152, 156, 201*n*1
Greer, Germaine 66
Greven, David 52, 60, 62, 144, 203*n*14
grim reaper 79–80, 204*n*5
Grimm 159
Groeneveld, Elizabeth 189
Grossman, Jennifer 149, 206*n*6
Grosz, Elizabeth 47, 51, 65
Gruner + Jahr 148–49
Guisewite, Cathy 13
Guthrie, Sharon R. 50–51, 55, 63

Hall, Stuart 16
Halloween 82–83, 120
Hallstein, D. Lynn O'Brien 197
Hano, Arnold 26–28
harassment 20, 54, 102, 107, 141, 147–48
Haraway, Donna 111, 113, 120, 176
Harding, Sandra 120
Harris, Charlaine 154
Haven 162, 166, 168
healing (power of) 4, 10, 159, 174
Heath, Stephen 70, 72, 86, 90, 93
Heaven Help Us 41
hegemony 3, 12, 15–16, 20, 22, 62, 65, 67, 120, 125, 127, 196, 199, 206*n*3
Heinecken, Dawn 8–9
Helford, Elyce Rae 9, 29–30, 202*n*8
Helms, Dorothea 64
Henner, Marilu 207*n*5
Hercules: The Legendary Journeys 202*n*2
Heroes 4, 151, 159, 164, 171, 173–75, 179–81, 184, 194, 199
Hewitt, Jennifer Love 198
Heywood, Leslie 189, 208*n*3
Highlander 202*n*2
Highlander: The Raven 42
Highway to Heaven 202*n*2
Hilgenberg, Holly 185
Hill, Anita 147–48
Hills, Elizabeth 7–8
Hirshman, Linda 180, 183, 185, 193
Holmes, Linda 208*n*2
housewife 1, 23–25, 27–30, 71, 198, 202*n*1
Hutchinson, Allan C. 125
Hyams, Joe 26–27
hysteria 86–87, 93

Index

I Dream of Jeannie 2, 24–25, 28–30, 32, 37, 187, 189
immortality 5, 10, 35, 52, 159, 161, 201*n*3
The Incredible Hulk 202*n*2
Inness, Sherrie A. 7–9, 13, 32–33, 35
invisibility (power of) 39, 108–10, 117, 173, 204*n*8
The Invisible Man 202*n*2, 204*n*8

Jackson, Michael 203*n*4
Jake 2.0 51–53, 58, 87–88, **115**–16, 140–41, 202*n*2, 205*n*11
Jenkins, Henry 17
Jenkins, Tricia 32–34
Jennifer Slept Here 37–38, 188
Joan of Arc 9, 51, 113, 134, 177
Joan of Arcadia 3, 43, 75–77, 84–88, **85**, 91, 193, 199
Jolie, Angelina 203*n*4
The Journal of American Culture 205–6*ch*5*n*1
Journeyman 158
judicial system **124**, 131, 146, 192
Justice League Unlimited 42, 125, 128, 130, 196, 203*n*12

Kaplan, E. Ann 195
Karlsen, Carol F. 138
Karlyn, Kathleen Rowe 6, 14, 91, 93, 201*n*6
Keck, William 169, 198
Kennedy, Kathleen 9
Kern, Brad 151
Kirby-Diaz, Mary 8
Klein, Melissa 208*n*3
Koerner, Brendan I. 93
Kournikova, Anna 64
Kramer, Matthew H. 150
Kreider, Jodie A. 9
The Krofft Supershow 202*n*3
Kyle XY 4, 158, 181

Lavery, David 8, 202*n*8, 204–5*ch*3*n*12
law 21, 44, 114–15, 122, 124–37, 139–50, 153, 178–79, 185, 191–92, 199, 202*n*9, 205*ch*4*n*1
Leave It to Beaver 24
Leaving L.A. 42
Leonard, Kendra Preston 9
Levine, Melissa 79, 206*n*4
Lewis, Richard Warren 26
Life on Mars 207–8*n*11
The Listener 159, 166, 175
Little Red Riding Hood 133
Logan, Michael 182, 206*n*6
Lois & Clark: The New Adventures of Superman 59, 90, 202*n*2

Look 26–27
Lorber, Judith 14, 16, 36, 201*n*5
Lost 207*n*11
Lotz, Amanda D. 63
Lyden, Julie R. 92
Lyon, David 106, 110

Machelidon, Véronique 77
MacKinnon, Catharine 126–27, 129–30
Magoulick, Mary 3
Maguire, Kerry 72, 78
makeover 65, 173
Manimal 202*n*2
Mann, Patricia S. 147
Mann & Machine 40–41, 203*n*11
Marsh, Earle 25, 31, 37–38, 41, 159, 187–88, 198, 201*n*1, 203*n*7, 203*n*8, 203*n*10, 204*n*8
Martha Stewart Living 149
Maschke, Karen J. 126–27
masculinity 9, 37, 49, 51, 60–61, 64–65, 70–72, 90, 110–11, 114, 117, 119, 121, 126, 128, 130, 149, 158, 174, 190, 204*n*6, 205*n*7
mask 19, 69, 70, 73, 78, 81–82, 90, 92–93
masquerade 19, 68–73, 77, 81–84, 86–87, 90–94, 190, 204*n*6, 204*n*9
matriarchy 29, 112, 130, 196
McCarver, Virginia 183–84, 186
McFadden, Patricia 120
McLean, Candis 92
McNeil, Alex 202*n*4
Medium 4, 43, 140, 142, 147, 152–53, 157, 168, 173–74, 193, 198
Mendlesohn, Farah 202*n*8
mental illness 92–93, 203*ch*2*n*1; depression 87, 93, 205*ch*3*n*13
metahuman 44–45, **49**, 51, 55, 61, 83, 203*n*14
Mighty Morphin Power Rangers 41, 188, 203*n*9
Millennium 202*n*2
Miller, Catriona 206*n*3
Millman, Joyce 204–5*ch*3*n*12
Minnelli, Liza 203*n*4
Misfits of Science 203*n*7
Missing 43, 88, 91, 113, 203*n*13
Mr. & Mrs. North 37
Mr. Ed 2, 24
Mitchell, Maria 66
Montgomery, Elizabeth (Liz) 18, 25–28, 198
Montgomery, Robert 25
Moonlight 158
Moore, Shemar 48
Mork & Mindy 202*n*2

Moseley, Rachel 65
mother 6, 14, 24, 27–**31**, 33, 35–**36**, 38–39, 43, 55, 61, 63, 69–71, 74, 76–77, 79, 84–85, 89, 91–94, 97, 101, 112, 125, 128, 130–33, 137–39, 152, 155–56, 161–62, 168–69, 171, 174, 179, 181, 184, 185, 199, 202n6
Moy, Suelain 7
Muir, John Kenneth 37–38
Mulvey, Laura 104, 205n3
The Munsters 24
Mutant X 42, 205ch4n12
My Favorite Martian 2, 24
My Life as a Teenage Robot 10, 43, 68–69, 72, 76–78, 82–**83**, 87
My Living Doll 24–25, 187, 201n2
My Mother the Car 24–25, 187
My Secret Identity 202n2

Nearly Departed 37–38
New Amsterdam 159
new domesticity 21, 185
The New York Times 75, 160
Nick at Nite 28
The Nine Lives of Chloe King 155–**157**, 164–65, 167–68, 172, 193, 207n6, 207n7, 207n8, 207n9, 208n13
No Ordinary Family 160, 168–69, 183

objectification 101, 104, 114–15, 120, 148, 162, 164, 175–76, 191, 197, 199
O'Donnell, Rosie 21, 148–49
Of Mice and Men 77
Once Upon a Time 208n12
The Onion 208n2
Ono, Kent A. 202n8
Othering 46–47, 58, 81, 99, 109, 111, 118–20, 157, 162, 202n8, 207n11
The Others 42
Out of This World 2, 38–40, 188
Oxman, Steven 48

Painkiller Jane 153–54, 156–57
Palin, Sarah 183–84
The Panopticon 16, 97–99, 101, 107, 110, 175; panopticism 16, 116–20, 190
Parenti, Christian 98
patriarchy 15–16, 18, 28–29, 32, 34, 38, 72, 81, 87, 94, 99, 107, 109, 111–12, 119–20, 125, 127–30, 144–46, 178, 188, 196, 205n7; patriarch 27, 38, 93, 160
Paulin, Tom 40
Paxil 93
Peay, Pythia 194–95
Pereira, Jennifer 207n3
Phelan, Peggy 81, 109, 204n7, 204n8

Pilato, Herbie J. 28
The Playboy Club 208n2
Point Pleasant 43
Poltergeist: The Legacy 203n10
popular culture 6–7, 9, 13–14, 28, 120, 197, 199, 202n10
The Powerpuff Girls 42
The Powers of Matthew Star 202n2
pregnancy 20, 118
premonition 2, 79, 113–14, 123, 136, 138–40, **139**, 140, 155, 205n9, 206n2
privacy 106, 117, 119, 173
Profiler 42
Projansky, Sarah 203ch3n2
psychic 9–10, 50, 57, 61–62, 88, 97, 104–**105**, 106, 134, 137, 151, 161, 174
psychoanalysis 7, 16, 70, 77, 81, 86, 190, 194
Psychology Today 7
Pushing Daisies 4, 158

Radway, Janice 17
Reaper 207–8n11
Reese, Stephen D. 15
Renegar, Valerie R. 197
representation 7, 9–15, 30, 37, 82, 104, 114, 117, 120, 124, 127, 188, 198–99, 201n6
"reverse" discourse 56
Riess, Jana 8
Rifkin, Janet 125, 127
Riordan, Ellen 202n10, 208n2
riot grrrls 6
Riviere, Joan 70–74, 77–78, 81, 83, 90
Rogers, Adam 13
Rome, Jim 64, 203n4
Rose, Matthew 148
Rosie 148
Roswell 42, 50, 53, 55–**56**, 66, 97, 99, 106–7, 113–14, 201n1
Rothenberg, Paula S. 125
Roush, Matt 198
Russo, Mary 52, 116

Sabrina, the Teenage Witch 2–3, 11, 42–43, 97, 99, 103, 122, 125, 128, 130, **135**–37, 143–44, 154, 189, 192, 197–98, 203ch3n2, 204n4, 206–7ch6n1
sacrifice 3–4, 21, 70–75, 77, 84, 86–87, 89, 91, 103, 109, 134, 137, 151, 153, 157, 165, 167, 169–**170**, 171, 177, 183, 190–91, 204–5ch3n12
Salem 122, **135**, 138
Samuels, Skyler 208n13
sanctuary 21, 151, 153, 180–81, 184, 194–95
Sanctuary 5, 161, 168, 182, 194
Sarafem (aka Prozac) 93
The Saturday Evening Post 26–27

Saving Grace 4, 153–54, 157, 167, 169–*170*, 171, 176–80, 183, 193
Scannell, Kara 149
Schneider, Elizabeth M. 126
scopophilia 104
Scott, Ashley 48
Scott, Joan W. 13, 15–16
The Secret Circle 155–57, 168, 193–94, 196, 198
The Secret World of Alex Mack 41–42, 188
The Secrets of Isis 31–32, 202n4
selflessness 4, 17, 19–21, 43, 68–74, 76–78, 80–84, 86–94, 100, 108, 114, 152, 166–72, 177–79, 185, 190–93, 199
Shazam!/Isis Hour 202n4
Sheena 42
Shields, Vickie Rutledge 119
Shoemaker, Pamela J. 15
Shugart, Helene A. 197
The Silence of the Lambs 7
Simmons, Rachel 199
The Six Million Dollar Man 32–34, 112, 154, 202n2
Small Wonder 2, 38–40, *39*, 188
Smallville 53, 59, 61, 79–*80*, 87–90, 114, 116, 141–42, 158, 171–72, 174–76, 202n2, 203ch2n3, 204n11, 206n5
Smith, L.J. 207n10
Sniegoski, Thomas E. 132
Something Is Out There 37–38, 40, 188
South, James B. 8
Sowards, Stacey K. 197
Spain, Daphne 20, 119
Spice Girls 5–6, 201n6, 202n10
Spider-Man (feature film) 204n10
Spigel, Lynn 18, 24, 28–30, 187
Stabile, Carole A. 184, 199
Stack, Tim 207n4
Stanley, Alessandra 75, 91
Star, Susan Leigh 92
Star Trek: The Next Generation 203n8
Stark, Steven D. 30, 200
Starman 202n2
Static Shock 202n2
Steinem, Gloria 94
Stewart, Martha 21, 149, 206n6
Stiehm, Jaime 21, 184–85
Storey, John 15–16
Strinati, Dominic 208n3
Superboy 202n2
SuperFriends 202n5
superhero 3, 10, 12, 19, 32, 36, 44, 50, 53–54, 61, 90, 130, 165, 171, 203ch2n3
Supernatural 158, 171, 175, 180
Superwoman (archetype) 11–12, 184–85
surveillance 3, 16–17, 20–22, 40, 43, 82, 95, 97–110, *100*, *105*, 114–22, 141, 152, 172–73, 175–76, 188, 191–93, 199, 205n5, 205n7; accompanying examination 101–3, 117, 191, 197, 205n1, 205n7; accompanying registration 102–3, 117, 191

Tabitha 31, 188
talk shows 65, 148
Tapping, Amanda 182
Tattooed Teenage Alien Fighters from Beverly Hills 41
Taub, Nadine 126
Teen Wolf 159, 166, 171–72
telekinesis 10, 57, 60, 155, 203n7
telepathy 4, 10, 57, 154, 159–60, 162–64, *163*, 171
That's So Raven 43, 57, 61–62, 65–66, 113–14
3rd Rock from the Sun 42
Thomas, Clarence 147–48
Thomas, Devon 169
Thomson, Rosemarie Garland 19, 47–50, 54, 58, 62–63, 165
The Tick 202n2
Tomb Raider 9
Topper 37, 201n2
Touched by an Angel 2, 41, 188
Tower Prep 151, 160, 166, 182
transgenic 54–55
transgression 8, 40, 50–52, 57, 60–62, 65–66, 137, 190–91
trial 3, 20–22, 122–23, 132–39, *135*, 141, 144, 146–52, 176–80, 183, 192–93, 205n11, 205–6ch5n1, 206n5
Tringali, Juliana 6, 189, 208n1
Tru Calling 3, 43, 68–69, 72–73, 75–76, 78, 87, 111–12, 203ch3n3, 204n5
True Blood 4, 154–55, 157, 162–64, *163*, 173–75, 193, 197–98, 207n3, 207n4
Tuchman, Gaye 201n7
Tucker, Ken 17, 76
Tucker's Witch 37, 188
TV Guide 26–28, 91, 161, 198
TV Land 28
TV Radio Mirror 27
Twilight 207n3

Unforgettable 35, 207n5

V 161–62
vampire 2, 4, 13, 45, 51, 55, 58–*59*, 63, 84, 101, 115–16, 128–29, 132, 154–55, 158, 160, *163*, 180, *182*, 189, 195, 204–5ch3n12, 205n6, 207n3
The Vampire Diaries 4, 159, 207n10
Vande Berg, Leah R. 203ch3n2

Ventura, Michael 7
visibility 82, 97–99, 109–10, 116, 152, 174–75, 191, 204n7, 204n8
voyeurism 46, 82, **100**, 107

Waggoner, Catherine Egley 197
The Wall Street Journal 148–49
Warehouse 13 162, 167, 175
Weird Science 42
Wenegrat, Brant 92, 205*ch*3*n*13
werewolf 4, 160–61, 163, 171, 181–**82**, 195
Whedon, Joss 8–9
Whelehan, Imelda 6, 66, 93, 198, 201*n*6
Wie, Michelle 64, 203*n*4
Wiegman, Robyn 117
Wilcox, Rhonda V. 8, 202*n*8
The Wild Thornberrys 42
Wilkie, Jane 26–27
Williams, Lauren 97, 99, 119
Williams, Raymond 15
Williams, Serena 63–64
Williams, Venus 63–64
Williamson, Milly 196
Winchell, Meghan K. 9
Winfrey, Oprah 21, 148
Wishik, Heather Ruth 125, 127, 133

witch 1, 11, 19, 24–25, 28, 30, 38, 45, 53, 60, 62, 74, 87, 103, 108, 122, 131, **135**–39, 144, 156, 163, 168, 206–7*ch*6*n*1, 207*n*10
Witchblade 3, 42, 45, 48, 51–52, 58, 60, 62, 66, 95, 97, 99, 104–**5**, 113, 125, 133–34, 144–45, 189, 202*n*9, 203*n*11, 203*n*14, 205*n*2
The Wizards of Waverly Place 161, 176–79
Wolf, Naomi 82
Wolf Lake 42
Wonder Woman 2, 18, 32, 34–37, **36**, 188–89, 202*n*5, 202–3*n*6; character as icon 12, 199, 205–6*ch*5*n*1
Wood, Julia T. 71, 169, 203*ch*3*n*2
Woods, Tiger 64
WordGirl 207*n*2

Xena: Warrior Princess 3, 7, 9, 43, 64, 201*n*3, 201*n*6

Young, Gig 26
Young, Mallory 183

Zeisler, Andi 6, 10, 13, 30, 34–36, 104, 205*n*3

www.ingramcontent.com/pod-product-compliance
Ingram Content Group UK Ltd.
Pitfield, Milton Keynes, MK11 3LW, UK
UKHW041940140426
5217IPUK00014B/587